Responding to Global Challenges

Editorial Board

Prof Paul Mbangwana, University of Yaounde I, Cameroon
Prof Dr Josef Schmied, Chemnitz University of Science and Technology, Germany
Prof John Nkemngong Nkengasong of blessed memory, University of Buea, Cameroon
Prof Jean-Paul Kouega, University of Yaounde I, Cameroon
Prof Njika Justina Atemajong, University of Yaounde I, Cameroon
Prof Michael Etuge Apuge, University of Buea, Cameroon

List of Reviewers

Prof Dr Josef Schmied (see editorial board)
Prof John Nkemngong Nkengasong of blessed memory (see editorial board)
Prof Jean-Paul Kouega (see editorial board)
Prof Njika Justina Atemajong (see editorial board)
Prof Ndongmanji John Niba, University of Bamenda, Cameroon
Prof Michael Etuge Apuge (see editorial board)
Prof Blossom Ngum Fondo, University of Yaounde II, Cameroon
Prof Adamu Pangmeshi, University of Bamenda, Cameroon
Prof Kelvin Ngong Toh, University of Buea, Cameroon
Prof Gilbert Tarka Fai, University of Bamenda, Cameroon
Prof Divine Che Neba, University of Yaounde I, Cameroon
Prof Gilbert T. Safotso, University of Dschang, Cameroon
Prof Lozzi Martial Meutem Kamtchueng, University of Maroua, Cameroon
Prof Eleanor Anneh Dassi, University of Yaounde I, Cameroon
Prof Fassé Mbouya Innocent, University of Douala, Cameroon
Prof Eunice Fonyuy Fondze-Fombele, University of Buea, Cameroon
Prof Comfort Beyang Oben Ojongkpot, University of Buea, Cameroon
Prof Mbu Martha Njui, University of Maroua, Cameroon
Prof James Tasah Ngoin, University of Maroua, Cameroon
Dr Terver Iorde Ahembe, The Federal Polytechnic, Mubi- Nigeria
Dr Adamu Usman, Nigerian Army University
Dr Meshach Terfa Zayol, Nasarawa State University, Keffi-Nigeria
Dr Shema'u Abubakar Umar-Ari, School of General studies and Pre-ND, Isa Mustapha Agwai I Polytecnic, Lafia, Nigeria
Dr Louisa Lum, University of Douala, Cameroon
Dr Eric Ekembe, University of Yaounde I, Cameroon
Dr Forti Etienne Langmia, University of Maroua, Cameroon
Dr Njimuwe Samson, University of Maroua, Cameroon

Responding to Global Challenges

Voices in Language and Literature

Edited by
Camilla Arundie Tabe
Ngong Joseph Sam

SPEARS ⓢ BOOKS
DENVER, COLORADO

Spears Books
An Imprint of Spears Media Press LLC
7830 W. Alameda Ave, Suite 103-247
Denver, CO 80226
United States of America

First Published in the United States of America in 2023 by Spears Books
www.spearsmedia.com
info@spearsmedia.com
Information on this title: www.spearsbooks.org/responding-to-global-challenges

© 2023 Camilla Arundie Tabe & Ngong Joseph Sam
All rights reserved.

No part of this publication may be reproduced, distributed, or transmitted in any form or by any means, including photocopying, recording, or other electronic or mechanical methods, without the prior written permission of the publisher, except in the case of brief quotations embodied in critical reviews and certain other noncommercial uses permitted by copyright law. For permission requests, write to the publisher, addressed "Attention: Permissions Coordinator," at the above address.

ISBN: 9781957296166 (Paperback)
ISBN: 9781957296173 (eBook)

Spears Media Press has no responsibility for the persistence or accuracy of urls for external or third-party internet websites referred to in this publication, and does not guarantee that any content on such websites is, or will remain, accurate or appropriate.

Designed and typeset by Spears Media Press LLC
Cover designed by Doh Kambem

Distributed globally by African Books Collective (ABC)
www.africanbookscollective.com

Contents

Foreword ix

Acknowledgements xv

Introduction xvii
Camilla Arundie Tabe & Ngong Joseph Sam

Part One
LANGUAGE AND GLOBAL CHALLENGES

ONE 1

Inside the Virtual 'State': A Speech Act Analysis of the Discourses of the Anglophone Problem in Cameroon
Camilla Arundie Tabe

TWO 22

Memes, Deep Fake Images of Public Figures and Hate Captions on the Anglophone Crisis on Facebook
Fombo Emmanuel

THREE 39

The Pragmatics of Greeting and Face Management in the Covid-19 Era in Northern Cameroon
Faissam Warda

FOUR 54

Conceptualisation of Covid-19 Metaphors in the Printed Word in English
Michael Etuge Apuge & Abba

FIVE 71

An Analysis of the Communication Strategies During the Covid-19 Pandemic: The Case of Apostolic Faith Church West and Central Africa
Ngonjo Victor Fuh

SIX 84

Linguistic Undertones of (Mis)apprehension, (Mis)trust, Panic and Assurance: A Pragma-Stylistic Reading of Stances on Covid-19 Vaccines
Joseph Nkwain

SEVEN 108

Language Shift amongst Refugee Children in Koza
James N. Tasah

EIGHT 124

Addressing Global Challenges from a Linguistic Perspective
Julius Nguafac & Gilbert Tagne Safotso

Part Two
LITERATURE AND GLOBAL CHALLENGES

NINE 137

Freedom Fighters or Terrorists? Terrorism in Helon Habila's *Oil on Water*
Ophilia A. Abianji-Menang

TEN 161

Post-Apartheid Multiracial Democracy and 'New' Patterns of Social Inequality in Nadine Gordimer's *The House Gun* and Nicholas Mhlongo's *Dog Eat Dog* and *After Tears*
Etienne Langmia Forti

ELEVEN 184

Politics of Gender in African and African American Dramaturgy A Study of Selected Plays by Athol Fugard and August Wilson
Ngong Joseph Sam

TWELVE   200

The Intricacies of Racial Stigma: A Self Reconstruction of the Sublime in Maya Angelou's *I Know Why the Caged Bird Sings*
Nye Grace Nformi

THIRTEEN   213

On the Margins of National Heritage: Colonising Conspiracy and Economic Misery in Helon Habila's *Oil on Water*
Koubli Nouanwa

FOURTEEN   229

Santa Claus on the Cross: A Postmodernist Reading of John Nkemngong Nkengasong's *God Was African* and Salman Rushdie's *Fury*
Ethel Joffi Molua-Ewusi

Appendices	243
List of Contributors	247
Index	251

List of Illustrations

Figure 1.1.	Samples of some screenshots from Facebook and Twitter	10
Figure 2.1.	Images showing producers' beliefs about some Cameroonians	28
Figure 2.2.	Images showing producers' beliefs about some Cameroonians	29
Figure 2.3.	Images representing Paul Biya as the genesis of the Anglophone crisis	31
Figure 2.4.	Image representations and communicating acts	31
Figure 7.1.	Pressure and resistance in language endangerment	112

List of Tables

Table 1.1.	Corpus composition	9
Table 1.2.	Percentage of offensive speech on Facebook and Twitter	15
Table 2.1.	Data statistics	27
Table 3.1.	Statistical distribution of greeting gestures directed to H's positive face	44

Table 3.2.	Statistical distribution of greeting gestures directed to H's negative face	48
Table 4.1.	Covid-19 is a war	57
Table 4.2.	Covid-19 is a pandemic	59
Table 4.3.	Covid-19 is an alien	60
Table 4.4.	Covid-19 is an enemy	61
Table 4.5.	Covid-19 is a Foreign Virus	63
Table 4.6.	Covid-19 is a Killer	64
Table 4.7.	Covid-19 is a Thing	65
Table 4.8.	Covid-19 is a New Land	65
Table 4.9.	Covid-19 is a Phenomenon	66
Table 4.10.	Covid-19 is an Airborne	67
Table 4.11.	Distribution of Conceptual Metaphors and their Occurrences	68
Table 6.1.	Distribution of bloggers' reactions	91
Table 7.1.	Number of respondents from the selected schools in Koza	115
Table 7.2.	Language use with parents at Home	116
Table 7.3.	Language used with Neighbours	116
Table 7.4.	Respondents' knowledge of languages spoken in Koza	117
Table 7.5.	Respondents' degree of Comfort with the host community's languages	118
Table 7.6.	Respondents' Adaption into the linguistic and cultural traditions of Koza	118
Table 7.7.	Language use in communicating with classmates in school	119
Table 7.8.	Respondents' parents plan to return to their original country	120

Foreword

Responding to Global Challenges: Voices in Language and Literature seeks to demonstrate how issues of global challenges can be assuaged and alleviated through language and literature.

Camilla Arundie Tabe, in *Inside the Virtual Stage: A Speech Act Analysis of the Discourses of the Anglophone Problem in Cameroon*, shows how the power of language can make or mar a peaceful and antagonistic society. When it is used as a virtual instrument where censorship acts as a watchdog and is hard to control, it can be fraught with hate speech, generating terror, horror and violence. But a healthy society will require a monitoring agency that can sanitise cyberbullying of offensive language directed to individuals, groups or systems of governance. She also shows how well-managed usage can be a boon to social living.

Fombo Emmanuel, *in Memes, Deepfake Images of Public Figures and Hate Captions on the Anglophone Crisis on Facebook*, analyses memes and deepfake images with hate captions. They are used principally to fuel the fire of the Anglophone crisis on Facebook. These artificial intelligence devices or artefacts are used to create illusionary images to depict reality. They portray something as if it appears in real-life situations, when it never occurred. Images are used to befuddle the reader, negatively or positively, as if it existed. Memes and deepfake images may be elements of abuses used to create tension, chaos and violence in times of crisis. These may also heighten disinformation and hate speech. In certain cases, the producers combine the visual designs and linguistic elements to unveil their intentions toward the target persons and situations to heighten the Anglophone crisis' tension.

Faissam Warda in *The Pragmatics of Greeting and Face Management in the Covid-19 Era in Grand North Cameroon* in the manner of Victor Ngonjo and Joseph Nkwain, portray politeness conveyed by gestures in the Fulbe society. Through creativity and adaptability, the Fulbe develop new strategies to cope with their interlocutors' positive and/or negative faces. What technique do the

Fulbe from the Grand North use to carry out greeting rituals adapted to the emergence of the Covid-19 pandemic? Strict observance of Covid-19 barrier measures undermines the traditional greeting patterns, yet greetings are still practised in one form or another.

Michael Etuge Apuge and Abba in *Conceptualization of the Covid-19 metaphors in the printed Word in English* unlike Joseph Nkwain who uses pragma-stylistic strategy to conceal meaning by implication, use the metaphor to conceptualise a deeper and concrete image through down-to-earth expressions pregnant with meaning, such as Covid-19 is an invisible enemy, a contagious virus, a killer disease and a global phenomenon. All the conceptualizations above help people and world leaders convey the exact message they intended to their listeners for their better understanding and image building.

Ngonjo Victor Fuh in *Analysis of the Communication Strategies during the Covid-19: The Case of Apostolic Faith Church West and Central Africa* describes Communication strategies of the Apostolic Faith Church developed at the advent of the Covid-19 pandemic. During the shutdown in West and Central Africa, the church members sought to maintain contact and fellowship through greetings by bowing the head, waving the hand, raising the right leg to touch the right leg of the fellow Christian, tapping the back of a person by elbow nudging. All these strategies replaced the conventional greeting methods, namely shaking one's hand, embracing a friend, hugging and kissing. People responded creatively to the new methods of greeting which managed to keep life and solidarity among fellow Christians in all they did.

Joseph Nkwain in *Linguistic Undertones of (mis)apprehension (mis)trust, Panic and Assurance: A Pragma-stylistic Reading of Stances on Covid-19 Vaccines* like Camilla Arundie Tabe, tries to use intended and not expressed meaning in portraying what people want to say. These novel words or neologisms finding their way into the lexical economy of mainstream English constitute a new way of talking. People are vaccinated but still need boosters to be sustainable, sometimes as many as eight boosters. Rhetorical questions like, who is WHO? is asked, WHO is rebranded to World Sick Organisation or World Hallucinated Oppression. All these doublespeak expressions make people flabbergasted and bemused on the efficacy of the vaccines. Yet, many remain and nurse immense hope in eradicating this frightful pandemic which threatens as the malady of the century.

James N. Tasah in *Language Shift as an Outcome of Migration of some Refugee Children in Koza* probes into a linguistic phenomenon of Language shift whereby some Nigerian refugee children in Koza (in the Grand North) are triggered by Boko Haram insurgency. The study seeks to find out if the language of the refugee children is still vital among them or gradually undergoing a shift in the course of their stay in the host country, Cameroon. Language shift, a recurrent phenomenon in Africa, is very much alive in Koza which is enhanced by Nigerian refugee children who need to be sociolinguistically integrated into the life of the host community. In Koza where three languages are spoken, the respondents can understand and be able to respond to a certain extent fairly in Mafa, Fulfulde or French. The Nigerian refugee children whose parents migrated to Koza are shifting gradually to languages spoken in the host community, not necessarily for the love of integrating themselves in the host community, but also for their survival. Though the Nigerian refugee children integrated into their host community linguistically and socio-economically, they for the moment, still maintain their mother tongue within the family transactions with no symptoms yet of language endangerment.

Nguafac Julius and Gilbert Safotso in *Addressing Global Challenges from a Linguistic Perspective* observe the mountain of problems assailing the world and suggest that language and dialogue may be creatively used to address these global challenges through cooperation and collaboration among the state and non-state actors. Language and dialogue can be a solution or a panacea to the global issues of climate change, Covid-19 and related variants, unemployment, ethnic conflicts, food security, to name only these few, if used appropriately, and the truth around the issues is revealed and not presented as a hoax or controversy as it sometimes happens.

Ophilia A. Abianji-Menang in *Freedom Fighters or Terrorists? Terrorism in Helon Habila's Oil on Water* discusses how sensitive the response of the public authorities to the people's basic demands, through negotiation and not violent repression, may be a productive solution to peace and harmony.

Etienne Langmia Forti in *Post-apartheid Multiracial Democracy and 'new' Patterns of Social Inequality in Nadine Gordimer's The House Gun and Nicholas Mhlongo's Dog eat Dog and After Tears* examines South Africa after 1994 as a divided nation socially and economically. Racism which was the bedrock of the official policy of social inequality before 1994 has now become aggravated by the legacy of apartheid which continues to thwart South Africa's attempt to re-invent itself. The two authors outline the new nation's problems as homelessness, poor prison conditions, high rate of unemployment, and a growing divide between classes under Black majority rule. Why are these dehumanizing legacies of apartheid still lingering and entrenched in Black South Africa's governance after 1994? The answer blows in the wind.

Ngong Joseph Sam in *Politics of Gender in African and African American Dramaturgy: a Study of Selected Plays by Athol Fugard and August Wilson* presents the authors Fugard and Wilson who (mis)represent women by making them play secondary roles. At the same time these authors reclassify women as they hold strategic roles in their plays, thus making gender a global issue. The invisibility and the inequality of the black woman in the United States continues to be the norm in other parts of the world even in the black continent of Africa. The plays show that no man can succeed without a woman behind or beside him. The plays reveal that men and women play complementary roles in life, that women should not be excluded from societal mainstream issues, for what men can do, women can do even better. These authors contributed to feminine political discourse as gender remains a captivating global issue.

Nye Grace Nformi in *The Intricacies of Racial Stigma: A Self-reconstruction of the Sublime in Maya Angelou's I know Why the Caged Bird Sings* outlines how solidarity in search for happiness will be sustainably fulfilling for the Negro race. The basic human essence of being kind and helpful towards others is of prime importance and a driving force.

Koubli Nouanwa in *On the Margins of National Heritage: Colonizing Conspiracy and Economic Misery in Helon Habila's Oil on Water* describes the unpatriotic leaders of the Third World whose activities and gullibility of their people with no hope to develop and liberate them from the yoke of the exploiters and neo-colonialists. The neo-colonialist regimes become demagogues using alluring expressions like: 'your situation is receiving national attention.' Yet the situation does not change as life is rife with rural exodus, juvenile delinquency, unethical and unorthodox practices. Through these deceitful fraternity relations, the neo-colonialist stays in power for life and the capitalist succeeds in improving and wielding its hegemony.

Ethel Joffi Molua Ewusi in *Santa Claus on the Cross: A Post-modernist Reading of NKengasong's God was African and Salman Rushdie's Fury* discovers that when symbols are juxtaposed and new histories are grafted, they must be negotiated in the third space, otherwise there will be a cacophony of cultures that may end up in fragmentation, ignoring their different circumstances originating from a variety of social, historical and political contexts. Rushdie's *Fury* paints the protean American society in which Indians and other nations cohabit. Various religious beliefs exist and people can navigate in any space they desire. Nkengasong's *God was African* describes how theses cultures which used to be different and distinct, took attributes of each other without completely losing their previous cultural identity nor fully adopting the new culture. There is a mixture of both the colonised and coloniser's cultures. The people of Nweh use hybrid lenses to view the changing society. During the church service in Nweh, songs were sung in English, Nweh and Latin. In this way a third space provides possibilities to open fluid spaces and reconsidering identity not as pre-given by history but as socially and discursively negotiated.

The authors of this book have crafted the various global challenges facing the world painfully and yet with some relish. Those who approach and respond to them with a literary slant present the issues to the reader so that they can be captured emotionally and understood with curiosity and concern. Those who outline and describe the challenges using certain captivating linguistic techniques cannot leave us indifferent to analyse the thrilling way people perceive and discuss the challenges at stake. These burgeoning young scholars' contributions to the troubling challenges that assail, bedevil and overwhelm our contemporary world of wonders should be savoured and saluted by their stakeholders.

Prof Paul Mbangwana
University of Yaoundé I

This book was published with partial financial assistance from the Faculty of Arts, Letters and Social Sciences of the University of Maroua.

Acknowledgements

The authors are grateful to the Scientific Committee of the Faculty of Arts, Letters and Social Sciences of the University of Maroua for funding the seminar during which the papers in this volume were presented and for partially financing this book's publication.

We equally express our special gratitude to all the colleagues who reviewed the papers published in this book.

Introduction

CAMILLA ARUNDIE TABE

NGONG JOSEPH SAM

The 21st century has recorded numerous challenges. Many issues are centred on transnational organised crime, health crisis, (notably the outbreak of cholera and Covid-19 variants), migration, global ethics, sustainable development and climate change, the status of women, democratisation, education, racism and wars. The responses to the aforementioned issues are multidimensional in that scientists, doctors, psychologists, philosophers, anthropologists and people from all walks of life have different approaches and solutions to these crises. The problems cannot be addressed by any government or institution alone. They require collaborative efforts from governments, international organisations, individuals, and scholars. Researchers in language and literature are not apathetic. They tackle these issues from their own ontological and cosmological views. In this vein, this book reacts to global challenges from the language and literature standpoints, bringing out the political, social, economic and cultural stakes and perspectives. It draws examples from Cameroon, Africa, Europe and America to highlight the importance of language and literature to solve some of the global challenges.

The contributions are grouped into two parts. Part one focuses on language and global challenges and part two centres on literature and global challenges. In the initial part devoted to language and global challenges, the first two papers emphasize the Anglophone crisis in Cameroon. Camilla Arundie Tabe writes on the role of the internet and social media in shaping and fuelling the Anglophone crisis in the English-speaking regions of Cameroon. For instance, hate speech and fake news from social media such as Facebook, WhatsApp, Instagram, YouTube and Tik Tok have driven many young men and women from the aforementioned regions to carry firearms against the Francophone-dominated regime. The youths have been brainwashed and misinformed about national cohesion by the digital setting. Fombo Emmanuel also examines the discourses of the above-mentioned crisis in Cameroon to find out the interpretation of the messages, signals and the part they play in the overall comprehension of the issues addressed by contending factions.

The following four contributions cover the Corona virus crisis. Faissam Warda observes that the Covid-19 preventive measures have been in friction with the traditional ways of behaving in Grand North Cameroon. The work examines the new face-saving techniques adapted during the Covid-19 period in greeting rituals in the Grand North of Cameroon. Michael Etuge Apuge and Abba examine Covid-19 metaphors in the printed word in English. The authors assume that metaphor is a linguistic code used by Covid-19 stakeholders in their speeches and debates to transmit messages to their audience. This chapter contends that instead of achieving the primary purpose of transmitting messages concerning the pandemic, these metaphors could create a certain psychosis to the population. Ngonjo Victor Fuh examines communication strategies used by some Christian denominations during Covid-19. Due to the coronavirus pandemic, some Christian institutions had to develop new communication strategies to strengthen a cordial relationship with their members. Joseph Nkwain illustrates many conspiracy theories concerning vaccines which have largely been acclaimed and recommended as a prompt response to the remedy. Despite this laudable scientific breakthrough, reservations from nonconformists and conservatives continue to cast doubt both on the suitability and efficacy of the vaccines and the intentions of the benefactors.

In the seventh contribution, James N. Tasah concentrates on migration as an ideal domain for investigating language dynamics that can shed light on language shift and change. In migratory contexts, migrants' language repertoires and cultural identities are often challenged as they face new socioeconomic environments and sociolinguistic needs to enhance their position in the host community. Migration as a result of the Boko Haram insurgence and the ensuing refugeeism in the Far North Region produced social and linguistic changes as some Nigerian migrants who settled in Koza had to establish a sense of belonging in the host community by adapting not only to the language(s), but also to the local cultures while remaining loyal to their Mother Tongues (MT). It is both a product of globalisation itself, and the presence of migrants in a new locality usually triggers complex linguistic and socioeconomic issues that may lead to language shift.

Moreover, Nguafac Julius and Gilbert Tagne Safotso examine major challenges facing the world today and stress the necessity of language and sincere dialogue as a solution to solve global issues if it is used suitably.

The book's second part, which focuses on literature and global issues, has six contributions. Ophilia A. Abianji-Menang dwells on critical perspectives on terrorism and freedom fighting in Helon Habila's *Oil on Water*. She reveals that a freedom fighter is often associated to a terrorist, a rebel and an insurgent by government agencies, to denote a lack of legitimacy and morality. Although these two words are used interchangeably to describe groups of people who fight for their rights and the liberation of their people through an armed struggle or conflict, this categorization continues to divide the academia over militant groups in countries where they exist.

In the following article, Etienne Langmia Forti focuses on social inequalities in South Africa. South Africa is still a divided nation due to the continued appalling socio-economic conditions of a cross section of its population. Against this backdrop, the critic thinks that such multidimensional challenges could have devastating consequences on the political endeavour to construct a multiracial democracy.

Gender inequality as a global challenge is also examined as an ongoing debate by Ngong Joseph Sam. The author thinks it may take over a hundred years for gender equality to be achieved. Most women in Africa and America have been psychologically and physically mutilated in the socioeconomic, political and cultural spheres. He postulates how male dramatists reclassify women to hold strategic positions in their plays as time is no longer on their side. The position towards women has changed drastically as examined in apartheid and post-apartheid plays. African American playwrights handle women with mixed feelings. Thus, it is observed that the conspiracy to annihilate women in male fiction functions unabated. Therefore, African and African American male writers have contributed immensely to feminist political discourse because gender remains a global challenge.

Similarly, Nye Grace Nformi reconstructs the misinterpretation by African American fictional characters from the corrosive stigma of racism in contemporary America. She assumes that the hope in the American dream is embedded in the philosophy of hard work and determination through education. Furthermore, she identifies various ways and measures African Americans seek to rebuild their identity.

Koubli Nouanwa analyses neo-colonial conspiracy. The essay is a denunciation of the western world's use of colonising multinational corporations and financial empires to establish power structures that continue to marginalise Third World countries in the name of capitalist commerce to the detriment of the colonised masses. The author holds that the colonising empires have plunged the colonised societies into chronic economic subalternity and dependency via the dominance of the International Monetary Fund and the World Bank, regarded as neo-colonialist projects and institutions. The paper further observes that what occurs to Nigeria's economic development is also the root cause of contemporary underdevelopment in the whole colonised world. Through brotherly deceitful relations, the capitalist world succeeds in impoverishing and dominating the economy of poor nations by establishing international hegemony.

The final contribution by Ethel Joffi Mulua Ewusi presents another critical view of shifting identities and characters who find it difficult to maintain a particular trend after a particular time frame. There is a cacophony of cultures as people feel free to mix cultures to an extent where some cultures lose their original connotations. However, some cultures blend perfectly while others do not. Therefore, there is a problem of identity where characters try to adjust to various shifting contexts to fit into contemporary societies.

The individual contributions highlight global challenges like terrorism, the Corona virus pandemic, migration, gender inequality and racism. The authors emphasize and analyse the issues in an agreeable style using data from specific contexts. This collection of essays is an appropriate response to global challenges by divergent and emerging voices in language and literature.

Part One

Language and Global Challenges

ONE

Inside the Virtual 'State'
A Speech Act Analysis of the Discourses of the Anglophone Problem in Cameroon

CAMILLA ARUNDIE TABE

Language is a vital tool in human interactions. It is an inseparable part of everyday life because it allows us to share our ideas, thoughts, feelings, and opinions with others as quickly as possible. Van Dijk (2014) explains that all discourses or language are produced and understood in specific communicative situations. Some groups may treat what the speakers or writers say as the truth, but for others, it may not be. In daily life, people use language to do something or influence others to do something, commonly known as the speech act. Language has the power not only to build society but also to tear it down. Nowadays, many people use language on social media to pour out their anger and melancholy, and this incites violence like in the case of the Anglophone crisis in Cameroon (see Farrington & Ttofi, 2011; Spieker et al., 2012; Bauman et al., 2013; Donoghue et al.; 2014; Maughan, & Arseneault, 2014). Language has been instrumental in expressing and displaying the various facets of the Anglophone problem on social media.

Political Background

Since the end of World War II, the nature of conflict and war has dramatically transformed and drastically increased worldwide. Some of these conflicts have been due to religious intolerance, ethnicity, struggle for political power, secession, terrorism, and the struggle over scarce natural resources (Duffield, 2014; Kaldor, 2005; Nyadera & Bincof, 2019). While conflicts have been widespread across the globe, Africa has been the victim of some of the deadliest conflicts, with some spanning over decades (Nyadera, 2018; Kacowicz, 1997; Deng, 1996).

Indeed, postcolonial African states continue to experience the challenges of establishing single national identities mainly due to the diverse nature of African societies and their colonial heritage that either exploited these differences or attempted to change the indigenous cultural identities.

The Anglophone separatist movements and claims go back to the 1970s and 1990s and re-emerged in a precarious socioeconomic and political context in Cameroon in 2016. The 11th of October 2016 marked the peak of the political crisis in the English-speaking parts of Cameroon as lawyers protested in Bamenda. The lawyers set the pace, followed by the teachers who came out on the 21st of the same month, all with sectoral demands, namely the 'intrusive appointment' of Francophone colleagues in their respective professional sectors (Okere, 2018). Their common arguments indicated that the French-speaking lawyers, magistrates, and judges lacked mastery of the English language and the sub-justice system, which is based on common law, inherited under British trusteeship. Teachers came in to assist, claiming that the French-speaking teachers were inundating the English-medium education in the two regions. These are the two corporatist demands that headed the lists of demands that rapidly grew in number (International Crisis Group, 2017; Konings & Nyamnjoh, 2015; Okere, 2018). Free thinkers believe that the lawyers' and teachers' grievances served as mechanisms for the execution of a political agenda which was then unknown until time unveiled it through the violent quest for separatism a few months later. This tested Cameroon's diplomacy as international pressures and outrage were visible. Another thing that widened the understanding of the evolution of the crisis was that there were ready-made leaders for the aspired independent Southern Cameroons who made the architecture of the movement before lawyers appeared on the street in Bamenda.

Konings and Nyamnjoh (2015, p. 207) assert that: "The political agenda in Cameroon has become increasingly dominated by what is known as the 'Anglophone problem', which poses a major challenge to the efforts of the postcolonial state to forge national unity and integration and has led to the reintroduction of forceful arguments and actions in favour of 'federalism' or even 'secession'.

From this statement, the reader may understand that the crisis was far from stopping at its embryonic stage because the Anglophone consciousness has deepened due to the erosion of some resolutions taken at the Foumban Conference in July 1961. This crack gave a chance to the uprising despite quick government responses such as the ad hoc committee to provide solutions. The ad hoc committee's task was to promote talks between the parties and bring about the Federal United Republic. Since then, the committee worked to meet that goal which to date is not fulfilled, not because it was unable to do so but because of the nature of the French colony, which always refuses federation. Other quick measures included the immediate translation of some legal texts into English, the special recruitment of one thousand bilingual teachers, and the imminent creation of the Bilingualism and Multiculturalism Commission (International Crisis Group, 2017). What followed was the declaration of independence of Ambazonia on October 1st, 2017, barely a year after the crisis re-emerged (Agwanda et al., 2020; BBC Africa, 2017).

Social media is used by the conflicting parties in the Anglophone crisis to make incongruous and competing claims. Since the outbreak of the crisis, the twist of discussions and claims has been permanent on social media. Some Cameroonian netizens have created a 'virtual state' or Ambazonia which is still imaginative or not a physically existing state but made by social media to appear so. Pro-activists have referred to it as the 'Facebook or social media republic' (see Fombo, 2021, 2022, p. 13). On these virtual platforms, individuals share the same ideas; target the ruling class with limitless verbal bullying or hate speech. The Internet brings the noises and images of the war right to the homes of the civilians who become psychologically hurt. This fuels the tensions among the population and lends a hand to the fighters who are cheered or lambasted on the screens via Facebook, Twitter, WhatsApp and somehow, Facebook Messenger.

Social media and the Anglophone problem in Cameroon

The motivation for this research stems from the Anglophone crisis, which is still raging with social media playing some influential roles wherein citizens are taking over the traditional duties of journalists in collecting and disseminating news stories (see Agwanda et al., 2020). These authors say social media has become a key component in the Anglophone conflict. They believe so because Anglophones, both at home and abroad, have used social media to advance political discussions. The diaspora based in countries such as the USA, South Africa, England, Germany, and Belgium have created chat groups that have drawn millions of Anglophone Cameroonians into disobedience towards the central government and obedience to their calls for a secession scheme (Agwanda et al., 2020). "The platforms are also used to galvanise other Anglophone Cameroonians to support the armed separatist fighters using financial donations through campaigns such as 'Adopt a Freedom Fighter' for a monthly minimum of $75 or 'Free the Nchang Shoe Boys" (Agwanda et al., 2020, p. 8).

As a medium for online communication, the internet poses challenges to privacy and security as we witness the use of hate language targeting groups and individuals. The emergence of social media and the Anglophone crisis have increased the use and spread of hate speech across Cameroon. Activists and some civilians have made Facebook and Twitter tools to spread hateful messages which erode social ties. The said users do so in the name of freedom of speech (Ngange & Tchewo, 2017; Barclays, 2018; Kweitsu & Bessong, 2019; Ngange & Mokondo, 2019).

Social media has enabled users to share their thoughts, everyday business, and personal and intellectual ideas effectively without restriction (Auwal, 2018; Darya, 2019; Mäkinen, 2019; Williams et al., 2009). However, through these tools, supporters of the Anglophone separatists are encouraged to fight not only through language but also to go to the battlefield. The fact that social media is a threat to security cannot be undermined. Revolutions have happened before the advent of social media, but what makes recent revolutions unique is how citizens communicate in moments of socio-political crisis. The media they use and how messages are broadcast instantaneously, free of deadlines and censorships typical of traditional news sources (Beaumont, 2011). In keeping with this, Agwanda et al. (2020, p. 8) note the following about the Anglophone problem:

> the extent to which social media is influencing the conflict is not yet comprehensive enough and requires further research; this entry observes that the social media platforms such as Facebook, WhatsApp, Twitter, and YouTube, have been exploited to amplify violence. The failure by the state to ensure justice for those who have been documented perpetrating violence against civilians, the state, and separatist groups have facilitated the emergence of a culture of retaliatory violence, thereby fuelling insecurity and conflict in the region.

Understanding the role of the Internet in social movements in general and the Anglophone crisis, in particular, can be helpful in our analysis. In keeping with this, Fekete and Barney (2013) found that the technologies helping distribute information and the internet have democratised the public debate in the Arab world. Their framework can help us to understand how the availability of social media and the internet has democratised the debate about secession in the Anglophone crisis. The above remark from Agwanda et al. (2020) shows that there need to be more studies on the role of social media in the conflict. Studies around the pragmatic analysis of the discourses on the Anglophone problem are also rare, so this research focuses on it.

Theoretical considerations

This study employs speech act theory to analyse social media discourse on the Anglophone problem. In any speech act, there is a message that the speaker wants to convey; it serves as a function in communication. Language use does not only produce a sentence but also performs an action. Since language is an instrument of action, this study is based on Austin's (1962) and Searle's (1969) speech act theory. The concept shows how speakers and writers "do things with words," both from locutionary, illocutionary and perlocutionary perspectives and how a written text is a discursive source of violence, discrimination, and bias.

Since the theory of speech act displays how speakers (and writers) "do things with words," Austin (1962) identifies three essential acts that are performed by speakers, namely locutionary act, uttering a sentence with no ambiguous meaning, through the grammar, phonology and semantic of a language; illocutionary act, performing an act by uttering a sentence where the real intention of the speaker is encoded either to promise, condemn, invite, incite or sentence to prison; perlocutionary act is the effect the utterance might have. The pragmatic content of any utterance relies on the illocutionary act because that is where the speaker's intention is demonstrated. This study focuses on the illocutionary and perlocutionary acts to analyse the discourses on the Anglophone problem.

Searle (1969), a student of Austin, modified Austin's speech act theory and described utterances from a slightly different perspective from his predecessor's trial of locution, illocution and perlocution. They hold that a speaker typically does four things when saying something: the utterance act, which is the act of uttering words (morphemes or sentences). Prepositional act is the act of referring and predicating, illocutionary act which includes acts of questioning, stating, ordering, and wishing and perlocutionary act which is an act of persuading or getting someone to do something.

Moreover, the theory of speech act is partly taxonomic and partly explanatory. It systematically grades types of speech acts and how they can succeed or fail. Searle (1969) also modifies Austin's classification of speech acts and comes up with five acts that may be an extension of Austin's illocutionary acts. The acts include representative, declarative, directive, expressive and commissive.

Representative or assertive speech acts commit a speaker to the truth of the expressed proposition, such as reciting, asserting, claiming, describing, concluding, reporting, suggesting, predicting, stating, etc. An example of this speech act in the context of Cameroon is: Anglophone Cameroonians got tangible solutions to their problem.

Declarative speech acts are words and expressions that change the world by their very utterance, such as 'I declare', 'I resign'. We can consider an instance related to the Anglophone crisis in Cameroon: 'I wonder whether the Anglophone problem is genuine.'

Directive speech act cause the hearer to take a particular action, such as requesting, commanding, advising, questioning, pleading, inviting, warning, etc. It is also known as imperative which Cruse (2011) says that the prototypical use of the imperative is to direct or to ask an addressee to do something. An example of this in the context of the Anglophone problem is as follows: (Please) stop the war.

Expressives include acts in which the words state the speaker's feelings, such as 'praising', 'congratulating' and 'regretting'. In Cameroon and other English-speaking contexts, we often say *Sorry* or *I am sorry* to indicate that we regret something we have done to someone.

Commissives are speech acts that commit a speaker to some future action, such as promising, threatening, offering, guaranteeing, vowing, betting, challenging and volunteering (Cutting, 2002). For example, if you encourage Cameroonians to stop the crisis, I will appoint you to a superior position.

Verdictives are speech acts in which the speaker makes an assessment or judgement about the acts of another, usually the addressee. These include ranking, assessing, appraising, and condoning. For example, 'You are first!

Performatives are acts that require the hearer to perform or do something a speaker orders. For instance, 'I order you to go out.' Behabitive speech act includes the notion of reaction to other people's behaviour and fortunes and of attitudes and expressions to someone else's past conduct or imminent conduct (Austin, 1962).

The analysis of data focuses on these speech acts. We will show how they are employed through certain expressions to signal accusations, threats, verbal bullying, hate speech inciting violence and intimidation. Their use in this study enables the reader to understand the discourse of the Anglophone crisis in Cameroon.

Literature review

This work examines how people use social media language to talk about the Anglophone problem in Cameroon. Several researchers have investigated the crisis from different dimensions. The following paragraphs present the literature on the Anglophone crisis in Cameroon.

The outbreak of the socio-political upheaval sparked the use of hate speech targeting individuals and the elite, and this was of interest to some researchers

(Barrack-Yousefi, 2018; Fombo, 2021, 2022; Kweitsu & Besong, 2019; Sawalda, 2020; Sombaye, 2018; Tasah & Sawalda, 2021). The researchers collected social media posts from activists and other Cameroonians living at home and abroad. In addition to internet posts, Sombaye interviewed Cameroonians living at home and in the diaspora. The researchers found the spread of hate speech and fake news related to the crisis on the internet. The researchers' findings show that hate speech is seen as a powerful tool with which the Cameroonian diaspora and separatists threaten national cohesion and development. Their results are similar to that of Alakali, Faga and Mbursa (2016); Elliott et al. (2016), Okpara and Chukwu (2019), who hold that hate speech has negative impacts on national unity. Elliott et al. (2016) argued that the issue of hate speech becomes more salient and prevalent during political and/or economic upheavals. Alakali et al. (2016) show that many people understand the implications of hate speech. However, they do not understand its legal consequences, such as loss of credibility, diverting media from fulfilling their primary role of serving the public interest and increasing moral decadence. All the scholars hold that hate speech has taken on xenophobic, political, religious and cultural forms.

In addition to the above, researchers (Kweitsu & Besong, 2019; Chukwuebuka, 2015; Salome & Barrach-Yousefi, 2018) have noted that violence attributed to online hate speech has increased not only in Cameroon but also worldwide. Hate speech has caused a global increase in violence towards minorities, including mass shootings, lynching and ethnic cleansing (Kweitsu & Besong, 2019; Chukwuebuka, 2015). Salome and Barrach-Yousefi (2018) found that social media is a fertile field where hate speech is increasingly being used; its contribution to the escalation of protests, such as the Anglophone crisis, is tremendous as the success of online activism greatly relies on offline action. The use of small media greatly complements social media use as platforms for alternative discourse. Moreover, it has been revealed that hate speech in Cameroon, as in other contexts, is used as a tool to achieve political ends such as polarising opinions, dehumanising opponents, exacerbating feelings of frustration and hate, and enticing violence (Barrach-Yousefi, 2018). All the researchers on hate speech discussed so far have recommended that there should be awareness as to what constitutes hate speech and that a monitoring mechanism agency should be put in place to identify and remove hate speech content from social media platforms.

Furthermore, the language used to report the socio-political crisis in the two English-speaking regions of Cameroon in newspapers motivated Tabe and Fieze (2018) and Ouamba (2018) to analyse newspaper headlines and articles critically. Through Critical Discourse Analysis (CDA) of 130 headlines from 16 private newspapers and one public newspaper (*Cameroon Tribune*), Tabe and Fieze (2018) suggest that the crisis reverberates in the media landscape through a war of words. On one side, the private newspapers are using boosters, verbal bullying and metaphors to discredit the leadership of the elite and tarnish the images of some individual political figures. The headlines on news-making stories are coined to create terror, horror, and violence in the minds of the readers or viewers; this aims to set the people against the government, which is accused of mishandling not only the armed conflict but also the mismanagement of the affairs. On the other side, *Cameroon Tribune* uses soft speech and mild language to downplay the outrage in the discourse, calm public opinion, and promote dialogue. Their data indicate that this government mouthpiece is the only newspaper with the highest use of words suggestive of dialogue. This interaction between physical and verbal tension, they think, worsens the unrest. The researchers suggest that fixing the language used by the competing and influential claims in the narratives on the situation can take some miles forward to its solution.

Moreover, the language used to present the Anglophone crisis in newspapers in the Northwest and Southwest of Cameroon motivated Ouamba (2018) to analyse metaphors. Through metaphor identification procedure (MIP) of 75 articles dealing with the Anglophone crisis, her study revealed that English-speaking Cameroonian newspapers mostly use the words *crisis, situation* and *conflict* as target domain-related words to refer to the events happening in those two English-speaking regions of Cameroon. Her study also unveiled the use of metaphorical expressions, among which the most predominant were *The Anglophone crisis is war, natural disaster, human being, disease* and *animal*. Regarding these metaphorical expressions, it could be said that newspaper owners are building in Cameroonians' minds the image of a destructive and disastrous crisis sponsored mainly by diaspora Cameroonians.

The Anglophone problem has also been studied from an educational perspective (Akame et al., 2021), geopolitical and rhetorical perspective (Ascone & Renaut, 2019; Ekah, 2019). These studies reveal that for children in the Anglophone zones to continue their education amidst the violence and disruption, they were relocated to neighbouring towns in the French-speaking parts of the country or to other relatively safe urban areas of the Anglophone regions. Moreover, the strategic location of the Northwest and Southwest, the presence of natural resources, demographic considerations and other geopolitical parameters are proving to be responsible for the heightening of the Anglophone crisis in Cameroon and in favour of the quest for an independent 'Ambazonia.'

The above review shows that some scholars have investigated hate speech related to the Anglophone problem, and some have studied newspaper headlines and articles on the crisis. However, linguistic works on the crisis, especially from the pragmatics dimension, still need improvement. The present study will, therefore, be a necessary addition to the literature.

Data and method

The corpus for this study comprises e-messages collected through screenshots of Anglophone Cameroonians' online communication from Facebook (FBK) and Twitter (TWT). These messages were sampled and collected between 2016 and 2021. Table 1.1 presents the corpus composition.

Table 1.1. Corpus composition

Platforms	Participants	2016	2017	2018	2019	2020	2021	Total number of e-messages
Facebook	150	56	60	58	35	40	51	300
Twitter	100	43	41	20	40	21	35	200
Total	250	99	101	78	75	61	86	500

Table 1.1 shows that 500 e-messages were collected from 250 informants by male (150) and female (100) users in the selected platforms. The messages were collected through screenshots. The researcher collected some of the messages herself and others with the help of field assistants. We contacted some Anglophone Cameroonians and pleaded with them to screenshot their messages related to the Anglophone problem and send them to us for research purposes. The majority accepted and sent us the data.[1] Samples of the collected screenshots are presented in Figure 1.1, and more are found in Appendix I.

The extracts used as examples are presented the way they appeared on the chats or e-messages, and some indiscretions in spelling and usage are not those of the researcher. In addition, names on screenshots have been blotted for ethical reasons. The messages were also coded for ease of reference in the analysis. Those from Facebook were coded as FBK01 to FBK300; those from Twitter had TWT01 to TWT200. This study follows a thematic analysis, considered appropriate for any study that seeks to discover the use of interpretations, particularly the pragmatics of the discourses, which is needed to analyse the language of

---

1 No Twitter or Facebook collection tool was used to obtain data. It was not possible for fear of not having appropriate data related to the Anglophone problem. In addition, the researcher is not familiar with the tools.

the Anglophone crisis. The researcher examined the expressions and categorised them following what they indicate and the speech acts they portray. The analysis of data considers the quantitative and qualitative approaches. The former deals with the statistical presentation of the screenshots (messages), and the latter describes the expressions and their functions. MS Excel was used to calculate the percentages of the recorded items.

Figure 1.1. Samples of some screenshots from Facebook and Twitter.

The extracts are presented as they appeared on the chats or e-messages

It is New Year! Cameroon still remains a tinderbox with regional crisis at its door steps. Biya the dictator and his junta sitting steadfast recruiting over 5000 thugs to "protect" the Cameroon territory. Absolutely false! This move is to strengthen his grip on power! What most Dictators don'... See More

Batibo takes to Street as 5 are shot in Mamfe, 2 in Santa. Reports of two killed so far from gun shots. Paul Biya must stop fooling himself. Guns will not resolve this problem.

We are not Francophones; we are not cowards. We are not Bamis; we will never give up. We are Ambazonians! We rise, we resist and we fight! - with **Yannick Sicot** and **5 others**.

Banana republic of Biya turns our young pipo into sex entertainers 😭 😭. @UN watches n celebrate while we are pain?! #Ambazonians must definitely be freed!

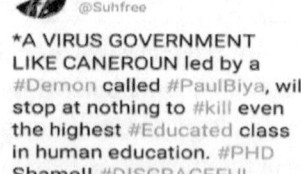

@Suhfree

*A VIRUS GOVERNMENT LIKE CANEROUN led by a #Demon called #PaulBiya, will stop at nothing to #kill even the highest #Educated class in human education. #PHD Shame!! #DISGRACEFUL

Mimi Mefo Info @Mimimefo237 · 1d
Police officials in Y'de #Cameroon have brutally descended on striking Doctorates and PhD holders in front of the ministry of Higher Education.

Tweet your reply

All these atrocities happen because of one man, Paul Biya the terrorist. Your days are numbered. You will be hanged in front of your family. You killed my sister & brother. You will have no peace, Biya. We shall see where you will be buried.

22:55 · 16 May 18 · Twitter for iPhone

Analysis

The data reveal that the discourses on the Anglophone problem on Twitter and Facebook are full of hate speech (HS) that signals the following: verbal bullying, accusation, threats, intimidation, violence and tension. These are captured through directive, verdictive, commissive, assertive and performative speech acts. There was also offensive language directed at individuals and groups of people. More on the speech acts found in the data is given in the following sub-sections.

Directive Speech Act

The directive speech act is depicted in the data through hate speech that signals verbal bullying, and it is the most prevalent with 38.40%. Following the directive speech act, which posits that an utterance causes the hearer to take a particular action, it should be noted that directives are issued with the desire that the hearer should do what is proposed; should change the world according to the uttered propositional content. Directives such as orders and requests cannot be true or false but can be obeyed, disobeyed, complied with, granted, and denied. The threads of discussions below show instances of hate speech that indicate verbal bullying:

> *Those idiots who said there is no Anglophone problem.... Hmmmm...* (December 1, 2016-FBK26-Male)
> *The vampire was caught by the camera doing what we all know he knows best.* (October 8, 2016-FBK62-Male) *Shameless Mousonge and other sell out Southern West elites stand next to a murderer deciding their own destiny.* (September 26, 2019-FBK229-Male)
> *A virus government like Cameroon led by a Demon called Paul biya, will stop to nothing to kill even the highest educated class in human education. PHD Shame!!* (September 29, 2018-TWT78-Male) *Stupid! instead of calling for massive bullets, idiots want massive ballots.* (April 15, 2018-TWT112-Female)

Words or expressions like *Those idiots, The vampire, Shameless, A virus government, Demon, Stupid* are some utterances from Anglophone Cameroonians to express that they have been disappointed by political leaders. They use these words on social media to intimidate individuals and the government.

Verdictive Speech Act

The verdictive speech act is seen in the corpus through hate speech related to accusations, and it comes in the second position with 32.80%. Bearing in mind the claims of the verdictive speech act, which says that we can do an action with a word, it can be said that the utterers of the samples of hate speech below call for actions from both the audience and the persons targeted. To an extent, they act as judges and bring opinions to conflict and people to dive into tensions. The messages indicate more actions than simple utterances; a close look at the excerpts shows that the persons or individuals targeted by the hate language are either nicknamed or qualified in exaggerated terms; more importantly, the sentences seek to give bad images to the people targeted and incite the readers to commit violence. See the examples below:

>(6) *Biya the dictator and his junta sitting steadfast recruiting over 5000 thugs to «protect» the Cameroon territory. Absolutely false! This move is to strengthen his grip on power! Dictator* (January 1, 2016-FBK14-Male) (7) *The brutal Paul Biya regime is causing havoc in Buea and its environs.* (November 10, 2016-FBK28-Male) (8) *Dictator Paul Biya and his brutal soldiers are killing southern Cameroonians with no remorse.* (February 12, 2017-TWT28-Fale)
>(9) *Dictator Paul Biya has shutdown internet 4 more than 1 month* (January 5, 2017-TWT32-Male) (10) *Paul Biya's Election Rigging Machine ELECAM using Uni. of Buea Students as a Disguise for Registration* (August 18, 2017-TWT76-Male) (11) *The Catholic Church is a criminal enterprise and guilty for 600 years of rape and genocide!* (September 4, 2018-TWT119-Male) Words like *dictator, brutal soldiers, havoc, killings* and *genocide*, are examples of inciting terms pushing the accumulation of tensions and the inflammation of the Anglophone conflict. The individuals or organisations targeted are accused of various mischiefs.

Commissive Speech Act

The commissive speech act is portrayed through offensive language that signals threats which is the third highest in the data with just 8.80%. It is worth mentioning that the commissive speech act commits the speaker to perform some future course of action. The speech act of threatening differs from promising in that the undertaking is not to do something for the benefit of the hearer but instead to his detriment. It can be understood that the speakers of the samples of hate speech below are threatening and frustrating the readers or hearers of these utterances:

>(12) *Southern Cameroon holding top position in Biya's gov't are the cause o tour mesiry. I therefore suggest that there should be given 3days*

maximum to resign and return home or may there never comeback. In this case, their homes should be burnt and their families exile if not kil. We can't be feelings the pains all alone. I Oscao approve this message (December 10, 2016-FBK17-Male) (13) *Paul Biya must stop fooling Amba. Guns will not resolve this problem.*
(September 22, 2017-FBK37-Male)
(14) *Paul Biya is an old dictator. He must leave Ambazonias alone if not Amba boys will deal with him.* (July 30, 2017-TWT60-Female)
(15) *This Paul is really a joke. Doing away from the problem and think it will just go away. You lie. The resolve of Anglophones is greater than those fake and baseless commissions you keep creating.* (December 3, 2018-TWT81-Male)
(16) *Paul Biya of la republic should know one thing British southern Cameroon Ambazonia will fight till end* (December 4, 2018-TWT39-Male)

Words such as *resign, burnt down to ashes, exile, kill, must stop fooling, must leave, fight till end* unveil the inclination of Anglophone separatists vis-à-vis the state of Cameroon, the leaders and their staff. To the Anglophones, how the leaders rule the country pushes them to violence and threats. As a result, some show their extremism and hostility against the state and political leaders. This can be read through the threads of discussions above.

Assertive Speech Act

The assertive speech act is perceived in the corpus through offensive language that shows intimidation, representing just 4% of the data. Assertive being a type of illocutionary point, states one's belief to be the case or not. Speakers achieve the assertive point when representing how things are (Kubo & Vanderveken, 2001). The following extracts exemplify the assertive speech act:

(17) *Let it be known that Elvis Ngolle Ngolle & Atanga Paul Nji are not representatives and do not represent the opressed and victimised people.* (November 29, 2016-FBK11-Male)
(18) *Mr. Biya we fought the Germans with all our might...defeated them in battles with meager resources! Reinforcement came from Germany and they wondered about our breed! we fought till the last man standing! This is 2016 and Southern Cameroon people will fight your French proxy «army» with even more sophisticated weapons ans we will win! We have the right to self Defense! We will not sit and watch*

> as our children are being massacred by your thuas. (December 10, 2016-FBK20-Male) (19) *ATANGA NJI YOU'LL GET A TASTE OF BAMENDA! COME OUT FROM YOUR HIDING PLACE NOW. NYAAM! STUPID COWARD!!!* (July 17, 2018-FBK122-Male) (20) *We are not Francophones; we are not cowards. We are not Bamis! We never give up. We are Ambazonians! We rise, we resist and we fight! –with Yanick Sicot and 5others.* (February 3, 2018-FBK199-Male)

Excerpts such as the ones above express the confidence of the Anglophone Cameroonians. In so doing, they threaten or intimidate the individuals and the government.

Behabitive Speech Act

With just 3.20% of the data, the behabitive speech act is portrayed through hate speech that hints at violence. Knowing that Behabitive speech acts are expressions of attitudes toward the conducts, fortunes, or attitudes of others, it is noteworthy to consider the following words or expressions as guns to shoot the hearer. They incite the reader to violence. See the excerpts below:

> (21) *Guinean president Alpha Condé wonders how on eath Camerooinans are putting up with an absentee president, who spends most of his time in luxury hotels and golf courses in Europe, and at times go for 6,7 months without holding a cabinet meeting. In his best attempt, president Conde tries to answer the puzzle as to why there has not been coup d'etat in Cameroon since 84.* (October 18, 2016-FBK8-Male) (22) *Beat him! Slap him!* (May 4, 2017-FBK47-Male) (23) *in Yaounde. If they refuse, we will come along with guns* (March 2, 2018-FBK99-Male)

When we consider words or expressions such as: *Beat him! Slap him!, I repeat that we shall march, we will come along with guns; it* can be said that some Anglophone Cameroonians incite violence and frustrate the hearer. It can be seen here that words and expressions are not only bearers of meaning but also used as guns to threaten individuals and the hearer.

Performative Speech Act

The performative speech act, which is 2.4% of the data, is seen through offensive language that signals tension. Through what the speakers say, they push the hearers to do something. Such hate language includes those given in examples (24) and (25):

> (24) *How can Atanga Nji sack Edith kah walla of the CPP and appoint his perferred president of that part?* (November 16, 2018-FBK244-Male) *(25) Horrible! Cameroon terrorists (soldiers of the Terrorist Biya Regime) shoot a house wife in her legs after breaking into her home in the city of Buea, Ambazonia.* (September 29, 2018-TWT121-Male)

The e-messages presented above can cause tension and adverse reactions from the public. The prevalence of offensive speech on both Twitter and Facebook to report the Anglophone crisis shows that the interactants are out to aggravate the crisis. A summary of the hate speech, what they signal, and the frequencies are presented in Table 1.2.

Table 1.2. Percentage of offensive speech on Facebook and Twitter

Platforms	Offensive language					
	Verbal bullying (directive speech act)	Accusation (verdictive speech act)	Threats (comissive speech act)	Intimidation (assertive speech act)	Violence (behabitive speech act)	Tension (performative speech act)
Facebook	15.20%	7.60%	04%	02%	3.20%	0.4%
Twitter	23.20%	25.20%	04.80%	02%	00%	02%
Total	38.40%	32.80%	08.80%	04%	3.20%	2.40%

Facts gleaned from Table 1.2 show that most of the messages collected from Facebook and Twitter for this research contain verbal bullying (38.40%), which is the most used hate language to promote conflictual relations on social media. This conflictual language is further followed in rate by accusations (32.80%); threats (08.80%); intimidation (04%); violence (3.20%), and tension (2.40%).

It is worth mentioning that out of the 500 e-messages sampled, 209 contain hate speech. One hundred and forty-seven of this offensive language were retrieved from Twitter, making it the platform with the highest rate of hate speech. 25.20% of the e-messages on Twitter signal accusations compared to 7.60% for Facebook. Verbal bullying registered 23.20% on Twitter and 15.20% on Facebook. 4.80% hate speech related to threats was also found on Twitter messages, as against 4% for Facebook. Hate speech directed to targeted groups and those focusing on individuals occurred only on Twitter, with 0.80% and 0.4%, respectively.

The analysis of the linguistic features indicates that most of the discourses on the Anglophone problem found on social media are fraught with hate speech; the discussions are propaganda of hatred, calls for disunity, calls to rampage, calls to kill or commit any other form of violence, insults, threats, intimidation and verbal bullying. Mafeza (2016), citing the American Bar Association, claims that most of the time, hate speech is based on disputes, tribal, racial, religious, political, and cultural differences targeting an individual or a group of people. It is a war of words that prepares for carnage, civil war or genocide, as in Rwanda's case, which was sparked by an incendiary radio broadcast (Mafeza, 2016; Scheffler, 2015). According to Scheffler (2015), it is an imminent threat to peace and security.

Biblically speaking, there is power in words; the world where we live was created and stands by the power of words (see Genesis Chap. 1). Therefore, it is subject to the effects of words that can tear it down or protect it. What people say can bless or curse, lead to death or life (Proverbs, 18:21). In the context of this inquiry into the discourses of the Anglophone problem on social media in Cameroon, we observed that all began with an increased screen time of the millions of subscribers in Cameroon while propagating violence and invectives towards the central government and some key figures in the management of the state affairs. This paved the way for the regrettable and horrendous bloodshed on the side of the separatist fighters and the state forces, with the population caught in the middle. The Anglophone crisis is fuelled by hate speech; studying the discourses on the crisis needs scrutiny on the use of hate language. The role of social media in the overall comprehension and evolution of the Anglophone problem cannot be overlooked. The masses are kept abreast of how the conflict is evolving through social media messages, images and videos. Most of the time, the crisis is fuelled by what is posted on social media. This includes hate speech, dehumanising language and outright incitement to tension and violence, which are some strategies that activists use intentionally to hurt people and incite them to war. They always use diction that propels people to revolt against the regime in power.

Conclusion

The analysis has shown that the architects of hatred and violence carefully select their words to overpower the reasoning of naïve readers. Without the inclusion of social media platforms and hate speech, the unwanted war in the said zones would not have imposed the calamity witnessed for many years. The hate messages have jeopardised national security and stability. Among some of the workable solutions to curb the spread of hate speech on social media from a linguistic perspective, there is the possibility that the government, in partnership with Facebook and Twitter authorities, could filter messages that contain HS and destroy them. The masses should also be educated on the appropriate use of words and expressions on social media to foster peace, stability and development in the country.

Abstract

Internet and social media have become fixtures in people's lives. They are believed to be tools for advancing freedom of speech, political participation and democracy. The digital setting is overloaded with tolerant and hate speeches, fake news, and facts. Against this background, this paper examines the discourses of the Anglophone problem in Cameroon to find out what the messages signal and their role in the overall comprehension of the problem. The author emphasises how speakers and writers do things with words from locutionary, illocutionary and perlocutionary perspectives. Data for this study are collected exclusively from English-speaking Cameroonians. Five hundred e-messages were collected from Anglophone Cameroonians - 300 from Facebook and 200 from Twitter. The quantitative and qualitative analysis showed that the discourses on the Anglophone problem signal verbal bullying, intimidation, and dialogue between the government and Anglophone Cameroonians among communities and individuals. It was discovered that Twitter and Facebook help disseminate hate speech nationwide. Social media spreads offensive, intimidating, denigrating, frustrating, and humiliating statements that can hurt the target persons or groups psychologically and emotionally. In conclusion, social media platforms serve as public hideouts where the inciters of mass atrocities operate and go unpunished; the propaganda of hate is seen to be an undeniable precursor of mass violence occurring in the two English-speaking regions of Cameroon. The study recommends that the government restrict social media use as a necessity for peace and stability.

Keywords: Anglophone problem, discourse, Facebook, Twitter, speech act.

References

Agwanda, B., Nyadera, I. N. & Asal, U. Y. (2020). Cameroon and the Anglophone crisis. In O. Richmond & G. Visoka (Eds.), *The Palgrave Encyclopedia of Peace and Conflict Studies*.

Akame, G.J, Crockett, J. & Awutarh, R. B.A. (2021). *Baseline research: Education in crisis in the Anglophone regions of Cameroon*. London: Solidarity and Development Initiative.

Alakali, T. T., Faga, H.P. & Mbursa, J. (2017). Audience perception of hate speech and foul language in the social media in Nigeria: Implication for morality and law. *Academicus International Scientific Journal, 15*, 166-183.

Allan, S. (2013). *Citizen witnessing: Revisioning journalism in time of crisis.* London: Polity.

Ascone, L. & Renaut, L. (2019). *How conflict is verbalized in counter-narratives to jihadist Discourse: A comparative approach to hate speech in Asia and Europe.* Paris: University of Paris.

Austin, J. L. (1962). *How to do things with words.* Cambridge: Harvard University Press.

Auwal, A. M. (2018). Social media and hate speech: Analysis of comments on Biafra agitations, Arewa youths ultimatum and their implications on peaceful coexistence in Nigeria. *MCC, 2(1), 54-73.*

Bauman, S., Toomey, R. B. & Walker, J. L. (2013). Associations among bullying, Cyberbullying, and suicide in high school students. *Journal of Adolescence, 36*(2), 341-350.

Barclay, D. A. (2018). *Fake news, propaganda and plain old lies: How to find trustworthy information in the digital age.* Washington: Rowman & Littlefield.

Barrach-Yousefi, N. (2018). *Social media and conflict in Cameroon: A lexicon of hate Speech terms.* Washington: US Institute of Peace.

BBC Africa (2017). Deaths in Cameroon Independence Pools, October 2. Retrieved from https://www.bbc.cm. world Africa-4161007

Beaumont, P. (2011). The truth about Twitter, Facebook and the uprising in the Arab world. *The Guardian*, February 25.

Chukwuebuka, E. C. (2015). *Hate speech and electoral violence in Nigeria.* Nsukka: University of Nsukka, Nigeria.

Cutting, J. (2002). *Pragmatics and discourse: A resource book for students.* London: Routledge.

Cruse, A. (2011). *Meaning in language: An introduction to semantics and pragmatics.* Oxford: Oxford University Press.

Darya, N. (2019). *Freedom of expression and hate speech in the law case of the European court of human rights and in the practice of social media.* (Unpublished Master's dissertation). Universität Wien.

Deng, F. M. (1996). *Anatomy of conflicts in Africa. In between development and destruction.* London: Palgrave Macmillan.

Donoghuea, C., Almeidab, A., Brandweinb, D., Rochac, G. & Callahana, I. (2014). Coping with verbal and social bullying in middle school. *The International Journal of Emotional Education, 6*(2), 40-53.

Duffield, M. (2014). *Global governance and the new wars: The merging of development and security.* London & New York: Zed Books.

Elliott, C., Chuma, W., El Gendi, Y., Marko, D. & Patel, A. (2016). *Hate speech: Key concept paper.* Working paper. MeCoDEM. (unpublished). http://eprints. whiterose.

ac.uk/117296/

Ekah, R. E. (2019). The Anglophone crisis in Cameroon: A geopolitical analysis. *European Scientific Journal, 15* (35), 141- 166.

Fekete, E. & Barney, W. (2013). Information technology and the Arab spring. *Arab World Geographer, 16*(2), 210-227.

Fombo, E. (2021). A speech act analysis of hate posts on the Anglophone crisis by Cameroonian activists. *International Journal of Humanitatis Theoreticus, 5(2), 62-79.*

Fombo, E. (2022). Aspects of hate speech on Cameroon social media. (Unpublished PhD thesis). Postgraduate School for Literatures, Languages and Sciences of Languages, The University of Maroua.

Fonchingong, T. (2013). The quest for autonomy: The case of Anglophone Cameroon. *African Journal of Political Science and International Relations, 7*(5), 224-236.

Giora, R. (1997). Understanding figurative and literal language: The graded salience hypothesis. *Cognitive Linguistics, 8(*3), 183-206.

Giora, R. (2003). *On our mind: Salience, context and figurative language.* Oxford: Oxford University Press.

International Crisis Group. (2017). Anglophone crisis at crossroads, crisis group Africa report No 250, 2 August 2017.

Kacowicz, A. M. (1997). 'Negative' international peace and domestic conflicts, West Africa, 1957-96. *The Journal of Modern African Studies, 35*(3), 367-385.

Kaldor, M. (2005). Old wars, cold wars, new wars, and the war on terror. *International Politics, 42*(4), 491-498.

Kecskes, I. (2010). Situation-bound utterances as pragmatic acts. *Journal of Pragmatics, 42*(1), 2889-2897.

Konings, P. & Nyamnjoh, B. F. (2015). The Anglophone problem in Cameroon. *The Journal of Modern African Studies, 35,* 207-229.

Kubo & Vanderveken, D. (2001). *Essays in speech act theory.* Amsterdam: John Benjamin Publishing Company.

Kweitsu, R. & Besong, B. M. (2019). *Hate speech and violent conflict in Cameroon.* Yaoundé: Local Youth Corner Cameroon Publication.

Lunn, J & Brooke-Holland, L. (2019). *The Anglophone Cameroon crisis.* London: House of Commons Library.

Mäkinen, E. K. (2019). Words are actions. More efficient measures against hate speech and cyberbullying. *Ministry of the Interior Finland, 27(8), 9-15.*

Mey, J. (2001). *Pragmatics: An introduction* (2nd ed.). New York: Blackwell.

Mutsvairo, B. (2016). *The Palgrave Handbook of media and communication research in Africa.* London: Palgrave Macmillan.

Nyadera, I. N. (2018). South Sudan conflict from 2013 to 2018: Rethinking the causes, situation and solutions. *African Journal on Conflict Resolution, 18*(2), 59-86.

Okpara, O. & Chukwu, E. M. (2019). Hate speech in Nigeria and its implication for national Cohesion. *International Journal of Humanities and Social Science, 9*(5), 184-190.

Okere, N. G. (2018). Analysing Cameroon's Anglophone crisis. *International Centre for Political Violence and Terrorism Research, 10*(3), 8-12.

Ouamba, T. S. R. (2018). *The study of Anglophone crisis related metaphors in some selected Cameroonian newspapers.* (Unpublished Master's Dissertation). Faculty of Arts, Letters and Social Sciences, University of Maroua.

Ngange, K. L. & Mokondo, M. S. (2019). Understanding social media's role in propagating Falsehood in conflict situations: Case of the Cameroon Anglophone crisis. *Studies in Media and Communication, 7*(2), 55- 67.

Ngange, K., & Tchewo, M. (2017). ICT use in teaching, research and outreach in the University of Buea, Cameroon. In K. Langmia, & T. Tia, (Eds), *social media: Culture and Identity*. Lanham: Lexington Books.

Nyadera, I. N., & Bincof, M. O. (2019). Human security, terrorism, and counterterrorism: Boko Haram and the Taliban. *International Journal on World Peace, 36*(1), 7-32

Sawalda, D. M. (2020). The use of online hate speech: A pragmatic perspective of the case of some Cameroonian diaspora activists. (Unpublished Master's Dissertation). FALSS, The University of Maroua, Cameroon.

Sombaye, J. R. E. (2018). *Inside the virtual Ambazonia: Separatism, hate Speech, disinformation and Cameroonian diaspora in the Anglophone Crisis.* (Unpublished Master's of Art Dissertation). Department of International Studies, University of San Francisco.

Salome, A. N. (2018). *Social media and small media use during the Anglophone crisis in Cameroon.* (Unpublished Master's Dissertation). Faculty of Culture and Society, Malmö University.

Searle, J. (1969). *Speech acts: An essay in the philosophy of language.* Cambridge: Cambridge University Press.

Sevasti, C. (2014). *Social media and political communication: Hate speech in the age of Twitter.* (Master of Arts Dissertation). Erasmus school of History, Culture and Communication: Erasmus University of Rotterdam.

Spieker, S. J., Campbell, S. B., Vandergrift, N., Pierce, K. M., Cauffman, E. & Susman (2012). Relational aggression in middle childhood: Predictors and adolescent outcomes. *Social Development 21*(2), 354-375.

Tabe, C. A. & Fieze, N. I. (2018). A critical discourse analysis of newspaper headlines on the Anglophone crisis in Cameroon. *British Journal of English Linguistics, 6*(3), 64-83.

Takizawa, R., Maughan, B., & Arseneault, L. (2014). Adult health outcomes of childhood bullying victimization: Evidence from a five-decade longitudinal British birth cohort. *American Journal of Psychiatry, 171,* 777-784.

Tasah, J. N. & Sawalda, M. D. (2021). Hate speech: A Pragmatic-stylistic reading of online Cameroonian activists. *Educational Research Journal*, 11(6), 102-108.

Ttofi, M. M., & Farrington, D. P. (2011). Effectiveness of school-based programs to reduce bullying: A systematic and meta-analytic review. *Journal of Experimental Criminology*, 7(1), 27-56.

Van Dijk, T. A. (2014). *Discourse and knowledge: A sociocognitive approach*. Cambridge: Cambridge University Press.

Williams, K., Boyd, A., Densten, S., Chin, R., Diamond, D. & Morgenthaler, C. (2009). *Social networking privacy behaviours and risks*. Pennsylvania: The Pennsylvania State University.

World Association for Christian Communication: Media and conflict in Cameroon today. Retrieved from https//:www/.waccglobal.org/articles/media-and conflict-in-Cameroon-today on 26 October 2021

TWO

Memes, Deep Fake Images of Public Figures and Hate Captions on the Anglophone Crisis on Facebook

FOMBO EMMANUEL

Words and images circulated on social media can be critical in shaping the public's attitudes and thoughts, especially in a crisis (Mahhyoop et al., 2020, p. 99). Memes and deep fakes (face swap) are artificial intelligence (AI) that producers create to represent reality. They portray something as if it appears in real life when, in fact, it never occurred (Graber, 2021, p. 4). Images are sometimes used to convince the receivers to believe something that does not exist or paint a negative or positive face of the target person. Such images seem to have been used in the context of this study to support the Anglophone crisis and the claim of the Southern Cameroons/Ambazonian independence struggle. The circulation of memes and deep fake images of President Paul Biya and others in the target situation may show how the country's democracy, peace and unity are threatened by artificial intelligence (AI) technology.

Research has revealed that deep fakes may harm democracy, including sowing division, undercutting public safety, constraining democracy and attacking national security (Chesney & Citron, 2021, p. 10). Therefore, memes and deep fake images may be abuses used to cause tension and violence or create chaos in times of crisis. Moreover, such images may cause distress and negative effects on those targeted. It may also heighten disinformation and hate speech both online and offline. Besides intensifying tension in crisis, it may even stimulate political tension, violence and mislead the general public (Nguyen et al., 2021, p. 1). They can also distort the viewer's memory. Ice (2019, p. 428) outlines eight potential harms to society resulting from deep fakes: distortion of democratic discourse, manipulation of elections, eroding trust in institutions, exacerbating social divisions, undermining public safety, undermining diplomacy, jeopardising national security, and undermining journalism.

The images disseminated on Cameroon social media landscape to target the Anglophone crisis seem to include the harms outlined by Chesney and Citron above. Concerning the potential harms mentioned above, the aim of the essay is to analyse the modalities (visual elements), hate captions and text description used to describe the images and to see how the linguistic elements used to describe the images can be a powerful tool used humorously to ridicule the target persons and how they have or may intensify the Anglophone crisis in Cameroon. From the above introductory highlights, this chapter is guided by the following questions:
1. What linguistic features are used through memes and deep fake images to provoke the disinformation campaign in the Anglophone crisis?
2. How are the modalities, text descriptions, visual contents and linguistic elements structured to shape and fuel the fire of the Anglophone crisis?

Background to the study

Meme and deep fake refer to ideas, behaviour, or styles that spread from person to person within a culture. The term meme was coined by the British ethnologist and evolutionary biologist, Dawkins in his landmark work, *The Selfish Gene*, (Ondřej, 2016, p. 8). Memes and deep fakes have gained massive popularity over the past years on Facebook. Even though memes and deep fakes are often regarded as harmless and generated especially for humour, they have also been used to produce and disseminate hate speech in times of crisis. Under such conditions, they attack target persons based on their personalities. Though the Cameroon social media landscape witnessed memes and deep fake images before the outbreak of the Anglophone crisis in 2016, the crisis has intensified its spread. The crisis has been at the root cause of such images, primarily targeting top personalities and other citizens associated with the Anglophone crisis.

Linguistic Features in Memes and Deep Fake Images

The linguistic features on memes and deep fakes cannot be ignored because they manifest the power of language for communication, value, beliefs and people's lifestyles. The language used on images is literal as the producer uses them and represents the language in which thoughts are expressed. This is because they allow us to identify the linguistic patterns of language represented differently in social space for different purposes. Moreover, an image generally is a mode of linguistic communication within a particular context, including specific linguistic levels and artistic ways to convey a message. This may provide data sources for linguistic analysis, including grammar, lexical words, and other linguistic patterns. In this study, one would likely see various visual communicative features accompanied by visual and linguistic features. Under such a situation, particular words are chosen for the desired purpose, which can influence the audiences' thoughts toward the images, persons targeted in the images and the situation the producer may indirectly refer to.

Related Studies and Theoretical Framework

Hate speech is a widely studied topic in the social sciences. This phenomenon has been monitored, tracked, measured or quantified several times. It appears in print media such as newspapers or magazines and traditional media such as radio broadcasts and TV news. Moreover, hate speech with remarkably diverse targets has appeared on social networks. In a study conducted on the meanings of lifestyle memes in English, Permata (2018, p. 90) holds that internet memes also have the power to influence social beliefs, ideas, perceptions and values significantly. The researcher analysed symbols conveyed by the memes' images to reveal their hidden meanings. From the analysis, the researcher found that the image and the caption have significant roles in creating the interpretation, which was completing and supporting each other.

Yang et al. (2019, p. 7) aim to investigate multiple modalities, such as text images and videos, to explore the deep multimodal fusion of text and photos for hate speech classification. They explored the challenge of automatically identifying hate speech with deep multimodal technologies, an extension of previous research which mainly focused on the text signal alone. The study concluded that augmenting text with images can lead to action. Conforming how internet memes have become a prominent method of communication across the internet, Sanchez (2020, p. 9) analyses the characteristics that have made internet memes a mainstay in online communication to propose a way in which to analyse the social influence of internet memes in their creation and diffusion. The researcher concludes that memes would benefit future research on societal desensitisation as it continues to be used as a commonplace form of language online.

Dasilva et al. (2021, p. 302) aim to analyse the conversation and the structure of relationships on the net arising around the term deep fake on Twitter using social network analysis technique. The analysis shows that half of the actors who function as bridges in the interactions that shape the network are journalists through their respective media. Graber (2021, p. 3) aims to discuss how deep fakes fit into the category of illusory speech, what they do in society, and how to deal with them. Classifying them into categories such as pornography, political misinformation and disinformation, deep fakes and the law of speech, the study realised that targets always feel exposed, ridiculed and defamed. Besides other harms, deep fakes resulted in the following: they reduce voters' faith in democracy and self-governance, attack the basic institutions of democracy through avenues other than the ballot box, discredit political opponents, sow division and deep fakes also pose a problem for the arbiters of truth in democracy.

To deal with deep fakes, researchers have argued for new civil and criminal penalties for deep fakers and new regulations and liabilities for internet platforms that host their work. Ka-WeiLee et al. (2021, p. 8) propose DisMultiHate, a framework that categorises multimodal hateful content. Specifically, they designed DisMultiHate to disentangle target entities in multimodal memes and to improve how hateful content classification is explained. They evaluated their proposed model on two popular publicly available hateful datasets: Facebook hateful memes (FHM) and Multi Off. The classification processes were discussed in different sections, such as text representation made up of text encoder and text-target disentanglement and visual representation made up of attention-based image encoder and visual-target disentanglement. Their experiment results show that DisMultiHate can outperform state-of-the-art unimodal and multimodal baselines in the hateful meme classification task.

Theoretically, this study is guided by Kress and van Leeuwen's theories and models of visual social semiotics, i.e., the grammar of visual design (1996). This grammar describes a social resource of a particular group (p. 3). It follows Halliday's theory of metafunctions (1994), which postulates that language fulfils three metafunctions simultaneously: ideational, interpersonal and textual (Stoian, 2015, p. 24). In addition to these three metafunctions, the researcher looked at three features of the language of images: language about images, images regarded as a language, and verbal language as a system informed by images. All of these are grouped as representational metafunction, interactive metafunction and compositional metafunction. Linking visual contents to grammar, the grammar of image, according to Kress and van Leeuwen (1996, p. 19), describe how words combine in clauses, sentences and texts, depict elements, people, places and things, combine in visual contents of greater or lesser complexity and extension. Visual language conveys information and ideas visually by visual means. The following tenets are central to this theory:

Representational Metafunction

This is similar to ideation, whose function is to show how an image conveys meaning and shapes the real world or their relationship in the world. In other words, representation requires that image producers choose forms to express what they have in mind, which they see as most apt and plausible in the given context (Kress & Leeuwen, 1996, p. 13). What precisely the image represents (modality) as producers use modality markers to give the viewers an impression of the truth or credibility (Hafifah & Sinar, 2020, p. 33). Different representational processes include action, reaction, speech, mental and conversion. The three found on the images used in this study are action (actors on the images), speech (dialogue using different linguistic features to link ideas) and symbolic processes (depicts what the producer means). The other kinds are not found on the memes and deep fakes presented in this study.

Interactional metafunctions

This is similar to interpersonal, whose function is to show how an image affects the viewer's perception. It has three dimensions: image act, social distance and point of view. Among the three dimensions, image act and point of view dimensions are found on the memes and deep fakes screenshot for this study. Image acts are emphasised by facial expressions and gestures. Interactional point of view or perspective comprises two types of images: subjective, i.e., presenting everything from a particular perspective dictated by the image producer. The image producer tells us what we have to know from one perspective, which is negative in this study's context. That is, any mode must represent a particular social relation between the producer, the viewer, and the object represented (Kress & van Leeuwen, 1996, p. 42). The objective image tells us what we must know about the target person and situation through the image, as they can be depicted from various angles through various text descriptions.

Compositional metafunction

This is similar to text, whose function is to show how the elements of an image are arranged or reproduced to achieve specific intentions and effects. In this case, meaning is built through three interrelated systems like information value (the visual areas of the image, which include left and right, top and bottom, centre and margin). All the areas have information to pass to the audience, receivers, target person, and situation. Salience (the attractiveness of the image), the visual elements indicating salience are the size of the image, sharpness of focus, and tonal and colour contrast, whose functions are within the producer's intention. Images used in this study featured the salience elements above. Framing (the connection and the disconnection of the elements found in an image).

Methodology

The research method used is descriptive qualitative to analyse the linguistic components found on memes and deep fake images. The components analysed included modalities, hate captions used to describe the images, text descriptions and the offensive linguistic features of both images (word classes, syntactic structures and word formation). This was done by classifying the different images to see their frequencies. Data and population for this study comprised 233 memes and deep fake images randomly screenshot from 14 Facebook profiles from 1st January 2020 to 31st December 2020. This period recorded several memes and deep fake images with hate captions related to the Anglophone crisis, which caught the researcher's attention. All the images analysed had modalities, hate captions, and text descriptions and were offensive. To get the data, Facebook profiles found with memes and deep fake images were followed (scrolled), screenshot and cropped for security reasons. The researcher used different criteria to edit the memes and deep fakes for security reasons; they were first reduced to 4x4 photo sizes to compress them into a page containing about four memes or deep fakes. To cover the producer's identity, the researcher double-clicked on the image and selected the image toolbar to trim the producers' identity. The trim technique helped the researcher secure data on mobile telephones and the computer. As a result, 233 memes and deep fake images were screenshot from different Facebook profiles, targeting top personalities and other civilians associated with the Anglophone crisis. The researcher used images captured from the platform to show examples in the analysis section. Out of the 233 images, 217 were memes, while 16 were deep fakes, as indicated in the table below:

Table 2.1. Data statistics

Data trace	Number identified	Percentages
Memes with hate captions and text descriptions	217	93%
Deep fake images with hate captions and text descriptions	16	7%
Total number of memes and deep fake images	233	100%

Data presentation, analysis and discussion

The data have been analysed by developing content, language and linguistic aspects. Based on these aspects, the meanings of the images have been interpreted to show how they are represented linguistically to fuel disinformation campaigns about the Anglophone crisis. This is done in relation to the taxonomies of the theory with more detail found in the data samples.

Images with linguistic representation to fuel disinformation campaigns about the Anglophone crisis

Images are represented to address various themes ranging from a belief and representations of some target persons responsible for the delayed solutions to the Anglophone crisis. These included producers' beliefs, targets represented with different narrative structures, Paul Biya represented as the genesis of the Anglophone crisis, mage representations and communicative acts and hate captions on the images. From these, images disseminated with similar features were grouped, as seen in the subsequent presentations.

Producers' belief

The images collected from the profiles of some producers showed their beliefs about the struggle for the independence of the Southern Cameroons. It was found that the producers believe that the Southern Cameroons is not achieving her dream of independence because of some Anglophone Cameroonians. This is revealed through the images on social media with similar linguistic features, which show their belief about the targets. See Figure 2.1.

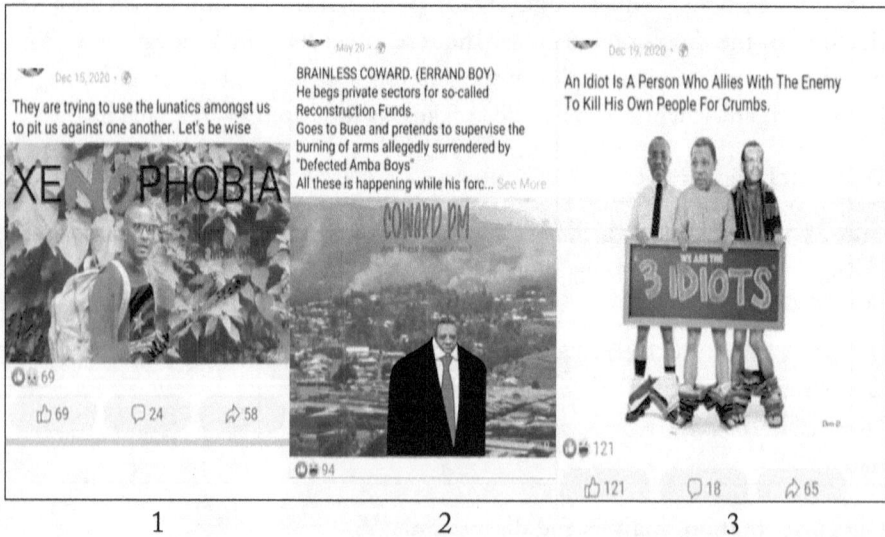

Figure 2.1. Images showing producers' beliefs about some Cameroonians

The three images in Figure 2.1 are screenshot from Facebook. They reflect the beliefs of the producers about the Anglophone crisis. The first metafunction involves different patterns used by the producers to represent the target persons, where the visual elements are encoded with catchy narratives. There are also different narrative processes in the above images: action and speech. Both images have action and speech, presenting unfolding actions and events surrounding the target situation (the Anglophone crisis). The represented target persons in the images are involved in an action and reactional process as producers looked directly at something outside the humorous aspects of the picture that can be identified as the producers' perceptions. Looking at the different catchy phrases like, let be wise (image 1), BRAINLESS COWARDS, COWARD PM (image 2) and 3 IDIOTS (image 3) are used by the producers to serve several linguistic and representational requirements.

Targets represented with different narrative structures

The producers use different narratives to represent the targets. The narratives include depicted elements, which form a gap between targets of different concerns. Kress & van Leeuwen (2006, p. 59) called these victors. See Figure 2.2.

Figure 2.2. Images showing producers' beliefs about some Cameroonians

The three images in Figure 2.2 are screenshot from Facebook. The images reflect the beliefs of the producers on the Anglophone crisis. The different narrative structures present unfolding actions and events, a process of change and transitory spatial arrangements, as indicated in images 1, 2 and 3. In image 1, for example, two victors are covered by two outstanding narratives: The Old

Man and The Blind Servant and MISSION: IMPOSSIBLE. The sub-narratives used to illustrate these are action and speech. The action narrative contains three elements: COMMISSION, STATUS and SPECIAL. In this narrative, SPECIAL is the target towards which the vector is directed through the second action indicated on the wheelchair directed through the narrative Bonne chance! (Goodluck!). In image 2, we find a reactional process where the image is produced through a combination of different target persons with glances of different directions of more participants. The represented participants in the image are involved in a transactional reactional process, with each actor looking directly at something outside the picture that can be identified as the viewer. Different linguistic features describe them: Southern Cameroon, enablers, ugly faces and misery. All of these depict the chain of the target process. Image 3, unlike images 1 and 2, included both action and speech. Outstanding narrative structures here are connected to the main participants in ways other than interaction. The intentions expressed by visual language are of different types: Locative participants of the image, generally referred to as BASTARDS, *are* the two left and right images used in action processes. Two phrasal features link the targets: REGIONAL RUBBISH and ENABLER IN CHIEF. These narratives are transactional because they are directed to pass across a message outside the image.

Paul Biya represented as the genesis of the Anglophone crisis

The images collected from the profiles of some producers showed through their language choices that Paul Biya is the genesis of the Anglophone crisis and the genocide enabler King Paul I of Biyameroun. They also used the opportunity to show their hatred toward Paul Biya, mainly through the language used to describe him, as seen in Figure 2.3.

The images here used a symbolic attributive process to picture the target (symbolic attribute of authority). The images represent reality through several processes, forming a complex pattern of representation. All the action processes in the images are linked with different descriptive and narrative features, which depict what the target does in each situation. All the narrative and descriptive features appear individually or together, just like a simple or complex sentence in language. Examples are King Paul I of Biyameroun, PHOBIYA'S IMPUNITY and ARSONIST. These narrative and descriptive features give the interactive meaning of the images in three dimensions: image act, symbolism and point of view. All the actions in the three images represent the target person and the situation emphasised by gestures. Image 1 symbolises dialogue; image 2 symbolises conflict and international interference, and image 3 symbolises war. The last dimension is a subjective point of view (as the producer tells the viewers everything from his own perspective) and objective (as the images tell the viewers what to know about the target person and the target situation). Moreover, the grammar of visual design (concept of modalities) is also outstanding in unveiling the linguistic features used by the producer since the above visuals represent the target and the situation as though they exist. Besides, modality is constructed through the above images by a complex interplay of markers, such as saturated colours, contextualisation of the situation, representation and brightness.

Figure 2.3. Images representing Paul Biya as the genesis of the Anglophone crisis

Figure 2.4. Image representations and communicating acts

Image representations and different communicative acts

The images below show how representations and communicative acts cohere to a meaningful message. Messages can be passed through different media and styles.

The images here have representative, interactive and compositional metafunctions that serve several communicational requirements to function as a complete communication system. All of these are the components of the grammar of visual design. The narrative structures used by the producer present the unfolding actions of the targets and the situation. The conceptual structure represents targets in terms of class, which is more of symbolism because the actions depict who the targets are and what the producer means. The interactive meaning of the images is seen through the image act direction of the targets and the image producer's subjective and objective points of view. Like the previous images, the concept of modality is also seen through the producer's display of a combination of modality makers like colour display and brightness. Moreover, the framing of the images also connects the representational meaning to the interactive one through the spaces between the different targets. This is further comprehended with hate captions such as CLUB MEMBERS, Grumpy Old Men, Dead men and DEAD MEN WALKING. The images here show how the encoding of artificial reality serves as a channel of expression.

Hate captions on the images

The samples presented above show that images have at least one or more multiple hate captions within a single post. In the images, we can see how the producers used adjectives to describe the target and actions in the images.

The use of adjectives

The main aim of producing images is to convey a message to the readers, receivers, or viewers. Image producers used concise and attractive words presenting descriptive information about the target persons and situations. In the images, adjectives are used to give a description of the target persons and the target situations and also to shape receivers' thoughts toward the targets. Some of the adjectives from our sample are evident in Figure 2.1 image 2 (BRAINLESS COWARDS, ERRAND BOY and COWARD PM); see Figure 2.2 image 1 (Old MAN and BLIND SERVANT), image 2 (ugly faces), image 3 (REGIONAL RUBBISH); Figure 2.4 image 1 (Grumpy old Men), image 2 (constitutional succession, Laripublik Wicked Generation and dead men).

The adjectives are used intentionally to provoke the target persons.

BRAINLESS COWARDS and COWARD PM, as seen in Figure 2.1 image 1, are synonymous with stupid, foolish or unintelligent and ERRAND BOY is a sarcastic reference to the target. Old MAN and BLIND SERVANT, as seen in Figure 2.2 image 1, are adjectives used by the producer to describe the two target persons. The adjectival phrase the ugly faces behind the misery of our people is used to describe the general picture as seen in image 2 of Figure 2.2. In addition, grumpy old men, as seen in image 1 of Figure 2.4, means bad-tempered and irritable people, DEAD MEN as seen in the phrase dead men walking in Figure 2.4 image 2, is used to refer to the two target persons in the images as dead people still living. Constitutional succession and Laripublik wicked generation are messages passed to the two target persons, implying the producer seems not to be satisfied with their stay in power. The adjectives used by image producers revealed their intents, which appeared to capture more attention of image readers to make them aware of the target situation (the Anglophone crisis). Similarly, image producers have used the adjectives symbolically to satirise the target persons and to create an impact on the receivers.

Discussion

This study presents and analyses how memes and deep fake image producers use images accompanied with linguistic features to fuel a disinformation campaign concerning the Anglophone crisis in Cameroon. The findings of this study corroborate and complement those of many other previous ones in several ways. It provides evidence to support the view that memes and deep fake producers use hate captions to express their thoughts and beliefs on social media concerning the Anglophone crisis. These are achieved through visual communication (the grammar of visual design).

Stoian (2015, p. 29) shows that visual encoding is carried on either by narrative and/or conceptual structures. The narrative structures present unfolding actions and events. The conceptual structures represent targets regarding their class, structure or meaning. From a semiotic perspective, it shows that circumstances expressed by visual language are of different kinds encoding reality such as locative, means and accompaniment. Just like Permata (2018, pp. 44-86) demonstrates how the language used on memes has the power to influence significantly social beliefs, ideas, perceptions and values of the people, this study identifies memes and deep fake images and tries to see how producers' beliefs and perceptions are associated with the Anglophone crisis through their hate captions. Jagadish & Pratiksha (2019, p. 73) submit that image producers use multiple vectors such as signs, symbols, colours, and words with images and stylish writing structures. Applying these vectors in image analysis discovers the following: Contents represented in images, Cultural identity, Gender equality, Politics in images etc. Apart from cultural identity and gender equality, this study identifies similar trends with features such as representation, politics in images, interaction and composition. Fombo (2021, p. 76) confirms some derogatory adjectives associated with the Anglophone crisis on social media, such as French Cameroun terrorists, genocidal killers, genocidal brutes, high-profiled terrorists, gang Republic!!! A bunch of sick wackos! Etc. This study equally identifies such derogatory adjectives used on memes and deep fakes to give a vivid description of the target persons and to fuel the fire of the Anglophone crisis. This also complements Chesney and Citron (2019, p. 67), who conclude that words and images could cause significant harm to individuals and organisations, exploitation, sabotage, distortion of democratic discourse etc.

Even though most audiences look at memes and deep fake images with humorous lenses, producers of such images produce them far beyond what the audience may see. However, the context of image dissemination, like the case of the Cameroon social media landscape on the Anglophone crisis, is clear as the producer's intention is shown through the choice of language to describe the targets on the images. In this context, producers combine visual designs and linguistic elements, sometimes conveying their intentions directly toward the target persons.

Conclusion and implications

This is a qualitative descriptive study conducted to present and analyse the linguistic features used by image producers to disseminate images on Facebook concerning the Anglophone crisis in Cameroon. The findings show that words and images are used not only on social media to entertain the audience, but other strategies like representation, interaction and compositional metafunctions have provided the grammar of visual design a comprehensive mode. The findings also indicated that focusing solely on a normal mode of information like written or spoken texts may remove our possibility of finding meaning in other forms, just like the samples used in this study for the analysis. The language on the images contains image act, point of view, modalities and other information values that indicate the reality encoded in them. The interaction and the narrative structures established between producers and target persons compose all of the metafunctions and visual resources that could be described, observed, and interpreted. Based on the above findings, it is concluded that images disseminated on Facebook carry multiple linguistic features, which are used intentionally to ridicule the target persons and to fuel the fire of the Anglophone crisis.

Memes and deep fake images on Cameroon's social media landscape reflect societal problems faced in our contemporary society. In an attempt to propose solutions to such a problem, since the majority of the people exposed to such creative activity on the new technologies are the youths, emphasis should be laid on the adverse effects of this creative art, especially images produced during crisis such as the Anglophone crisis in Cameroon. People might think memes and deep fakes are only about jokes; there is something behind it, which can reveal the producer's ideology and implicature through the image captions. Researchers and professionals should help readers understand the effect of such a communicative strategy and show how it can be used to convey useful information and solve societal problems. If not, continuous exposure of the active youth age to such content and its misuse may remain one of the major causes of offline problems in our society. Moreover, several approaches have not been explored to use research to solve this problem on Cameroon social media landscape. For instance, a critical discourse analysis of memes and deep fake images, memes and deep fake producers' perception for producing such content using both English and French and the narrative and communicative strategies used to produce such images. The above are some possible areas that have not been researched to see their implications on the Anglophone crisis.

Abstract

This paper presents and analyses memes and deep fake images accompanied by hate captions on Facebook concerning the Anglophone crisis. The chapter aims to present and analyse images with linguistic representation to fuel the disinformation campaign of the Anglophone crisis. This study's data comprises 233 memes and deep fake images collected from activists' Facebook profiles from 1st January 2020 to 31st December 2020. All the analysed samples had hate captions (text descriptions). The qualitative analysis method identifies the representatives (metafunctions) and linguistic features used by the producers to justify the images. Kress and van Leeuwen's (1996) theories and models of reading images, i.e., the grammar of visual design, help the researcher to identify the metafunctions used to represent the images. The samples analysed show that the producers use different metafunctions of representational, interactional and compositional accompanied with hate captions to accomplish the memes and deep fake images. In effect, they have been used to fuel the fire of the Anglophone crisis on Facebook.

Keywords: Memes, Deep fake images, social media, Anglophone crisis, hate captions.

References

Agarwal, S., Farid, H., Gu, Y., He, M., Nagano, K., & Li, H. (2019). Protecting world leaders against deepfakes. *CVPR Workshop on Media Forensics, 1*, 38-45.

Arazna, M. (2015). Conflicts of the 21st century based on multidimensional warfare: 'hybrid warfare,' disinformation and manipulation. *Security and Defense Quarterly, 8*(3), 103-129.

Chesney, B., & Citron, D. K. (2019). Deep fakes: A looming challenge for privacy, democracy and national security. *California Law Review, 107*(6), 1753-1820.

Chesney, B., & Citron, D. K. (2019). Deep fakes and new disinformation war: The coming age of post-truth geopolitics. *Foreign Affairs, 98*, 147–155.

Dack, S. (2019). Deep fakes, fake news, and what comes next. Retrieved from https://jsis.washington.edu/news/deep-fakes-fake-news-and-what-comes-next.

Dasilva, J.P., Ayerdi, K.M., & Mendiguren T G. (2021). Deep fakes on Twitter: which actors control their spread? In *Media and Communication, 9*(1), 301-3012.

Dawkins, R. (1976). *The Selfish Gene*. Oxford: Oxford University Press.

Fish, T. (2019). Deep fakes: AI-manipulated media will be weaponised to trick military. Retrieved from https://www.express.co.uk/news/science/1109783/deep-fakes-ai-artificial-intelligence-photos-video-weaponised-china

Fombo, E. (2021). A speech act analysis of hate posts on the Anglophone crisis by Cameroonian activists. In *International Journal of Humanitatis Theoreticus, 4*(2), 62-79.

Graber, N. M. (2021). Artificial illusions: Deepfakes as speech. *Intersect, 14*(3), 1-19.

Hancock, J.T & Bailenson, J.N. (2021). The social impact of deepfakes. *Cyberpsychology, Behavior, and Social Networking, 24*(3), 149-152.

Ice, J. (2019). Defamatory political deepfakes and the first amendment. *Case Western Reserve Law Review, 70*(2), 417-455.

Jagadish, P &Pratiksha, N. (2019). Contents and the language used in graffiti: A case of Kathmandu Valley. *Journal of NELTA, 24*(1-2), 52-76.

Ka-WeiLee, R., Rui, C., Ziqing, F., Jing, J., & Wen-Haw, C. (2021). Disentangling Hate in Online Memes. In *Proceedings of the 29th ACM International Conference on Multimedia (MM '21)*, 20-24. Retrieved from https://doi.org/10.1145/3474085.3475625.

Korshunov, P, & Marcel, S. (2018). Deepfakes: a new threat to face recognition? Assessment and detection. *arXiv Preprint arXiv: 1812.08685*.

Kress, G.R., & Van Leeuwen, T. (1996). *Reading images: the grammar of visual design*. London: Routledge.

Matern, F., Ries, C, & Stamminger, M. (2019). Exploiting visual artifacts to expose deepfakes manipulations. *IEEE Winter Applications of Computer Vision Workshops (WACVW)*, 83-92.

Mahyoop, M., Algaraady, J., & Alrahaili, M. (2020). Linguistic-based detection of fake news in social media. *International Journal of English Linguistics,11*(1), 99-109.

Mirsky, Y, & Lee, W. (2021). The creation and detection of deepfakes: a survey. *ACM Computing Surveys (CSUR), 54*(1), 1-41.

Nagel, E. van der. (2020). Verifying images: deepfakes, control, and consent. *Porn Studies, 7*(12), 1-6.

Nicholls, C. (2020). Online humour, cartoons, videos, memes, jokes and laughter in the epoch of the Coronavirus. *A Journal of Literature, Theory and Culture, (10), 274-318*.

Nguyen, T.T., Quoc, V.H.N., Cuong, M.N., Dung, N., Duc. T. N., & Saeid, N. (2021). Deep learning for deepfakes creation and detection: a survey. *ArXiv preprint ArXiv:1909.11573v3[csV.CV]*.

Ondřej, P. (2016). Cohesive Aspects of humor in internet memes on Facebook: a multimodal sociolinguistic analysis. In *Ostrava Journal of English Philosophy, 38(8), 7-38*

Patrini, G. (2019). Mapping the deepfake landscape: deepfake labs. Retrieved from https://deeptracelabs.com/mapping-the-deepfake-landscape.

Permata, C.S. (2017). *Meanings of lifestyle memes in English: pragmatic-semiotic analysis.* (Unpublished Thesis), Sanata: Sanata Dharma University.

Sanchez, B. (2020). Internet memes and desensitization. *A Journal of Humanity and Social Inquiry, 1*(2), 1-11.

Shen, T., Liu, R., Bai, J, & Li, Z. (2018). Deepfakes using generative adversarial networks (GAN). Retrieved from http://noiselab.ucsd.edu/ECE228_2018/Reports/Report16.

Sontag, S. (1971). *On photography*. London: Penguin.

Stoian, C. (2015). Analysing images: A social semiotic perspective. *Scientific Bulletin of the Politehnica University of Timișoara Transactions on Modern Languages, 14*(1), 23-30.

Tolosana, R., Vera-Rodrigues, R., Fierrez, J., Morales, A, & Ortega-Garcia, J. (2020). Deepfakes and Beyond: a survey of face manipulation and fake detection. *Information Fusion, 64*, 131-148.

Tucker, P. (2019). The newest AI-enabled weapon: deepfaking photos of the earth. Retrieved from https://www.defenseone.com/technology/2019/03/next-phase-ai-deep-faking-whole-world-and-china-ahead/155944.

Villasenor, J. (2019). Artificial intelligence, deepfakes, and the uncertain future of truth. Retrieved from https://www.brookings.edu.

Yang, X., Li, Y, & Lyu, S. (2019). Exposing deepfakes using inconsistent head poses. *IEEE International Conference on Acoustics, Speech and Signal Processing (ICASSP)*, 8261-8265.

Yang, F., Peng, X., Ghosh, G., Shilon, R., Ma, H., Moore, E., & Predovic, G. (2019) Exploring deep multimodal fusion of text and photo for hate speech classification. In *Proceedings of the Third Workshop on Abusive Language Online, 1*, 11-18.

Zampieri, M., Malmasi, S., Nakov, P., Rosenthal, S., Farra, N., & Kumar, R. (2019).

Zampieri, M., SemEval-2019 Task 6: Identifying and Categorizing Offensive Language in Social Media (OffensEval). *Proceedings of the 13th International Workshop on Semantic Evaluation* (pp.75–86). Minneapolis, Minnesota, USA: Association for Computational Linguistics.

THREE

The Pragmatics of Greeting and Face Management in the Covid-19 Era in Northern Cameroon

FAISSAM WARDA

Rituals of greeting are essential habitual behaviours in enhancing harmony and considerateness in African societies. In Cameroon in general and the northern part of the country, greeting is particularly delicate as it is the nucleus of politeness in the community. Research in sociopragmatics (concerning speech or ritualistic acts) is flourishing (Duranti, 1997; Mulo Farenkia, 2016; Tabe & Faissam Warda, 2018). In Cameroon, however, very few works seem to be carried out in the domain compared to some countries in Asia or Europe. As regards the northern Cameroon speech community, to the best of the researcher's knowledge, except for a few papers, including Goron (2016) and Tabe and Faissam (2018), almost nothing has been done on the ritual acts of greeting. No work has been conducted to evaluate the relationship between greetings and face management in northern Cameroon. Thus, the current research explores the pragmatics of greeting and its relationship with face management in northern Cameroon in the Covid-19 era. In this respect, this paper attempts to answer the following questions. What traditional techniques do people from northern Cameroon use to carry out greeting rituals? What techniques are adapted to the advent of the coronavirus pandemic in that society? How do people from the northern Cameroon society relate their adapted greeting techniques to their addressees' negative or positive face? In order to provide answers to these questions, the elicited data will be analysed in line with Brown and Levinson's (1987) face-saving view. This is to show what types of greeting (gestures) are addressed to negative face or positive face in order to examine and describe how face management is carried out in northern Cameroon regarding greeting rituals in the Covid-19 era. The chapter is subdivided into three main sections: theoretical framework and literature review, methodology and data analysis and discussion under which the traditional greeting techniques in northern Cameroon and the Covid-19 era greeting techniques are discussed.

Theoretical Framework and Literature Review

The face-saving view, a theory elaborated and propounded by Brown and Levinson (1987), is one of the earliest theories framed to address linguistic/pragmatic politeness. This theory stipulates that any adult fluent language speaker has two main types of face in interacting with others, either verbally or non-verbally. For any interaction thus to hold successfully, each interactant (the speaker and the hearer, henceforth S and H) has to pay attention to and consider these two types of face (positive and negative face). Otherwise, any interactant must consider his or her hearer's positive or negative face to manage the communication appropriately. In this vein, Brown and Levinson (1987) developed the following assumption to clarify the notion of face, positive face and negative face:

> all competent adult members of a society have (and know each other to have)
> (i) 'Face', the public self-image that every member wants to claim for himself, consisting in two related aspects:
> (a) Negative face: the basic claim to territories, personal preserves, rights to non-distraction - i.e., to freedom of action and freedom from imposition
> (b) Positive face: the positive consistent self-image or 'personality' (crucially including the desire that this self-image be appreciated and approved of) claimed by interactants […]
> Brown & Levinson (1987:61)

The face-saving theory claims that every social interactant has a face and is cognisant that the other also has a face. In addition to having face and being aware of the other's face, any adult language speaker has to attend to that face.

Practically in pragmatics studies, the face-saving framework is mainly used by researchers to treat speech acts that have propositional content, including directive speech acts such as requests which are inherently face-threatening. One could hardly find any work that treats greeting from the face-saving view's angle. Unlikely, the current study applies the face saving view to greeting rituals. Some scholars, like Searle and Vanderveken (1985), claim that greetings do not have any propositional content. This is probably the reason that justifies the lack of studies that apply the face saving view to greeting acts. However, this view cannot be universally shared. Depending on the context of communication and the purpose of the greeting act, the greeting can have propositional content or not. It can be used to praise the recipient or show interest in his/her well-being, to introduce a request or remind something to the hearer, and in this context, it has propositional content (Homeidi, 2004; Tabe & Faissam, 2018).

Greeting is one of the most elementary linguistic behaviour any member of a society must have acquired from his/her childhood. It is an inherently polite linguistic act. Otherwise, politeness is enrooted in social greetings (Duranti, 1997). According to the latter, greeting determines whether this or that person is a socially acceptable member of society. In this same respect, Schleicher (1997, p. 334) asserts that "the more speakers understand the cultural context of greetings, the better the society appreciates them, and the more they are regarded as well-behaved." To these scholars, individuals have to internalise the greeting norms of their society. This implies that for a new member of a given society to be considered well-behaved and integrated, he/she must learn the basic greeting techniques of the society. This becomes more delicate in some communities, such as the Bororo speech community, where greeting is an essential part of traditional behaviour and habit, and a significant length of time is dedicated to it each time people are to greet one another (Goron, 2016). Staying tied to their tradition and customs, the Bororo people could hardly fail to greet any person they meet (familiar or non-familiar), following their greeting norms and taking all their time to show respect and consideration to their interlocutor(s) (Goron, 2016; Tabe & Faissam, 2018). The commonly well-shared saying 'time is money' is not the Bororo's portion when it comes to greeting.

Going from the view that every interaction participant has positive and negative face that has to be attended to as propounded by Brown and Levinson (1987), Nkwain (2016:230) declares that "when we approach a co-participant, we are entering his/her personal territory and this constitutes an FTA, especially if we fail to greet. Silence in such a case is usually considered as disconcerting and breaking the silence by greeting is a redressive act to save face." Nkwain (2016) demonstrated how Cameroon Pidgin English speakers show awareness of the positive and negative face needs through greeting rituals. Likely, the current study attempts to examine how Cameroonians of the Grand North struggle to attend to their co-interactants' face through greeting despite the Covid-19 demands of not shaking hands, a very recurrent phenomenon in greeting before the Covid-19 era in their society.

Tabe and Faissam (2018), when exploring politeness in the English spoken by the Fulfulde native speakers, have examined some acts and instances of greeting in their linguistic behaviour. Their findings show that there is a pragmatic transfer in the way Fulfulde speakers greet in English. There are sets of routinely Fulfulde-specific greeting behaviours in their linguistic greeting in other languages (English and/or French), especially when conversing among themselves (Tabe & Faissam, 2018). These findings have much in common with Goron (2016) and the traditional greeting techniques of Cameroonians of the Grand North slightly discussed in a subsequent section here. However, they are very different from the core of the current study, the greeting techniques adapted to the Covid-19 pandemic.

Methodology

Data for the study were collected from one hundred and twenty northern Cameroonians through participant and non-participant observation. The observation was conducted in schools, university campuses, travel agencies and marketplaces from March 2020 to November 2020. Fifty participants (41.67% of the sampled population) were female respondents, and seventy (58.33%) were male. The great majority of the population was made up of young people. Forty participants were about forty-five years old and above. Data were mainly obtained from 120 native inhabitants of the headquarters of the three Northern Regions of Cameroon: Ngaoundere in the Adamawa Region, Garoua in the North Region and Maroua in the Far-North Region. In this vein, the subject of the study is made up of people who are, by origin, from this part of the country and live there. They are fluent Fulfulde speakers. The researcher, being also a fluent speaker of the Fulfulde language, observed greeting instances and the gestures that accompanied them in the Covid-19 period and jotted them down in a notebook he used specifically for that purpose. The gestures accompanying the greetings are the greeting parts that are analysed here, for verbal parts of the greetings are not influenced by the advent of the coronavirus. The conversations are mainly held in Fulfulde and French, with recurrent instances of code-switching from French to Fulfulde and vice versa. In addition, the researcher administered unstructured interviews to a part of the population (thirty-five northerners) to inquire about how they behave when greeting concerning the coronavirus preventive measures such as social distancing and not shaking hands. This was also aimed at checking what greeting gestures Cameroonians from the Grand North were more inclined to use in their conversations in the Covid-19 era. Data gathered from these two techniques are pragmatically analysed and classified according to whether they are directed to negative or positive face of the interactants. They are categorised, classified and statistically presented in tables in the following section.

Data Analysis and Discussion

The data collection took place during the Covid-19 pandemic period. In this section, traditional greeting (i.e., norm-based greetings before the advent of the coronavirus) in Northern Cameroon is first presented, and then the Covid-19 adapted greeting behaviours are further addressed.

Traditional Greeting Techniques in Grand North Cameroon

The Grand North Cameroon was linguistically conquered by the Fulbe people. Thus, the Fulbe are dominant in terms of local language use because Fulfulde, the language of the Fulbe, has become a lingua franca. In this vein, as language is culture and language is behaviour, the behaviours of the Grand North Cameroonians are significantly impacted by the Fulbe ways of doing.

In Grand North Cameroon, traditional polite ritual behaviours are mainly characterised by serial greetings. Repetitive adjacency pairs, followed by repetitive handshaking in formal and informal conversations, are commonly observed (Tabe & Faissam, 2018). Let us consider the following greeting sample taken from Goron (2016):

S1: sannu ma! (Good morning to you)
S2: sannu Mal Bouba! Noy djam na? (Good morning Mal Bouba! Are you OK?)
S1: djam, djam mbandu? (Fine, fine health?)
S2: djam ni town. Djam saaré? (Fine for now, the home is OK?)
S1: djam ko dimé. Djam boukon? (Fine, there is no problem. Children are fine?)
S2: Allah hamdulilah! Djam naié? (Fine by the grace of Allah. Are the cattle fine?)
S1: djam ni town (Fine for now)
S2: Oussé ma! (Thank you)
S1: Ousséko! (Thanks)
Adapted from Goron (2016:275)

In this conversation extract, a typical greeting from Grand North Cameroonians, repetitive adjacency pairs are observed. In face-to-face communication, these serial greetings are continuously and repetitively accompanied by handshakes when interactants are physically close to each other. In the pre-Covid-19 era, waving hands at a distance when greeting could also occur in this speech community. However, this was not well preferred. Interactants could prefer getting closer to shake hands and show warm consideration to their interlocutors even when one of them or both were in haste to go somewhere or for business. This obtains in Grand North Cameroon, especially in the Fulbe community under normal circumstances. Nevertheless, the coronavirus pandemic exigencies have imposed other behaviour on Grand North Cameroonians. The greeting techniques of the Covid-19 era are addressed in the following section.

Covid-19 Era Greeting Techniques in Grand North Cameroon

The advent of the Covid-19 pandemic has impacted many human activities, including social behaviour. In Grand North Cameroon, the pragmatics of greeting have been readapted to the coronavirus preventive requirements. Thus, the linguistic greetings and gestures accompanying them vary according to whether the speakers are acting with regard to the positive or negative face of the hearer. Greetings addressed to H's positive face and greetings addressed to H's negative face are respectively discussed in the following sections.

Greetings Addressed to H's Positive Face

Greeting in Grand North Cameroon is far beyond mere ritual behaviour. It determines the social acceptability and integration of interactants in line with being considered polite. Despite the Covid-19 demands of keeping social distancing and avoiding physical contact with other people (no handshaking), in Grand North Cameroon, a society where handshaking in complement to serial verbal greetings is the core of polite greetings, some new techniques of conveying the politeness embodied in the traditional ways of greeting have been coined out. In a positive politeness context, the verbal serial greetings are accompanied by the following gestures: elbow knocking, foot shaking, back-of-the-hands tapping and forearm crossing. The frequency of occurrence of these greeting gestures is presented in Table 3.1.

Table 3.1. Statistical distribution of greeting gestures directed to H's positive face

Greeting gestures	Elbow knocking	Foot shaking	Back-of-the-hands tapping	Forearm crossing	Total
Number	20	6	18	12	56
Percentage	35.71%	10.71%	32.15%	21.43%	100%

Elbow knocking

Simple elbow knocking or elbow knocking and chest tapping are recurrently observed in Grand North Cameroon to show conviviality, friendship, familiarity and belonging to the same background. In this study, it is the most frequent greeting gesture in the Covid-19 period in the Grand North of Cameroon, with a frequency of 35.71%, as shown in Table 3.1. This positive politeness-related greeting gesture is observed among young male and female interactants. Nonetheless, its frequency is higher among male interactants. The tapping of the chest (heart) when greeting shows that the greeter has heartfelt warm consideration for the greeted person. Chest tapping can be done with a closed or unclosed hand. It is believed in Grand North Cameroon society (as some of the interviewees claimed) that when someone greets you with a closed hand on his/her chest, he/she means a tight relationship between him/her and you or that the consideration he/she has for you is critical.

Let us consider the following two male friends:
S1: Jo! (a slang term used among youngsters in the Grand North of Cameroon)
S2: Ouais! Noy tone way? (yeah! How there?)
S1: Walay sam goddo am. Noy gal maa? (Nothing, my person. How on your side?)
S2: Sey djam. Noy saaré? (Only fine. Is the home fine?)
S1: Djam ko dimé. Noy gal maa boo? (Fine, there is no problem. How on your side too?)
S2: Allah hamdulilah! A done? (Fine by the grace of Allah. You are there?)
S1: Nda yam way! (Here I am)
S2: Woddy! (Good)

In the instance above, the interactants knock their elbows repetitively after each question (sequence of greeting) in a sign of conviviality. Many words like *jo, goddo am, way, ouais*, show conviviality, friendliness, familiarity, etc., but analysing them is beyond the scope of the current chapter since we are just looking into the aspects of the behaviour imposed on by the advent of the Covid-19.

To keep as much distance as possible to prevent the spread of Covid-19, people can be greeted just by tapping their chest with closed hands without knocking elbows. This is mainly used to manage positive face among people with less tight, less intimate and less close relationships. There is also a notion of trust that is at stake at this level. In Grand North Cameroon, social distancing is easily minimised when we trust someone as if a trustworthy person could not contract or transmit the coronavirus. Thus, people can quickly greet others they trust - people to whom they are very close, with less regard to social distancing. However, social distancing is visibly respected with people they are not very close.

Back of hands tapping

Handshaking, a pragmatically forbidden greeting technique in the Covid-19 era, consists of holding someone's hand in the palm to say hello, good morning or goodbye. In Grand North Cameroon, interactants sometimes accompany their serial greetings with 'back-of-the-hands' tapping or shaking' during the Covid-19 period. This is the second most frequent greeting gesture directed to a positive face, with a frequency of 32.15% in this study. Is the coronavirus transmitted only through the palms of the hands or the hands as far as the notion of handshake avoidance is concerned in preventing the spread of the virus? Providing an answer to this question is far beyond the current study. However, from some Covid-19-related advertisements, the following was recorded: 'avoid touching your eyes, your nose and your mouth'. A pragmalinguistic analysis and interpretation of this sentence could make us infer that people should avoid touching their eyes, nose and mouth to prevent the spread of the virus through any of these organs should they come in contact with an infected person. This advertisement does not give room for interpretation as 'do not touch your eyes, your nose and your mouth with the palm of your hands'. This means that there is a possibility of carrying the coronavirus even with the back of the hands. Nevertheless, as one always tends to continue doing what has already become one's habit, Grand North Cameroonians find it challenging to greet without making any contact (especially hand contact) with their interlocutor(s). They think that, if they should not shake hands to prevent the spread of the coronavirus when greeting, at least they can tap the back of their hands as in the following conversation:

> S1: (Tapping S2's back-of-the-hand) bonjour bro! (good morning, bro!)
> S2: Ouais man! On dit quoi? (yes, man! What's up?)
> S1: Gars, on est là. Et toi? (Guy, we are there. And you?)
> S2: Ça va brother. Noy lekol? (Fine, my brother. How is school?)
> S1: On pousse seulement. Noy gal maa boo? (We are just pressing ahead. How on your side too?)
> S2: Allah hamdulilah! Ça essaie d'aller quand-même. (Fine by the grace of Allah. It is kind of ok)
> S1: Ah là c'est bien! (Ah, that is great)
> S2: Ok bro, aa mi dogga way (Ok bro, let me run, i.e., I have to leave)
> S1: (Tapping S2's back-of-the-hand) Woddi way, sey yesso! (Good, only next time)
> S2: Ouias, à la prochaine. (Yes! next time)

In the extract above, the tapping of the back of the hand occurs at a moment where handshaking would have strictly been observed in a normal pre-Covid-19 greeting situation in Grand North Cameroon. This is a socio-contextual adaptation to greeting gestures in this speech community.

Forearm crossing

The forearm crossing is one of the most convivial and friendship-showing greeting techniques in Grand North Cameroon in the Covid-19 era. The latter indicates a great friendly attachment among interactants tempted to hug each other but impeded by the coronavirus anxiety. It is mainly observed among friends, mates or very close people who have not met for a long time.

From my observation, forearm crossing mainly occurs throughout the whole greeting series. Otherwise, forearms are maintained, crossed from the beginning to the end of the serial greeting. This draws from the fact that, before the advent of the coronavirus, Grand North Cameroonians held each other's hand in certain greeting circumstances from the beginning to the end of the greeting process. Let us consider the following (a greeting between two former classmates who had not met for a long time):

>S1: (crossing the greetee's forearm with his right arm) Le Faissalo! (a vocative nickname)
>S2: ouais! (Yeah!)
>S1: L'homme perdu. On dit quoi ? (The lost man. What's up?)
>S2: Ça va man, comment tu vas ? (Fine man, how are you?)
>S1: Ça va mon frère. (Fine my brother)

In the interaction above, though the interactants have not met for a long time, they still have a certain degree of intimacy.

Foot shaking

Just like elsewhere in the country, foot shaking as a literal equivalence of handshaking is commonly observed in greetings in Grand North Cameroon. This new greeting habit frequently occurs among school students, young people in crowded meetings or parties and occasionally among older people during friendly encounters. Foot shaking is a jocular greeting that enhances the degree of friendliness, intimacy and confidence among the interactants. It indicates that the interactants are co-operators. See the following greeting sample between classmates on the first day of school resumption:

>S1: My dear classmate!
>S2: Hi! (knocking S1's foot)

S1: How are you? (knocking S2's foot)
S2: I'm fine. You see what Corona has done to us.
S1: What?
S2: I missed you, and I want to kiss you now, but we are obliged just to knock feet.
S1: (laughing)

All these Covid-19-adapted greeting techniques, elbow knocking, foot shaking, back-of-the-hands tapping and forearm crossing, are concomitant to the peculiar Grand North Cameroon serial verbal greetings that are not laboriously elaborated on here. Covid-19 has dramatically impacted the non-verbal greetings or non-verbal concomitants of greetings in the Grand North, but the long, repetitive and serial verbal part of greetings remain unchanged.

So far, greeting techniques addressed to the positive face of H have been discussed. The following sub-section discusses how Grand North Cameroonians manage their interlocutors' negative face in greetings during the Covid-19 period.

Greetings Addressed to H's Negative Face

A negative face is a more delicate face to be managed in interpersonal conversation. Its poor management likely leads to social discomfort, frustration and, to some extent, interpersonal conflict (Leech, 2014). In Grand North Cameroon, specific greeting gestures, including self-handshakes, nodding (reciprocal), simple hand on chest, attention-like standing/ bowing and namastes are used to save or enhance the addressee's negative face. These greeting gestures are presented in Table 3.2.

Table 3.2. Statistical distribution of greeting gestures directed to H's negative face

Greeting gestures	Self-handshaking	Nodding	Simple hand on chest	Attention-like standing	Namastes	Total
Number	18	9	16	11	10	64
Percentage	28.13%	14.06%	25%	17.19%	15.62%	100%

Self-handshakes

Whilst positive politeness is concerned with demonstrating closeness and affiliation, negative politeness is concerned with distance and formality (Mills, 2003, p. 59). In the sense of greeting in Grand North Cameroon, keeping the sociological distance is keeping the physical distance. Therefore, when greeting a person from whom we are socially distant and whose negative face has to be attended to, we should keep physical distance from the person. In this respect, as shaking hands is a typical Grand North Cameroon greeting gesture, the greeter has to shake his/her hands to show consideration and politeness to the greeting recipient. Self-handshaking is the most frequent greeting gesture directed to H's negative face in Grand North Cameroon during the Covid-19 period, with a frequency of 28.13% (as seen in Table 3.2). This way of greeting existed before the advent of the coronavirus pandemic but has been privileged in the Covid-19 era as social distancing has become a necessity in preventing the disease. As observed by the researcher, it is used by greeters of a low social class to greet their superiors. It is generally accompanied by slight bowing. Let us observe the following greeting sample:

>S1: (shaking his own hands) Allah hokou djam! (May God give health!)
>S2: Allah seyné (May God bring peace)
>S1: (shaking his own hands) Djam mbandou moun? (Are you having good health?)
>S2: djam ko dimé (Fine, there is no problem)

Simple hand on chest

Since negative politeness or negative face is avoidance-based, physical contact is hardly observed in negative politeness situations. The simple posing of the hand (the right hand) on the chest as one utters a greeting to a person is a sign of respect and wholehearted consideration. This greeting gesture is the second most recurrently observed technique in the Covid-19 era in Grand North Cameroon. In this study, 25% of the elicited data are simple hand on the chest. In traditional greetings in the Grand North, this gesture was accompanied by repetitive handshaking. In the Covid-19 era, this has been reduced to simple hands on the chest to avoid contact. It is used by a speaker of a lower social class or a speaker of equal social class as the recipient but hardly used by a speaker of a higher social class. Let us see the following:

>S1: (putting his right hand on his chest) Je vous salue chef! (I am greeting you, chief!)
>S2: Bonjour! (Good morning!)
>S1: Comment allez-vous ce matin? (How are you doing this morning?)
>S2: On remercie Dieu. (We thank God.)
>NB: In Grand North Cameroon, being in a high social class means having more wealth or earning a larger salary.

Nodding (reciprocal)

Nodding is another way of greeting that came into existence in Grand North Cameroon during the Covid-19 period. It is a reciprocal behaviour between two or more interactants of equal social status who must attend to each other's negative face. Social distancing (physical distance people keep between each other to avoid contact) and social distance (a sociological variable that indicates whether people are close/familiar or not close/unfamiliar) are both respected in such a context of communication. Social distancing and social distance condition the use of reciprocal nodding in a context of communication where both interactants deserve negative face maintenance in the Covid-19 period. In most greeting contexts, nodding is generally accompanied by furtive verbal greetings.

Attention-like standing/ bowing

Attention-like standing is another pragmatic greeting technique in the Covid-19 period in Grand North Cameroon. This is generally observed amongst male interactants of the same social class. In most cases, attention-like standing as a greeting is followed by slight or total bowing as a sign of great respect. The deeper the bow, the politer the greeter is. This greeting gesture is observed with a frequency of 17.19% in the data collected for this study. The attention-like standing position can be a furtive greeting gesture or be maintained as long as the serial verbal greeting. This depends on whether H's status over S is very high: the higher the status of H, the more the attention-like standing lasts.

Let us consider this sample:
> S1: (standing in an attention-like position) Bonjour ce grand! (Good morning the big!)
> S2: Bonjour! Noy tone? (Good morning! How is it?)
> S1: Ça va grand et Vous? (Fine, the big and you?)
> S2: Ça va, ça va (Fine, fine)

Namaste greeting

Namastes originate from the Indian traditional greeting: saying 'namaste' with folded hands followed by a slight bow. In the Grand North context of greeting in Cameroon, as it has been observed, the Namaste greeting consists in making a slight bow with folded hands while uttering the traditional repetitive serial greeting words. This greeting technique started emerging in 2020 as Covid-19 barrier measures were to be strictly observed. It currently occurs with a frequency of 15.62% in this speech community. It is mainly used when greeting members of royal families (princesses, princes, queen, king or Lamido (chief)).

Namaste greetings can occur occasionally among people of the same social class (high social class) or when a speaker addresses a highly superior person:

> S1: (folding his hands, followed with a slight bow) sannu moun yerima! (Good morning to you, prince)
> S2: sannu Mal Daouda! Noy djam na? (Good morning Mal Daouda! Are you fine?)
> S1: (with folded hands) djam, djam mbandu moun yerima? (Fine, fine, your health, prince?)
> S2: djam ni town. Djam saaré? (Fine for now, the home is fine?)
> S1: (with folded hands) djam ko dime yerima. Djam boukon? (Fine, there is no problem, prince. Children are fine?)
> S2: Allah hamdulilah! (Fine by the grace of Allah.)
> S1: (with folded hands) Allah barketiné yerima! (May God bless you, prince!)
> S2: Amina! (Amen!)

Grand North Cameroon is a region where positive face is not neglected, but negative face is highly paid attention to. From the observation, jocular gestures can occur in any context of positive face-saving. However, the context of negative face-saving is considered with maximum seriousness in the subjects' behaviour. This is a typical reflection of the Grand North Cameroonians' mindfulness of keeping their distance and behaving in specific contexts according to social norms.

Conclusion

The current investigation examined the new face-saving techniques adapted to the Covid-19 period in greeting rituals in Grand North Cameroon. Data were collected through observation (participant and non-participant) and interviews to attain the objective. The face-saving view, a linguistic politeness theory propounded by Brown and Levinson (987), was used to process the elicited data. The study shows that in Grand North Cameroon, serial greetings accompanied by specific gestures constituted greeting norms before the advent of the coronavirus pandemic. In addition to this, the essay contends that namastes (bowing with folded hands), attention-like standing (with right hand on chest/heart), self-hand shaking, simple hand on chest, etc. (followed by repetitive serial verbal greeting utterances that are not fully described in this essay because of the scope limit) are new greeting strategies directed to H's negative face and forearm crossing, 'foot shake', closed hands or back-of-the-hands knocking are gestures that accompany greetings directed to H's positive face. Social behaviours in the

Covid-19 era, as far as greeting techniques and face management are concerned, have demonstrated the human capacity for contextual-situational adaptation. Strict observation of Covid-19 barrier measures hindered society's traditional greeting and politeness gestures. However, people did not lack the creativity to come up with new strategies to enhance or maintain their interlocutors' positive and negative faces.

This chapter contributes to the pragmatic study of the Covid-19 challenges in general and greeting rituals in Cameroon. However, the scope of the study is limited to greeting acts (especially non-verbal greeting gestures) in the Covid-19 era. Further studies can handle other linguistic or non-linguistic behaviours, such as welcoming, congratulating, etc., that can more or less be influenced by the advent of the coronavirus pandemic.

Abstract

The advent of the coronavirus pandemic has brought about many challenges and behavioural changes around the world, as strict measures to curb the pandemic had to be scrupulously observed. As the case might be in other parts of the world, the Covid-19 preventive measures have been in friction with the traditional ways of behaving in the Grand North of Cameroon. In this speech community, like in many African societies, greeting rituals and practices constitute an indispensable social behaviour that enhances and strengthens interpersonal relationships and face maintenance. In this community, people are easily considered well-behaved or not based on their way(s) of greeting and the frequency of greeting they utter each time they meet others. The chapter examines the new face-saving techniques adapted to the Covid-19 period in greeting rituals in northern Cameroon (precisely in Ngaoundere, Garoua and Maroua). Data for this study are elicited from Grand North Cameroonians of every social class through (participant and non-participant) observation and (unstructured) interviews. The data were analysed based on Brown and Levinson's (1987) theory of face. The study shows that in Grand North Cameroon, serial greetings accompanied by specific gestures constituted greeting norms before the advent of the coronavirus pandemic. In addition to this, the essay contends that namastes, attention-like standing (with right hand on chest/heart), bowing with folded hands, self-hand shaking, simple hand-on-chest, etc., (followed by corresponding verbal utterances) are new greeting strategies directed to H's negative face, and forearm crossing, 'foot shake', closed hands or back of the hands knocking are gestures that accompany greetings directed to H's positive face. Social behaviours in the Covid-19 era, as far as greeting techniques and face management are concerned, have demonstrated the human capacity for contextual-situational adaptation in the Grand North of Cameroon.

Keywords: Greeting, pragmatics, Covid-19, face management, Grand North Cameroon.

References

Brown, P., & Levinson, S. (1987). *Politeness: Some Universals in Language Usage.* Cambridge: Cambridge University Press.

Duranti, A. (1997). Universal and Culture-Specific Properties of Greeting. *Journal of Linguistic Anthropology,* 7(1), 63–97.

Goron, A. (2016). Les rituels de salutation chez les Bororos du Nord-Cameroun. In B. Mulo Farenkia (Ed.), *Im/politesse et rituels interactionnels en contextes plurilingues et multiculturels* (pp. 269-279). Frankfurt am Main: Peter Lang.

Homeidi, M. (2004). Arabic Translation across Cultures. *Babel,* 50(1), 13-27.

Leech, G. (2014). *The Pragmatics of Politeness.* New York: Oxford University Press.

Mills, S. (2003). *Gender and Politeness.* Cambridge: Cambridge University Press.

Mulo Farenkia, B. (Ed.). (2016). *Im/politesse et Rituels Interactionnels en Contextes Plurilingues et Multiculturels.* Frankfurt am Main: Peter Lang.

Nkwain, J. (2016). The socio-pragmatics of Greeting Ritual in Cameroon Pidgin English. In B. Mulo Farenkia (Ed.), *Im/politesse et rituels interactionnels en contextes plurilingues et multiculturels* (pp. 227-245). Frankfurt am Main: Peter Lang.

Schleicher, A. (1997). Using greetings to teach cultural understanding. *Modern Language Journal,* 81(3), 334-343.

Searle, J., & Vanderveken, D. (1985). *Foundations of Illocutionary Logic.* Cambridge: Cambridge University Press.

Tabe, C. A., & Faissam, W. (2018). Politeness in the English of Fulfulde Native Speakers in Maroua. *International Journal of English Language and Linguistics Research,* 6(3), 11-31.

FOUR

Conceptualisation of Covid-19 Metaphors in the Printed Word in English

MICHAEL ETUGE APUGE & ABBA

Covid-19 is a world health concern causing tremendous harm to human existence. Some organisations, critics and especially world leaders have used figurative language to represent and discuss the disease. Language is not only the best means of communication but also provides an appropriate landscape for analysing societal pulsation. Communication about Covid-19 produced by various organisations and world leaders is propounded through non-literal expressions known as metaphors. In fact, metaphors have long been considered an extraordinary way of using language. This is notwithstanding the point raised by some researchers like Lakoff & Johnson (1980) about the key place of cognition in producing metaphors. Thus, with that connection to the mind, metaphors have been conceived as constituents of daily conversations. They are studied as the surface manifestation of a deeper system through which everyday issues are conceptualised.

Believed to have originated in Wuhan, China, in December 2019 (WHO's report, March 11th, 2020), SARS-CoV-2 is the third most highly pathogenic human coronavirus (HCoV) after the 2002 SARS-CoV (renamed SARS CoV-1) and the 2012 syndrome CoV (MERS-CoV) outbreaks. The current Covid-19 pandemic caused by severe acute respiratory syndrome coronavirus-2 has affected the world population. Among the several pathogenic viral epidemics in the past is the 1918 "Spanish Flu" or la Gripe Espanola, which adversely impacted human health and the global economy. According to the International Committee on Taxonomy of Viruses (ICTV), all known viruses are classified under three orders, 56 families, nine subfamilies and 233 genera of more than 1550 species.

After a few months of the first emergence of the virus in December 2019 and its rapid global spread in the northern and the southern hemispheres, its transmissibility was not significantly affected by seasonal variation. Covid-19 has a high primary reproductive number (R0), ranging between 2.0 to 2.5 days. The R0 measures the average number of infections from one infected individual in a susceptible population. R0 has been, however, estimated with varying results and interpretations. The current estimation of the mortality rate for Covid-19 is 3.4%, which is significantly higher than that of seasonal flu (0.02%) but lower than that of SARS-CoV-1 (9.6%) and MERS-CoV (34%). The disastrous effects of Covid-19 have brought world leaders and organisations operating in the healthcare domain to prescribe necessary and preventive messages to limit the spread of the virus. These messages were transmitted through the use of metaphors as they constitute a significant strategy concerning issues of global concern.

This chapter therefore sets out to analyse the metaphorical conceptualisation of Covid-19 by some heads of state and global opinion leaders in the printed word in English.

Literature Review

Though a recent phenomenon, Covid-19 metaphors have drawn the attention of many writers. Most of the works in this light are published online in different avenues. Salamurović's (2020) article analyses metaphors used to represent SARS-CoV-2 and other aspects of the pandemic. In this article, Salamurović discusses many metaphors used to describe the virus. Salamurović concludes that metaphors are ubiquitous in language use because they facilitate the explanation of something abstract or less known by referring to something more concrete or familiar. For instance, the pandemic is framed as a genuinely *global phenomenon*, "China and the rest of the world... in the same river," including a *journey* "sailing", with an implicit time reference, because every journey has its start and end point, with some obstacles in terms of natural phenomena which are not so extreme, but asking for caution - "storms and waves," "dangerous water" and appealing to general solidarity beyond national borders.

Also, Nerlich (2020) published an article, "Metaphors in the time of coronavirus." Her blog was inspired by the article written by Kenan Malik, another blogger, for *The Observer*. In his article, Malik states, "The coronavirus is both a *physical threat* and a metaphor for everything from the failures of globalisation to the menace of foreigners." The purpose of Nerlich's article was to display a random collection of metaphors caught on the fly, a quick overview of metaphors and metaphorical analysis. She states that metaphors create meaning and acknowledges that war metaphors have been primarily used to represent

Covid-19, as evidenced in the UK discourse by the government and printed media - *The Sun, The Guardian*.

Semino (2021), in the article "Not Soldiers but Fire-fighters" – Metaphors and Covid-19" presents metaphors used by world leaders during the outbreak of Covid-19. Semino chronicles the speeches of some heads of state and/or world leaders on Covid-19, fraught with metaphors. These leaders used metaphors to address the issue, especially as they were unanimous about the fact that it was a dangerous disease. Semino asserts that the leaders employed metaphors to draw the attention of their citizens to and/or influence their attitudes toward the pandemic. According to the author, most of the communicators use metaphors such as "enemy" to be "beaten," a "tsunami" on health services; they also use expressions like "glitter" that "gets everywhere" to refer to Covid-19. Semino further intimates that *war metaphors* were the most used. She suggests that *fire metaphors* are particularly appropriate and versatile in communication about different aspects of the pandemic. Therefore, lexes related to evil serve as a substantial avenue for the emergence of phenomenal concepts on the global stage.

Methodology

The linguistic corpus used in this chapter comprises 19 conceptual metaphors drawn from 57 metaphorical expressions from some heads of state and opinion leaders during their speeches and debates on the pandemic. The data were obtained through an online search. Focus was paid to speeches and briefings made by some world leaders. Utterances carrying metaphorical expressions were then underlined alongside the context of their production and grouped under various conceptual metaphors, namely: Covid-19 is a war, Covid-19 is a disease, Covid-19 is a phenomenon, Covid-19 is an enemy, Covid-19 is a killer, Covid-19 is a thing, and Covid-19 is a new land. This will be elaborated in the tables below.

Theoretical Framework

The theory used is Lakoff and Johnson's Conceptual Metaphors Theory (CMT) (1980). Lakoff and Johnson (1980:460), cited by Meutem (2019), uphold that "linguistic expressions are containers for meaning [and that] aspects of the metaphor entail that words and sentences have meanings in themselves independent of any context or speakers." The theory states that the "essence of metaphor is understanding and experiencing one kind of thing or experience in terms of another" (Lakoff and Johnson, 1980, p. 455). They further establish that metaphorical concepts "involve understanding fewer concrete experiences in terms of more concrete and more highly structured experiences" (Lakoff and Johnson, 1980a, p. 486). Briefly, metaphors are not mere linguistic stuff used in communication but are manifestations of language and thoughts, part of everyday language. Metaphors describe how people conceive things in the environment through the equivalences they establish between different domains. The central tenet of the theory stipulates that "metaphors are not only a matter of language but of thought and reason" (Lakoff & Johnson, 1980, p. 3).

Data Analysis and Findings

As noted in the previous sub-section, conceptual metaphors are grouped as follows: Covid-19 is a war, Covid-19 is a disease, Covid-19 is a phenomenon, Covid-19 is an enemy, Covid-19 is a killer, Covid-19 is a thing, and Covid-19 is a new land. The data are presented in tables. In each table below, the first column shows the instances or source domain words used to conceptualise Covid-19. The target expression that carries a metaphoric constituent is marked in bold. The second column provides information about the utterer of the excerpt, as well as the date.

Table 4.1. Covid-19 is a war

	Covid-19 is a war	Utterer and venue
1	"This is a "darkest hour" of Second **War** World" using Winston Churchill's words".	Italian Prime Minister, Giuseppe Conte, March 9th 2020.
2	"We are **at war** with a virus-and not winning it…This war needs a war-time plan to fight it"	UN Secretary-General, Antonio Gutiérez: G-20 Virtual Summit on the Covid-19. March 26th, 2020.
3	"I'm a **wartime** president"	Donald Trump, March 2020
4	"…We all should be confident that we will win this **war**".	Chinese president, XI-Jinping: Wuhan, March 10th 2020.
5	"…the Republic of Serbia, as of today Serbia has been at **war** against an invisible enemy (…) that our country must defeat."	Serbian President, Aleksandar Vučić, 15th March 2020.
6	"We will win this **war**. When we achieve this victory, we will emerge stronger and more united than ever before!"	Donald Trump, News interview. March 28, 2020.
7	"We are **at war**, admittedly a **health war**: we're **fighting** neither an army nor another nation".	Emmanuel Macron, Élysée March 16, 2020.

	Covid-19 is a war	Utterer and venue
8	"Estamos en **la Guerra**"- "We are **at war** (trans)".	Spanish prime minister, Pedro Sanchez April 5th, 2020.
9	"We are **at war** with Covid-19. We need to fight it like **a war**"	Donald Trump: The *Globe and Mail*, April 6th, 2020.
10	"China was mobilizing the nation in a "people's **war**" in China announcing a total **war** against Covid-19.	Chinese President, Xi Jinping, August 13, 2020.
11	"It's a **medical war**. We have to win this war. It's very important."	Donald Trump, White house conference. March 18th 2020.
12	"To this day, nobody has seen anything like what they were able to do during **World War II**". Now it's our time. We must **sacrifice** together because we are all in this situation together and we will come through together"	Donald Trump, White house conference: March 18th 2020.
13	"We **will meet again**" evoking a **Second War World song**".	Queen Elisabeth II, BBC News address: April 5th, 2020.
14	"Covid-19 to be the most challenging **serious challenge** facing Germany since **World War II**	German Chancellor, Angela Merkel, TV address 18th March 2020.

Table 4.1 reveals that the conceptual source domain "war" maps the conceptual target domain "Covid-19." The expressions "will meet again," "World War II," "sacrifice," "serious challenge," "wartime," "health" "war," "fighting," and "medical war" represent the values used in the conceptual source domain to map the conceptual target domain. It is worth pointing out that a war is referred to as "any situation in which there is strong competition between opposing sides or a great fight against something harmful" (Cald, 2008, p. 456). By using the source domain of WAR to discuss Covid-19 in their speeches and debates, the heads of state and opinion leaders build the image of a fight against a vicious enemy. For instance, Donald Trump and other speakers used the concept of war to name Covid-19 in their speeches based on their similarities and because military expressions may help increase people's morale. Covid-19 is therefore conceptualised as war. What accounts for this linkage is that WAR engages the life of protagonists in nefarious consequences such as terror, damages, injuries, and death. These consequences are also manifest in Covid-19 situations: people are terrorised, the world acknowledges economic, financial, societal damages and

many deaths. This mapping eases the understanding of the closeness between Covid-19 and war. It can therefore be concluded that Covid-19 is a war.

Table 4.2. Covid-19 is a pandemic

	Covid-19 is a pandemic	Utterer and venue
1	"We have therefore made the assessment that the Covid-19 can be characterized as a *pandemic*"	WHO Director-General, Tedros Adhanom Ghebreyesus, March 11, 2020.
2	"I felt it was a *pandemic* long before it was called a *pandemic*."	Donald Trump, News briefing, March 17, 2020.
3	"The encouraging lessons learnt from our Covid-19 response strategy enabled us (…) persons most affected by the *pandemic*".	Paul Biya, Unity Palace, 19th May 2020.
4	"Most have already been implemented and are certainly to slowing down the spread of the *pandemic*."	Paul Biya, Unity Palace, 19th May 2020.
5	"It is scary but fulfilling to be at the forefront of the fight against this *pandemic* through volunteering."	U.N volunteer, Christine Mouaha, Yaoundé, 2020.
6	"(…) I would like to express my condolences. This *pandemic* is a serious global challenge for all of us."	Danish Prime Minister, Mette Frederiksen, 5 Nov 2020.

In Table 4.2, the declarations of presidents Trump, Biya, the WHO Director-General and others indicate that they conceptualised Covid-19 as a pandemic. The use of the *pandemic* is not a linguistic decoration but more an indication that Covid-19 is a global concern with a high transmission risk and a sharp spread in the vast majority of the world. Early official information (WHO report, 11th January 2020) about Covid-19 reported that it emerged in December 2019 in China and spread rapidly in the northern and the southern hemispheres with a high basic reproductive number (R0), ranging between 2.0 to 2.5 days. Therefore, nations, institutions, and people must collaborate to fight or at least impede this global enemy. Presidents Donald Trump, Paul Biya, Emmanuel Macron, Prime Minister Boris Johnson and other officials resorted to strong language by conceptualising Covid-19 as a pandemic after the WHO declared it as such since they saw the link between both phenomena. Following Lakoff and Johnson's (1980), Conceptual Metaphor Theory, when a concept "A" (target domain) establishes a mapping with a concept "B" (source domain), Covid-19 can be conceptualised as a pandemic. This conceptualisation sends a powerful message to various populations that Covid-19 has become a large-scale and dangerous threat to the world.

Table 4.3. Covid-19 is an alien

	Covid-19 is an alien	Utterer and Venue
1	"Brits would see off the virus like every other *alien* in 1,000 years"	The Brits Prime Minister, Boris Johnson, March 2020.
2	He added: "(…) we will succeed, just as this country has seen off every *alien invader* for the last thousand years"	Boris Johnson, March 2020.
3	"As coronavirus has *invaded* the world and is threatening the humanity…"	Nerlich, February, 2021
4	"And we will succeed by collective effort, by following the guidance and with the help of weekly (…) the science we will defeat this *alien*."	Boris Johnson, March 2020

The expressions "alien," "alien invader," "other alien" have been used metaphorically in Table 4.3 to form the conceptual metaphor of Covid-19 as an alien invader. As a harmful and invasive enemy, Covid-19 has pushed Nerlich and Prime Minister Boris Johnson to use the word "invaded" and the concept "alien invader", respectively, to name the pandemic. An invader can be considered a devourer or a destroyer, while an alien is a strange creature from a different planet than the one where humans live. Boris Johnson used this expression concerning glorious victories over specific invaders in the history of England: "(…) we will succeed, just as this country has seen off every alien invader for the last thousand years" (Boris Johnson, March 2020). "England has had victory over those epic aliens and will therefore survive in the era of Covid-19"; this is what the prime minister said during his conference with the Conservatives. Conceptualising Covid-19 as an alien invader, Boris Johnson is first and foremost drawing the attention of his countrymen and giving them hope to come out victorious, as they have in past battles.

Covid-19 effects actually correspond to those of an alien invader. These characteristics are evident in the global impacts of the Covid-19 pandemic because it destabilises human freedom and peace, weakens health capacity, and kills dreams. Following the phenomenon of mappings proposed by Lakoff and

Johnson (1980), conceptual metaphors denote that an unfamiliar concept can map into a more understandable reality. Thus, the conceptualisation of Covid-19 as an alien invader is therefore valid.

Table 4.4. Covid-19 is an enemy

	Covid-19 is an enemy	Utterer and venue
1	"We have an *invisible enemy*."	Donald Trump, News conference, March 16, 2020
2	"[…], but the **enemy** is there, *invisible*, elusive, and it's making headway. And that requires our widespread mobilization".	President Emmanuel Macron, Élysée, March 16th, 2020.
3	"Yes, this **enemy** can be deadly"	Boris Johnson, 16 March 2020
4	"Ladies and gentlemen, dear citizens of the Republic of Serbia, as of today Serbia has been at war against an **invisible enemy**…"	Serbian president, Aleksandar Vučić, 15th March 2020
5	"We're *fighting* against *an invisible enemy*".	USA president Donald Trump, News briefing, March 17th, 2020.
6	"No matter where you look, this (Covid-19) is something—it's an **invisible enemy**".	USA president Donald Trump, News briefing, March 17th, 2020.
7	"I just say this: We have an **invisible enemy**."	Donald Trump, March 17, 2020
8	"The Cabinet Office would continue to marshal all the resources of the government in the fight against this **invisible enemy**".	Michael Gove, England Cabinet Officer. April 2020
9	"[…] today, the context is different. Cameroon, like most countries in the world, has been affected by Covid-19. Our health system is mobilized to combat this **terrible enemy**".	Cameroonian President, Paul Biya, Yaoundé 19th May 2020
10	"[…] to fight this **terrible** and horrible **enemy**"	Donald Trump, Fox News, 16th March 2020
11	"[…] Let us channel all our energies towards *fighting* this **common enemy**."	Paul Biya, Yaoundé, 19th May 2020

	Covid-19 is an enemy	Utterer and venue
12	"We should join our forces to combat this **global enemy** to its ultimate rest"	Antonio Gutieres, 26th March 2020
13	Serbia has been at war against […] a **dangerous enemy** that our country must defeat."	Aleksandar Vučić, 15th March 2020
14	"The government must act like any war-time government while facing a **deadly enemy**".	Boris Johnson, 15th March, 2020
15	"[…] this thing (Covid-19) is a **horrible enemy**"	Donald Trump, Fox News 16th March 2020.
16	"This **horrible enemy** is alleviating the life of past generation"	Boris Johnson, 15th March, 2020.

The abundance of metaphorical expressions in Table 4.4 relates to the domain of "enemy" that are part of the world's realities. They establish a correspondence between the more visible and less concrete domains of Covid-19. In this light, Covid-19 is perceived as an *enemy* with what it entails. An enemy is a person or something that hates or opposes another person and tries to harm them or deter them from succeeding or progressing in life. The enemy is dangerous as he seeks to destroy or kill his opponent. All these qualifications emphasise the source domain (enemy), and Covid-19 symbolises the aforementioned deadly roles; it is invisibly fatal, common, vicious, global, terrible, and dangerous. It has afflicted considerable damage to the world, leading to the stoppage of business and movement worldwide, limited sociability and face-to-face interaction, deprived citizens of leisure and pleasure, and led to millions of deaths, among others.

Before the advent of Covid-19, the world was not suffering from the aforementioned misfortunes; people were somehow living peacefully, having access to their leisure and desires with no such unbearable restrictions; they were free in their movements and businesses. Once Covid-19 appeared, everything broke down and fell apart. Covid-19 is not only an enemy but also something abstract and difficult to deal with. This justifies why it is conceived as an invisible, common, vicious, terrible and dangerous enemy. So, it is important to make people aware of the harmful effects of the illness in order to take appropriate measures to *fight* that enemy. Therefore, conceptualising Covid-19 as an (invisible) "enemy" intends to enlighten people and rally humanity for a constructive discussion.

Table 4.5. Covid-19 is a Foreign Virus

	Covid-19 is a Foreign Virus	Utterer and Venue
1	"It's one person coming in *from China*, and we have it under control. It's going to be just fine."	Donald Trump, News briefing January 22th 2020.
2	"This is the most aggressive and comprehensive effort to confront a *foreign virus* in modern history."	Donald Trump, News briefing, March 11, 2020.
3	"This is a very *contagious virus*. It's incredible. But it's something that we have tremendous control over."	Donald Trump, News briefing, March 15th 2020.
4	"I always treated the *Chinese Virus* very seriously, and have done a very good job from the beginning, including my very early decision to close the 'borders' from China."	Donald Trump, News briefing, March 18th 2020
5	"We continue our relentless effort to defeat the *Chinese virus*,"	Donald Trump, News briefing, March 18th, 2020
6	Trump used the phrase "our war against the *Chinese virus*."	Donald Trump, News briefing, March 18th 2020
7	(…) and we will ultimately and expeditiously defeat this *virus*.	Donald Trump, March 11, 2020
8	"We're using the full power of the federal government to **defeat the** *virus*, and that's what we've been doing."	Donald Trump, 14thMarch, 2020
9	"We don't want people to be together so that this *virus* doesn't continue onward."	Donald Trump, March 19th 2020
10	"I can tell you that your government is working night and day to repel this *virus*."	Boris Johnson: 29 April, 2020

In Table 4.5, stakeholders conceptualised Covid-19 as a "virus." Evidence that different speakers above realised that the disease had become a large-scale and dangerous threat to the world abound. Framing Covid-19 as a virus means that Covid-19 and a virus may have some point of resemblance. This is obvious when the comparison is made on some of their features. Some viruses are dangerous micro-organisms that affect a large-scale of people; they are invisible, contagious and move through the air. Covid-19 is also dangerous, not visible, and it also affects a large-scale of the population. Lakoff and Johnson (1980) hold that metaphors are based on similarities and the conceptualisation of everyday reality through acts and thoughts. Through the principle of conceptualisation,

Covid-19 is used to map the concrete concept "virus." President Donald Trump and British Prime Minister Boris Johnson located the origin and the identity of Covid-19 using the locative adjective "foreign" in the expressions "foreign virus," "Chinese virus." This is to emphasise the idea that China is responsible for the outbreak of Covid-19. President Trump linked the origin of Covid-19 with ethnicity or identity, which is China. It can be concluded that Trump's metaphorical use of language intending to release himself from domestic responsibilities and to blame an external factor for this foreign enemy is calculative. While Boris Johnson represented Covid-19 as a virus that builds confidence and hope in the Brits so that fear should be curbed in them, his ultimate goal was to let his people know that Covid-19 is a beatable virus.

Table 4.6. Covid-19 is a Killer

	Covid-19 is a Killer	Utterer and Venue
1	"(…) that the fight against that *killer disease* should be collective."	Boris Johnson, Friday, 5th March 2021
2	"Health Secretary of Britain reported that his country is fighting a "war against an *invisible killer.*"	Katie McCallum's Telegraph, March 16, 2020

In Table 4.6, the speakers represent Covid-19 as a killer. In these utterances, Covid-19, the target domain, is mapped into the source domain, killer. It is worth mentioning that a killer is widely understood as someone or something that kills people or things, especially a disease or an illness. Like a killer that kills people, Covid-19 also kills. Reports from WHO say that victims are counted in dozens of millions. Conceptual Metaphor Theory stipulates that people use everyday knowledge of the world to discuss fewer concrete issues. In this light, the killer seems more concrete than Covid-19 to people. The conceptualisation of Covid-19 as a killer helps to establish a set of mappings between the killer (source domain) and Covid-19 (target domain). The set of mappings underscored through the mappings of shared characteristics between Covid-19 and a killer is that both kill people. Following Conceptual Metaphor Theory, these mappings implement a set of correspondences from which similarities are drawn. Thus, some parallels can be observed between both domains. Also, the conceptual metaphor constructs under the domain of killing to denote Covid-19 as a killer looks much more understandable to people, and as a result, they will set up a strategy to fight it.

Table 4.7. Covid-19 is a Thing

	Covid-19 is a Thing	Utterer and Venue
1	[...] "No matter where you look, this is *something*".	Donald Trump, March 16th, 2020
2	"I have faced everything; it is not that your *thing* that will stop me".	Emile Bouin, France
3	"We're in the middle of *something* none has faced before."	Danish PM, Mette Frederiksen, 12th 2020

The conceptualisation of Covid-19 as a "thing" is discussed in the preceding excerpts in Table 4.7. Donald Trump and Emile Bouin (the late former French education Minister) used the source domain concept "thing" to map the conceptual target domain "Covid-19." A thing is "used to refer in an approximate way, to an idea, subject, event, action, etc." The conceptual metaphor referring to Covid-19 as a thing can be paraphrased as Covid-19 is something that people cannot fathom. This means that Covid-19 is an abstraction; it is like a thing that happens in a vacuum or is unclear in people's minds. Covid-19 has caused much trouble in people's minds; people strive to characterise it without success. The US President attributed Covid-19 to names like "enemy," "Chinese virus," etc., in his preceding speeches before using the concept "thing." One of the tenets of Conceptual Metaphor Theory is that a "metaphor can be based partly on similarities" (Lakoff and Johnson, 1980). This justifies the conceptualisation of Covid-19 as a thing or something in the speeches of Donald Trump and Emile Bouin.

Table 4.8. Covid-19 is a New Land

	Covid-19 is a New Land	Utterer and Venue
1	"This is our *new home*".	Queen Elisabeth II, 5th April 2020
2	"Coronavirus is as a *new land* or a dangerous visitor."	Danish PM, Mette Frederiksen, 12th May 2020

The utterances in Table 4.8 above reveal that Queen Elisabeth II and the Danish PM coined the conceptual metaphor "Covid-19 is a new land," signifying that Covid-19 is new territory, a common home, or a new challenge. Both speakers conceptualised Covid-19 (target domain) as a new land (source domain). As pointed out in Conceptual Metaphor Theory (CMT), using metaphors implies the mapping of correspondences between features of the source domain and those of the target domain. In these utterances, the modifier "new" is the value used with the source domain "land" to map the conceptual target domain "Covid-19." That is, the elements used in the conceptual source domain refer to the concrete thing "land." Land can be understood as a large territory where many people can settle. Like the (new) land that can host many people, Covid-19 is a world concern. Admittedly, this virus's devastating damages have affected people worldwide. Definitely, it is something that is creating a new world of horror and requires a joint effort to confront it since it kills children, youth, and the old indiscriminately. Therefore, like a land where people live, the Queen and Danish Prime Minster conceptualise Covid-19 as a product of the global village.

Table 4.9. Covid-19 is a Phenomenon

	Covid-19 is a Phenomenon	Utterer and Venue
1	[...] "We must sacrifice together because we are *all in this together* and we'll come through together."	Donald Trump, 19th March 2020
2	"As the Covid-19 pandemic rages across the world, one thing is clear: this epidemic, like all others, is a *social phenomenon*."	Parker Melissa, 20th march 2020
3	"Covid-19 –a social *phenomenon* requiring diverse expertise."	Haylay McGregor, March 20, 2020

Table 4.9 describes Covid-19 as a phenomenon of concern to everybody that needs a common front to fight it. US President Donald Trump and other speakers consider Covid-19 as a strange event or an act that necessitates answers. That is probably why he said, "we are all in this together and we'll come through together." Conceptual Metaphor Theory by Lakoff and Johnson (1980) indicates that speakers can shape people's understanding and attitudes towards the world by emphasising neutral or less negative features of a particular concept, while the potentially offensive features are overlooked. Based on this, Trump attempts to highlight the nature of Covid-19 to Americans so that they link the image of Covid-19 to a circumstance borne by the entire population. Covid-19 is a strange event to people, and even America (a powerful country in science with military might) could not easily understand the virus and has to bear it like other less-privileged nations. That is why Trump represents Covid-19 through the image of a phenomenon.

Covid-19 is perceived as a social phenomenon when examples in which the target domain (Covid-19) is conceptualised either by using "lexical items associated with the phenomenon or ascribing characteristics only human beings can possess" (Vuorinen, 2014:58). This metaphorical construction is built with the modifier "social," implying that Covid-19 is an issue to the society, a societal concern. The strangeness and extreme severity of the Covid-19 pandemic in the U.S. and other parts of the world have made some leaders perceive it as a phenomenon.

Table 4.10. Covid-19 is an Airborne

	Covid-19 is an Airborne	Utterer and Venue
1	"(…) there's increasing evidence that Covid-19 is *airborne* in certain situations, particularly in enclosed, poorly ventilated spaces":	CDC Director-general Dr. Connolly Wednesday, 15th April 2021
2	"People can protect themselves from the virus that causes Covid-19 by staying at least 6 feet away from others, *wearing a mask* that *covers their nose* and mouth, washing their hands frequently, (…) and staying home when sick".	Julia Ries, Oct 7, 2020

Table 4.10 reveals that the word *airborne* has been metaphorically used to refer to the Covid-19 pandemic in the excerpt of speeches. Airborne is a word that describes something carried by the wind or by an aircraft. In the medical domain, airborne refers to an illness that can be transmitted to another person by air. Covid-19 is *airborne* in certain situations, particularly in poorly ventilated spaces. From the foregoing, it is assumed that Covid-19 is compared to an airborne based on the aspect of correspondence. The correspondence between Covid-19 and "airborne" lies in their medium of transmission. Both elements are transmitted through air, wind and aircraft. Like Lakoff and Johnson's theory established the mappings between love and journey, mappings can also be found between the target domain (Covid-19) and source domain (airborne). Covid-19 is transmitted through the air, wind and aircraft like airborne diseases get into people. That is why people are requested to wear masks, cover their noses and adopt social distancing (people can protect themselves from the virus that causes Covid-19 by staying at least 6 feet away from others). These are some of the measures that people should adopt to protect themselves from Covid-19. If Covid-19 has as its vehicle, air and wind, it can therefore be referred to as

"airborne." It is meaningful to recall that Covid-19 started in China and later spread to many countries worldwide. This shows that Covid-19 uses air, wind or an infected agent to travel from one country to another. This assertion is shared by the CDC Director-general, who conceptualised Covid-19 as an airborne virus in his April 15th, 2020 statement.

Table 4.11. Distribution of Conceptual Metaphors and their Occurrences

Conceptual Metaphors	Number of Occurrences
Covid-19 is a war	14
Covid-19 is a pandemic	6
Covid-19 is an alien	4
Covid-19 is an enemy	16
Covid-19 is a foreign virus	5
Covid-19 is a killer	2
Covid-19 is a thing	3
Covid-19 is a new land	2
Covid-19 is a phenomenon	3
Covid-19 is an airborne	2
Total	57

The table above presents the various conceptual metaphors along with their occurrences. It can be observed that the conceptual metaphor which has registered the highest number of values is that Covid-19 is an enemy (16 occurrences), followed by Covid-19 is a war (14 occurrences), Covid-19 is a pandemic (6 occurrences), Covid-19 is a foreign virus (5 occurrences), Covid-19 is an alien (04 occurrences), Covid-19 is a thing, a phenomenon (3 occurrences) and Covid-19 is a new land, a killer (2 occurrences). It can therefore be admitted that Covid-19 stakeholders conceptualise Covid-19 most as an enemy in their speeches.

Conclusion

This paper set out to analyse the conceptualisation of Covid-19 in the printed word in English. The data analysed were collected from speeches and debates of some heads of state obtained online. The data were analysed within Lakoff and Johnson's (1980) Conceptual Metaphor Theory (CMT). The work is based on the hypothesis that metaphors comprise a communication strategy used by Covid-19 stakeholders in their briefings to discuss the ramifications of the pandemic and pass the message around the world. The analysis reveals that stakeholders conceptualised Covid-19 as a war, a pandemic, an alien, an enemy, a foreign virus, a killer, a thing, a new land, a phenomenon and an airborne disease. Furthermore, the conceptualisation of metaphors of Covid-19 played an essential role in the message delivered by heads of state and opinion leaders as this strategy helped the population to understand the pandemic and to seek solutions to curb it.

Abstract

This chapter examines the conceptualisation of Covid-19 metaphors in the printed word in English. The work is discussed from the standpoint of cognitive linguistics, using Lakoff and Johnson's (1980) Conceptual Metaphor Theory (CMT). The study posits that metaphor is a linguistic code used by Covid-19 stakeholders in their speeches and debates to transmit messages to their audiences. The findings reveal that the stakeholders conceptualised Covid-19 as follows: Covid-19 is a war, Covid-19 is a pandemic, Covid-19 is an alien, Covid-19 is a foreign virus, Covid-19 is a phenomenon, Covid-19 is an enemy, Covid-19 is a killer, Covid-19 is a thing, Covid-19 is a new land, and Covid-19 is airborne. This paper contends that instead of achieving the primary purpose of transmitting messages concerning the pandemic, these metaphors could create fear within the population.

Keywords: Covid-19 Metaphors, Speeches and Debates, Cognitive Linguistics, Fear.

References

Aristotle (1909). *The Poetics*. Cambridge, MA: Harvard University Press.
Cambridge advanced learner's Dictionary, 3rd edition. (2008). Cambridge: Cambridge University Press.
Ghebreyesus, T. A. (2020). WHO Director-general's opening remarks at the media briefing on COVID-19. March 23, 2020, Geneva.
Lakoff, G. and. Johnson, M. (1980 a). Conceptual metaphor in everyday language. *Journal of Philosophy* 77(8), 453-486.
Lakoff, G. & Johnson, M. (1980 b). *Metaphors we live by*. Chicago: The University of Chicago Press.
Lakoff, G. (1994). The contemporary view of metaphor. In A. Ortony (ed.), *Metaphor and thought*, 2nd ed., (pp. 202-251). Cambridge. Cambridge University Press.
Meutem Kamtchueng, L. M. (2019). On the conceptualisation of corruption metaphors in Cameroon online media. In L. M. Meutem Kamtchueng, C. A. Tabe & D. Nkemleke (Eds.), *Language, media and technology: usages, forms and functions* (pp. 108-123). Muenchen: LINCOM GmbH.

Nerlich, B. (2020). Metaphors in the time of coronavirus. Making Science Public. University of Nottingham Blogs

Salamurović, A. (2020). Metonymy and the conceptualisation of nation in political discourse *Yearbook of the German Cognitive Linguistics Association* 8(1), 181-196.

Semino, E. (2021). Not Soldiers but Fire-fighters – Metaphors and Covid-19. *Health Communication, 36*(1), 50-58.

World Health Organisation (2020). *Covid-19 press briefing*. Geneva.

FIVE

An Analysis of the Communication Strategies During the Covid-19 Pandemic
The Case of Apostolic Faith Church West and Central Africa

NGONJO VICTOR FUH

The world, West and Central Africa in particular woke up towards the end of the first quarter of 2020 to experience a terrible pandemic unprecedented in recent memory. Cucinotta and Vanelli (2020, p. 157) state that the coronavirus outbreak started in Wuhan, China, in December 2019 and became a global pandemic on March 11, 2020, as declared by the World Health Organisation. Some world leaders like Donald Trump rhetorically called the disease an "invisible" enemy. This virus struck the entire world so hard that governments took draconian measures to curb its spread. Due to the ravaging nature of this invisible monster, the World Health Organisation came up with some preventive measures which governments worldwide adopted and even went beyond them. Some of these measures include:
1. Limiting large gatherings.
2. Limiting activities involving physical contact and only allowing sports that allow for physical distancing.
3. Limiting the number of people at funerals, baptisms, weddings, birthday parties and cultural ceremonies.
4. Drivers and passengers should avoid using non-medical masks or cloth face covering.
5. Passengers should sit apart from each other such as using every other seat on buses and taxis.
6. People should stay home and only go out if needed.
7. People should report to a nearby hospital when they feel sick.
8. Hands should be constantly washed with clean water and soap. They

should be sanitised.
9. Objects and surfaces, such as toys, phones, toilets, and door handles, should be cleaned and disinfected.
10. Keep two metres away from each other outside your home.
11. Avoid greetings that include physical contact, such as handshakes.
12. If you start to develop symptoms of Covid-19, isolate yourself from others and contact your healthcare provider or local public health authority.
13. Avoid touching your face with unwashed hands.
14. Cough and sneeze into a tissue or the bend of your arm.
15. Wash your hands often with soap and clean water for at least 20 seconds or use an alcohol-based hand sanitiser containing at least 60% alcohol.

It is worth mentioning that while individual governments laid down rules on how their populations should live, respective organisations also did the same on how they could better function during the pandemic. This chapter investigates the communication strategies that AFC West and Central Africa developed during the Covid-19 pandemic to maintain contact with their members.

Organisational Structure of Apostolic Faith Church (AFC) West and Central Africa

The Apostolic Faith Church (AFC) West and Central Africa is a religious organisation whose main objective is to win Africa for Christ. To accomplish this mission, the church in Africa has been divided into the Southern Africa zone, the East Africa zone and the West and Central Africa zone. This chapter analyses the communication strategies of this organisation in West, and Central Africa adopted during the Covid-19 pandemic for its better functioning.

The Apostolic Faith Church in West and Central Africa (WECA) is structured as follows:

West Africa

The Apostolic Faith Church in West Africa is found in countries like Nigeria, Ghana, Liberia, Niger Republic, Gambia, Ivory Coast, Burkina Faso, Republic of Benin and Togo.

Central Africa

The Apostolic Faith Church in Central Africa has branches in Cameroon, the Democratic Republic of Congo, and Gabon.

It is important to note that the churches that make up our case study are headed by district, regional and country overseers. Furthermore, these overseers are led by a superintendent, the Superintendent of Apostolic Faith Church West and Central Africa (WECA), with headquarters at Anthony Village, Ikorodu Road, Lagos, Nigeria. The headquarters determines how this organisation should function in line with the word of God in all aspects of life, emphasising the spirituality of brethren and sisters. When this is done, directives are sent to district, regional and country overseers for implementation in their various congregations.

Research Problem

It should be noted that the church was not exempted from the devastating effects of lockdown, especially in Central and West Africa. Furthermore, according to Yunusa et al. (2021, p. 43), more than 87% of the world's student population - over 1.5 billion learners in 165 countries have been affected by the temporary closure of educational institutions. Amid this turbulent situation, Brien (2020, p. 242) poses two questions:

- Will the Covid-19 lockdown weaken the stability of modern religion?
- Can religion adapt to a vastly changed society?

Across the globe, people are bringing innovations in their religious practices. In the United Kingdom, for example, BBC One has returned to broadcasting Sunday morning services. In Iran, Muslims attend drive-in religious ceremonies during Ramadan, described by one participant as "creative and beautiful" (Brien, 2020, p. 244).

Given the challenges posed by the pandemic, AFC West and Central Africa developed innovative strategies to maintain contact with its followers during this period.

Review of Related Literature

Many critics and researchers have written a lot on the Covid-19 pandemic, as illustrated in the literature below. Reynolds and Quinn (2008, p. 138) state that, during a crisis, open and empathetic communication that engenders the public's trust is the most effective when officials attempt to galvanise the population to take positive action or refrain from a harmful act. Although trust is imperative in a crisis, public suspicions of scientific experts and governments are increasing for a variety of reasons, including access to more sources of conflicting information, reduction in the use of scientific reasoning in decision-making, and political infighting. Trust and credibility which are demonstrated through empathy and caring, competence and expertise, honesty and openness, and dedication and commitment are essential elements of persuasive communication.

On the other hand, Quinn et al. (2005, p. 207) state that in 2001, the United States experienced its first bioterrorism attack in the form of anthrax sent through the U.S. Postal Service, and public health professionals were challenged to communicate with a critical audience, U.S. postal workers. Postal workers, the first cohort to receive public health messages during a bioterrorist crisis, offer a crucial viewpoint that can be used to develop best practices in crisis and emergency communication. The results revealed that the social context and changing messages were among the factors that damaged trust between postal workers and public health professionals.

Furthermore, Reddy and Gupta (2020, p. 37) state that the impact of Covid-19 on vulnerable groups relies in part on the quality of communication regarding health risks and danger. Strategic planning should fully consider how life conditions, cultural values, and risk experience affect actions during a pandemic. The concept of educational communication changes social human behaviour, which is captured by technology and media. Ignorance of sociocultural, economic, psychological, and health factors can jeopardise communication at all levels. The authors show that understanding and practising various communication strategies is crucial for physicians and healthcare workers to develop therapeutic relationships with Covid-19 patients.

In the same light, symptom management and skilled communication with patients and families are essential clinical services amid the Covid-19 pandemic (Bowman et al., 2020, p. 98). Although palliative care specialists have training in these skills, many frontline clinicians from other specialities do not. All clinicians responding to the Covid-19 crisis must have access to clinical tools to support symptom management and difficult patient and family communication. Also, mandated face mask use by healthcare providers creates an additional communication barrier for older adults with cognitive, communication, and/or hearing challenges, asserts Porter and Burshnic (2020, p. 7). Face masks can soften a speaker's voice, conceal vocal tone, and hide facial expressions that relay essential non-verbal information. An inability to understand healthcare information or words of support can lead to frustration, anxiety and decreased quality of life. Thus, this work reviews the current research, provides clinical examples and highlights communication strategies (written, gestural, and picture support) and modifications to personal protective equipment that healthcare providers can implement, in isolation or combined, to improve communication with adults.

With effective Covid-19 vaccines in hand, we must now address the spread of information on social media that might encourage vaccine hesitancy

(Broniatowski et al., 2021, p. 1055). Although misinformation comes in different forms, including false claims (for example, deliberately false information) and rumours (for instance, unverified information), social media companies now seek to interdict this objectionable content, for the first time in their history by removing content explicitly containing conspiracy theories and false claims about vaccines. Social media users routinely disparage "anti-vaxxers" online, conflating a large group of vaccine-hesitant individuals who may be using social media to seek information about vaccination with a potentially much smaller group of "vaccine refuters." Both strategies could cause more harm than good, necessitating a change in communication strategy as demonstrated by scientific evidence that could enable more effective online communication about Covid-19.

The world's attention is rightly focused on measures to mitigate the transmission and economic effects of the Covid-19 pandemic (Dalton, Rapa & Stein, 2020, p. 346). In this rapidly changing situation, media and social conversations are entirely dominated by the outbreak, and children are exposed to large amounts of information and high levels of stress and anxiety in the adults around them. Simultaneously, children are experiencing substantial changes in their daily routine, fostering resilience to changing events.

Parents would do anything to protect their children from distress and might avoid talking about difficult feelings and events. However, research shows that even children need honest information about changes within their families; when this information is absent, children attempt to make sense of the situation independently. On the other hand, governments throughout the world can learn many critical lessons from examining instances of effective communication with the public during the global Covid-19 pandemic (Kim & Kreps, 2020, p. 398). Ineffective communication has resulted in a great deal of public confusion, misunderstanding, and severe errors in responding to this evolving health threat, leading to disastrous health and social outcomes for the public, thereby prolonging the pandemic, especially in the United States. The authors offer communication strategies that promote delivering relevant, accurate, and sensitive information to key public groups, minimising communication noise to guide desirable coordinated actions. These communication strategies can be applied locally, nationally, and internationally.

Vietnam is considered one of the countries with the earliest and most effective responses to the outbreak of the Covid-19 pandemic (Tam et al., 2021, p. 45). An essential contribution to the overall success is the effectiveness of governmental communication strategy in achieving the desired cognitive effect and behavioural outcomes. Results show that Vietnamese have adequate information about the Covid-19 pandemic, and most experience low emotional levels of anxiety, fear, dread, distress, and panic. In the same line, Martens' (2021, p. 1) study examines if the risk communication strategies in the state of Minnesota in its response to the Covid-19 pandemic align with the best practices described in the work above. The findings showed that Minnesota's risk communication strategies aligned with two-thirds of the best practices found in Martens' study. The state of Minnesota failed in its application of effective risk communication strategies in pre-planning tactics.

The Covid-19 pandemic has led to the infection of over 22 million individuals and resulted in over 780,000 deaths globally (Shih & Chi, 2020, p. 341). The rapid spread of the virus and the precipitously increasing number of cases necessitated the urgent development of accurate diagnostic methods, effective treatments, and vaccines. Shih and Chi (ibid) review the progress of developing diagnostic procedures, therapies, and vaccines for SARS-CoV-2, focusing on current clinical trials and their challenges. For diagnostic, nucleic acid amplification tests remain the mainstay diagnostics for laboratory confirmation of SARS-CoV-2 infections.

Similarly, the world is battling the novel coronavirus outbreak, which has caused a downward spiral in many nations' economies, particularly in higher education (Yunusa et al., 2021, p. 43). A growing number of universities have either postponed or cancelled academic activities. A few universities have intensified measures to prevent face-to-face interactions, intending to protect staff members and students from the highly contagious disease. The study shows that Covid-19 negatively impacted several universities. Also, Kamal and IIIiyan (2021, p. 311) state that the Covid-19 outbreak has affected catastrophically every sector of the economy throughout the world, and the education sector is not left out from the devastating effects of the lockdown, especially in South Asia. It has led to the prolonged closure of schools and universities; traditional teaching expeditiously transformed into online education. Also, Seak (2020, p. 388) states that Linkou Chang Gung Memorial Hospital, Taiwan, has been at the forefront of efforts to manage and mitigate the Covid-19 pandemic since 20th January 2020. Despite having one of the world's largest and busiest emergency departments, they have managed to maintain a "zero infection" rate among their emergency department healthcare workers through various systematic approaches. The measures implemented include establishing a clear flow chart with route planning, strict infection control policies and medical equipment regulation, and team-based workplace segregation.

From the above discussion, we can conclude that all the works carried out during the coronavirus pandemic are characterised by communication strategies with patients and health workers, lockdown of schools and businesses, the pandemic's impact and the pandemic's mitigation, to name a few. These works have yet to touch on communication strategies used by religious leaders in the religious realm to strengthen a cordial relationship with their congregational members which is the focus of this essay.

Data Collection

According to Olayinka, Taiwo, Raji and Farai (2005:77), data are "the symbols, numbers and or alphabetical characters used to describe one or more attributes such as age, sex, volume, growth rates, temperature, etc. of an entity." Data are obtained by observing, measuring, and counting, etc. Data were collected using the instrumentation of a questionnaire. A total of 20 questionnaires were sent to brethren and sisters in the Apostolic Faith Churches that make up WECA. The random sampling technique was used to get the views and opinions of respondents about the topic under study. The questions were formulated based on the different activities in AFC churches in WECA on Sundays. This was done to solicit information on the communication strategies they have been using during the Covid-19 pandemic. The questionnaires were sent online using the social media application WhatsApp to the different respondents in the other churches under study. A total of sixteen questionnaires were sent to Apostolic Faith Churches in West Africa as follows: four questionnaires to AFC Ghana, one to Gambia, one to Ivory Coast, one to Liberia, one to Togo, one to the Republic of Benin, one to Niger Republic and six to Nigeria. On the other hand, four questionnaires were sent to Apostolic Faith Churches in Central Africa: one to Cameroon, one to the Democratic Republic of Congo, one to Burkina Faso and one to Gabon. All the questionnaires were answered by the respondents, and copies were duly returned. The questionnaires were made up of the following four questions:
- How do you greet someone you meet in church on Sunday?
- Which medium is used on Sundays to teach you the word of God?
- How are announcements communicated to you in church on Sunday?
- How do the authorities of your church communicate with you out of the church?

Data Analysis

The collected data were analysed using the communication theory propounded by Shannon (1948, p. 379) and later elaborated by Weaver (1949, pp. 11-13), a media specialist with the Rockefeller Foundation. He extended Shannon's insights about electronic signal transmission and the quantitative measurement of information flow into a broad theoretical model of human communication. The effectiveness of human communication, Weaver asserted, may be measured by the success with which the meaning conveyed to the receiver leads to the desired conduct on his part. In general, for any messaging system - from computers linked by modems to tin cans connected by a string, we can identify and evaluate the following basic components:

1. Sender (or Encoder): An information source, a person or device that originates a message.
2. Receiver (or Decoder): The audience for a message, also known as the addressee.
3. Message: The information or signal sent from a sender to a receiver. The "content" of a communique.
4. Medium (or Channel): The method used to transmit a message (for example, print, speech, telephone, smoke signals, etc.).
5. Noise: Technical or semantic obstacles; that is, anything that interferes with the clear transmission of a message (for example, poor ink quality, low visibility, etc.).
6. Interpretation: All operations a receiver performs to decode and understand a message.
7. Feedback: Information about a message that a receiver sends back to the sender; the receiver's action or response to a communiqué.

The above theory has been adopted to identify those communication strategies used by our case study during the Covid-19 pandemic. This information was analysed in two parts: responses from questionnaires collected from AFC brethren in Central Africa and responses from AFC brethren in West Africa.

Responses from AFC Brethren in Central Africa

Responses to question one show that brethren in Central Africa greeted someone they met in church differently. They greet the person verbally, that is, good morning, brother or good evening, sister; they wave at the person, bow their head, tap the back of the person, by elbow nudging in line with Covid-19 guidelines, and use their legs too. That is, a person uses the right leg to touch the right leg of the other person.

Responses to question two show that brethren in Central Africa were verbally taught the word of God on Sunday by the teacher who stood some distance from the congregation. This was done during the Sunday School Service. This has been the practice in AFC churches in Central Africa before the advent of the Covid-19 pandemic. During this service, the teacher teaches the assembly using a microphone. When a congregational wants to answer a question, they are given a microphone to answer their question to the students' hearing in class. However, during the Devotional and Evening Revival or Evangelistic Services, the word of God is taught from the pulpit.

Regarding question three, respondents said announcements were communicated to them on Sunday from the pulpit several metres from the congregation. They were read out to them using microphones connected to loudspeakers.

Responses to question four showed that during the Covid-19 pandemic, AFC Central Africa authorities did everything to maintain contact with their brethren, even out of the church milieu. Thus, during this period, they made use of social media. For example, it was noted that WhatsApp groups were created during the Covid-19 pandemic, such as "Seek ye first the Kingdom of God and AFC CAM Youth Movement." These WhatsApp groups sent messages and happenings concerning the different congregations. Apart from e-mails sent to members of the other congregations, they also communicated with them on Facebook.

Furthermore, cells were created during this period in the quarters and homes of members of AFC Central Africa. Those heading these units were also responsible for implementing the church policies. For example, they coordinated evening prayers in their cells on Monday, Tuesday, Thursday and Friday from 6 pm to 8 pm and then Bible Studies on Wednesday from 6 pm to 8 pm.

Responses from AFC Brethren in West Africa

Responses to question one showed that the brethren of AFC West Africa used the same methods of greetings as their counterparts in Central Africa. For example, greetings are done verbally, with a wave of the hand and a bow of the head.

Responses to question two also revealed that preaching in AFC churches in West Africa on Sundays was done verbally by the teacher, who also stood some distance away from the students when it was the Sunday School Service. During this service, the teacher taught the students using a microphone. When a student wants to answer a question, they are given a microphone to answer their question to the students' hearing in class. This has also been the tradition in AFC churches in West Africa before the Covid-19 pandemic outbreak. When it was the Evening Revival or Evangelistic Service, the word of God was taught from the pulpit. Moreover, these services are always communicated online by streaming to those who cannot attend the in-person gathering for some reason.

Announcements are made from the pulpit several metres away from congregation members, with a population of not more than 50 Christians. These announcements were made via WECA's Public Address System: servicehub.afmweca.com. Furthermore, it is done virtually, and members can connect to YouTube, AFM Radio Heritage and Webcast. This activity was done online for those absent due to the Covid-19 pandemic guideline measures and for the benefit of the Internet audience. Apart from the above, announcements are also communicated to worshipers on notice boards in different church locations. It is essential to state here that the streaming of live services was done at WECA Headquarters, Anthony Village, Lagos, Nigeria.

Responses to question four showed that the church keeps pace with technological advancements and therefore uses the available means of communication like the aged-long telephone calls. More to this, authorities of AFC West Africa communicated with their brethren out of the church by using social media. It was noted that the brethren of AFC West Africa also have WhatsApp groups like "AFC Couples 3," "AFC Husbands," and "Applied Sunday School P5." These groups are used to reach out to brethren, either to preach the gospel or to inform the population about the church's activities. Furthermore, these leaders also used e-mails to reach out to the sheep of God. Several meetings were also held online via Zoom.

Given that WECA's headquarters is located in West Africa, precisely at Anthony Village, Lagos, Nigeria, it influenced the communication strategies used during this period, especially at the level of social media. For example, since the outbreak of this pandemic, Anthony Village has been broadcasting live online services watched by millions of AFC devotees worldwide using these channels: AFC FM Radio Heritage, YouTube and Webcast.

In addition, gospel material is also available online for the public.

Results

The findings of this study revealed that during the Covid-19 pandemic, members of Apostolic Faith Churches in West and Central Africa greeted one another in different ways. For example, they greet the person verbally, that is, good morning, brother or good evening, sister, wave at the person, bow their head, tap the back of the person, by elbow nudging in line with Covid-19 guidelines, and use their legs. That is, a person uses the right leg to touch the right leg of the other person. Furthermore, teaching the word of God on Sundays in the churches under study was done in two ways. First, teaching is done by the teacher in a class by standing several metres away from the students during the Sunday service and, secondly, from the pulpit when it is the Evening Evangelistic or Revival service. Also, announcements are communicated to members in two ways. The first way is when the announcements are transmitted from the pulpit on loudspeakers. The second way is when these announcements are pasted on notice boards in the different locations in the church compound. This practice was done mainly by churches in West Africa, especially AFC Headquarters. Furthermore, Sunday services were streamed online, especially at AFC Headquarters at Anthony Village. The analysis shows that the churches under study communicated with members outside the church by phone calls and text messages. However, when it comes to the use of social media, churches in Central Africa are limited to social media platforms like WhatsApp and Facebook. In contrast, churches in West Africa are more advanced as they use YouTube (AFC Headquarters), WhatsApp and Zoom to reach out to their members. Furthermore, communication is also done through Webcast and AFC Radio Heritage.

Conclusion

The world in general and West and Central Africa in particular experienced a dreaded disease that changed how the world and individuals in particular functioned. The whole world was in total lockdown. Businesses, transport companies and schools were shut down. Furthermore, people were restricted from carrying out their daily activities because of the number of people dying in the countries affected by the virus. The church, it should be noted, was not left out because the virus also affected churches in different countries. For example, not up to 50 people were supposed to worship together. Does this mean that churches will no longer operate? Certainly not. They have that obligation to operate. Faced with this ugly situation, religious authorities had to put in place measures that would make them always be in contact with their congregations. For example, in the United Kingdom, BBC One radio returned to broadcasting Sunday morning services, which this organisation had not done before the pandemic.

In AFC West and Central Africa, the church must continuously operate. For this reason, church leaders developed innovative ways of communication to maintain contact with their members during the pandemic. In the context of this work, it is established that during the Covid-19 pandemic, traditional methods of greetings like shaking one's hand, embracing someone, hugging and kissing were abandoned in favour of modern technology. Thus, the coronavirus era brought new communication methods, with each institution or organisation going in for strategies that could best serve its interest.

Abstract

This essay examines communication strategies the Apostolic Faith Church West and Central Africa (AFC WECA) used during the Covid-19 pandemic. The premise of this chapter is that because businesses, schools and other sectors of life were compelled to shut their doors due to the coronavirus pandemic, AFC WECA developed new communication strategies to maintain contact with its members. Data for this work were collected using questionnaires. Twenty questionnaires were sent online to various devotees who worship in Apostolic Faith Churches in West and Central Africa, regardless of gender. The collected data were analysed using the theory of communication. The findings revealed that during the Covid-19 pandemic, Apostolic Faith Churches in West and Central Africa adopted new strategies of communicating with brethren, such as a wave of the hand, a bow of the head and using social media such as YouTube. These measures did not only help to cement the bond between the church and its members but also went a long way to curb the spread of this pandemic.

Keywords: Communication strategies, Covid-19, pandemic, social media, congregation

References

Bowman, B., A. Back, A., L. Esch, A., E. & Marshall, N. (2020). Crisis symptom management and patient communication protocols are important tools for all clinicians responding to Covid-19. *J Pain Symptom Manage*, *60*(2), 98-100.

Brien, H., O. (2020). What does the rise of digital religion during Covid-19 tell us about religion's capacity to adapt? *Irish Journal of Sociology*, *28*(2), 242-246.

Broniatowski, D., A. Dredze. M. & Ayers, J., W. (2021). First do no harm: Effective communication about Covid-19 Vaccines. *American Journal of Public Health*, *111*(6), 1055- 1057.

Cucinotta, D. & Vanelli, M. (2020). World Health Organization declares Covid-19 a pandemic. *Acta Biomedica, Mattioli*, *91*(1), 157-160.

Dalton, L., Rapa, E., & Stein, A. (2020). Protecting the psychological health of children through effective communication about Covid-19. *The Lancet Child & Adolescent Health*, *4*(5), 346-347.

Kamal, T. & IIliyan, A. (2021). School Teachers' Perceptions and Challenges towards online Teaching during Covid-19 pandemic in India. An economic analysis. *Asian Association of Open Universities Journal*, *16*(3), 311-325.

Kim., D., K., & Kreps, G., L. (2020). An analysis of government communication in the United States during the COVID-19 pandemic: recommendations for effective government health risk communication. *World Medical & Health Policy, 12*(4), 398-412.

Martens, A., B. (2021). *Risk communication and Covid-19: An exploration of best practices* (Master's alternative plan paper, Minnesota State University, Mankato). Cornerstone: A collection of scholarly and creative works for Minnesota State University, Mankato.

Olayinka, A. L., Taiwo, V. O., Raji Oyelade, A., & Farai, I. P. (2005). *Methodology of basic and applied research.* Ibadan: Dabfol Printers.

Porter, K., & Burshnic, V., L. (2020). Optimizing effective communication while wearing a mask during the Covid-19 pandemic. *Journal of Gerontological Nursing, 46*(11), 7-11.

Quinn, S., C. Thomas, T. & McAllister, C. (2005). Postal workers' Perspectives on Communication during the anthrax attack. *Biosecurity and bioterrorism: biodefense strategy, practice, and science, 3*(3), 207-215.

Reddy, B. V. & Gupta, A. (2020). Importance of effective communication during Covid-19 Infodemic. *Journal of Family Medicine and Primary Care, 9*(8):3793-3796.

Reynolds, B. & Quinn, S., C. (2008). Effective communication during an influenza pandemic: The value of using a crisis and emergency risk communication framework. *Health promotion practice, 9*(4), 13-17.

Seak, C. J. (2020). Rapid responses in the emergency department of Linkou Chang Gung Memorial Hospital, Taiwan effectively prevents spread of Covid-19 among health-care workers of emergency department during outbreak: Lessons learnt from SARS. *Biomedical Journal, 43*(4), 388-391.

Shannon, C. L. (1948). A Mathematical Theory of Communication. *Bell System Technical Journal, 27(3),* 379-423.

Shih, H. & Chi, C. Y. (2020). Fighting Covid-19: A quick review of diagnoses, therapies, and vaccines. *Biomedical Journal, 43*(4), 341-354.

Tam, L., T. Ho, H., X. Nguyen, D., P. Elias, A., & Le, A., N., H. (2021). Receptivity of governmental communication and its effectiveness during Covid-19 pandemic emergency in Vietnam: A qualitative study. *Global Journal of Flexible Systems Management, 22*(1):45-64.

Weaver, W. (1949). *The mathematical theory of communication.* Urbana: University of Illinois Press.

Yunusa, A., A. Temitayo S. I. Dada, O., A. Oyelere, S., S. Agbor, F., J. Obaido, G., & Aruleba, K. (2021). The impact of the Covid-19 pandemic in higher education in Nigeria: University Lecturers' Perspectives. *International Journal of Education and Development using Information and Communication Technology (IJEDICT), 17*(4), 43-66.

SIX

Linguistic Undertones of (Mis)apprehension, (Mis)trust, Panic and Assurance
A Pragma-Stylistic Reading of Stances on Covid-19 Vaccines

JOSEPH NKWAIN

The Covid-19 pandemic remains one of the most traumatising global challenges humanity has had to grapple with over the past centuries. Its economic, psychological, religious, social, cultural and diplomatic ramifications continue as individual, collective and institutional strides to overcome it endure. Pitted with previous pandemics, the peculiarity of Covid-19 is the fact that from its outburst in Wuhan, China, in December 2019 and in Europe in February 2020, it was observed that human behaviour and habits shaped by hundreds of years of experience underwent radical changes in just a brief period. The "new normal" that emerged constitutes a drastic epoch characterised by socio-cultural, economic, and psychological stressors like decreased life satisfaction, irritability, disappointment, emotional discomfort, sadness, guilt, fatigue, boredom, insomnia, lack of concentration and indecision, detachment from others, and decreased work performance. All these are earmarked as the most common psychological and behavioural reactions caused by the pandemic.

The unparalleled interest accorded to the subject has dramatically enriched pandemics literature. However, reporting, describing, discussing, and meta-phorising this global demon has unfortunately led to another infodemic with the widespread dissemination of false medical advice, hoaxes, fake products and fake information about the virus. The situation has been exacerbated by the flooding of (mis)information in conspiracy theories meant to thwart, disapprove, discredit and undermine different strides towards collective, individual and institutional remedies to the prevailing situation. Amidst the present dispensation, when the masses are almost gripped by uncertainty, mistrust, apprehension and confusion, their language behaviour tends to accommodate these realities. Scientific endeavours culminating in producing vaccines against the virus have triggered controversial over-reactions and under-reactions, stances reminiscent of apparent distrust, disbelief and outright fear.

This chapter hinges on the hypothetical premise that during a pandemic, *nosophobia* - a type of psychological disorder in which a person is afraid of getting a particular disease is rife. People typically become hypervigilant about any bodily change that might suggest an infection (fear of the body), try to protect the body as a treasure that may be lost (fear for the body), experience themselves as being potentially dangerous to their loved ones (fear for significant others), and experience significant others as potential threats (fear of significant others). These experiences are often inherent in their linguistic idiosyncrasies and constitute the interest of this investigation.

Situational Background

The world was taken aback by the initial discovery of the virus in Wuhan, China, in 2019 and more astonished by its instant and rapid spread to almost all the nooks and crannies of the globe. This situation was met with instant travel bans from China to other parts of the world, and eventually, with the rapid spread of the disease, the bans were internationalised in a conscious effort to curb or significantly reduce the spread of the virus. This entailed closing national borders in many countries, and this restrictive measure was eventually extended to strict regulation of movements within national territories. The incessant spread of the disease later led to complete lockdowns of private and public institutions. Attendee numbers in educational, religious, political and sporting gatherings were significantly reviewed or completely proscribed. These measures were corroborated by the WHO's appeals to various countries worldwide to reduce the rapid spread rate and death toll, although it kept increasing daily.

Measures such as washing hands with water and soap for at least 20 seconds regularly (especially after going outside), wearing masks, implementing a social distancing of at least a metre with other people in public, sneezing and coughing into a bent arm, regularly gaggling the throat with warm water and seeking immediate medical attention in case of doubt were enacted by governments. Their implementation trickled down to local areas. A surge in death tolls, especially in European countries such as Spain, the UK, and Italy, as well as in the USA and some South American countries, sent incredibly shocking waves of fear around the continent. By mid-2020, the introduction of the first Covid-19 vaccines neither remedied the global situation nor assured the panic-stricken populace. Even before then, fake information, unreliable advice, misinformation and hoaxes about the origins, nature, curability, existence, types, mutation, strands, infection means, and many incongruities left many confused. The situation was still exacerbated by viral conspiracy theories that only enhanced and further triggered apprehension, distrust, disdain and disbelief. This state of affairs, therefore, elicited responses reminiscent of the different appreciations of stakeholders.

Methodology

The data set for this study was culled from a microblog – an online information dissemination platform put in place by the World Health Organisation (WHO) – *Covid-19 Information Centre* (at http://www.unicef.org) for vaccine resources, to inform the masses about developments related to the pandemic. The choice of the blog is explicated by the fact that, for one, it is (supposed to be) the most dependable world-accredited health institution that guarantees health provision (logistics, drugs and vaccines, health equipment, medical advice, supervision, health surveys, human resources, etc.), especially to the needy in regular and health crises situations. Besides, the expert, authoritative and trustworthy nature of its personnel assures the churning out of reliable information amidst fake news, hoaxes and other forms of information intoxication, which are particularly rife with netlore. It is therefore considered the most dependable and acceptable information resource at the disposal of the public.

The data set constituted a total of 300 reactions which were culled and analysed for this study. They included bloggers' reactions/responses to information provided by the WHO about the vaccines and the appreciation of their use and effectiveness. This was done between March and December 2021, when the first proposed vaccines were being produced and administered worldwide and when the second phase of the pandemic was being experienced in America in most European and South American countries.

The procedure involved systematically reading vaccine-related publications by accredited and mandated WHO resource officials. Such publications ignite reactions from bloggers who strive to appreciate information from differing perspectives. The reactions that ensued were randomly screenshot to constitute a database analysed through the Pragma-stylistic Approach. Also known as Speech Act Stylistics or Pragmatic Stylistics, Pragma-stylistics builds on Austin's (1962) Speech Act Theory and explains language use concerning context, the speaker's attitude and its effect on the hearer. The Pragma-stylistic approach to meaning is a linguistic approach that examines the speaker's intended meaning and distinctive style. These aspects are germane in understanding the entire meaning of utterances and their consequences. This is because every individual tends to have idiosyncrasies - a distinct mode of expression and linguistic features that characterise them. To Leech (1981), Pragma-stylistics seeks to investigate meaning not from the formal properties of words and constructions but from how utterances are used and how they relate to the context in which they are uttered. Mey (2009) agrees on situating Pragma-stylistics within the more prominent literary subfield of Stylistics, claiming that it is an established discipline which lies on the cusp of narrative studies within Stylistics. He characterises it as the study of the user's role in the societal production and consumption of texts and, alternatively, as the science of the unsaid. Thus, Pragma-stylistics, according to the tenets of Pragmatics, attempts to discover, analyse and formalise the implicit meanings of utterances. It is unified, however, by its emphasis on explaining existing interpretations of texts rather than generating new readings. The reactions were scrutinised to size up the linguistic and stylistic features underlying such usages. Bloggers' identities were blinded for ethical concerns, and only their posts were copied and cropped for eventual analysis.

Erstwhile Work

A natural health predicament has never engendered as much interest as the Covid-19 pandemic. The incessant interest in the subject is attested in the innumerable academic articles churned out daily. From different perspectives, with diverse motivations and approaches, concerned researchers continue to explore the subject laying bare fascinating and thought-provoking findings.

The advent of the pandemic has ushered in new linguistic behaviour with the proliferation of novel forms of usage and the redefinition of old ones. From a comparative perspective, Mustajoki, Zorikhina Nilsson, Guzman Tirado, Tous-Rovirosa, Dergacheva, Vepreva, and Itskovich (2020) examine corona-related neologisms in Finnish, Swedish, Russian and Spanish. Al-Salman and Haider (2021) develop novel words inspired by the pandemic and demonstrate how these neologisms are threatening their way into the lexical economy of mainstream English.

Piekkari, Tietze, Angouri, Meyer, and Vaara (2021) and Goddard and Wierzbicka (2021) insist on the fact that the role of language, far from constituting an immediate panacea for the pandemic, plays an irreplaceable role in facilitating communication during this crisis period. They demonstrate how effective communication is reassuring for the affected; the effective dissemination of vital information and intelligible exchanges between stakeholders ensure harmony and relief. Similarly, from a comparative perspective, Hua, Woods, Azman, Abdullah, Hashim, Rahim, Idrus, Said, Lew, and Kosem (2020) propose the application of a wide range of methods for different focus and perspectives that may be customised to the researcher's unique context. The study presents macro and micro-linguistic perspectives, ranging from corpus-based analysis to content analysis studies. It explores communication through official announcements, parliamentary proceedings and Covid-19-related corpora. Besides, they analyse selected corpora with lexical, semantic, and discourse foci and personal posts of short narratives and photos which encapsulate meanings from human life and experiences.

With regard to language use and communication among stakeholders (patients and doctors, for example), studies such as Harding, Aloysius, Bell, Edney, Gordon, Lewis, Sweeting, and Murphy (2020) envisage a situation where limited patient visits and communication, the consistent wearing of face masks by patients and staff might negatively affect the development of communication and its breakdown. Berg, O'Hara, Shortt, Thune, Brønnick, Lungu, Røislien, and Wiig (2021) provide insights and synthesise the existing evidence regarding different modes of communication used by health authorities in health risk communication with the public during a pandemic. Through a rapid scoping review, the study identifies three categories for modes of communication: communication channels, source credibility and how the message is communicated. Leyva-Moraga, Juanz-González, Barreras-Espinoza, Soualhi, Ocejo-Gallegos, Urquijo and Ibarra-Celaya (2020) and Reed, Ferrante and Oh (2020) are concerned about patients suffering from hearing loss, especially with isolated patients. They intimate that sign language has gained a unique role in communication in these contexts.

From a stylistic perspective, language has been seen as an effective remedy to the pandemic through humour for instant relief and relaxation. Whereas Olah and Hemplemann (2021) provide leeway for humour research during the pandemic crisis, Strick (2021), Chlopicki and Brzozowska (2021) and Seba-Elran (2021) examine the identity of humorous mechanisms in Poland and Israel and concur that humour can bolster the effects of moving messages to better facilitate emotion regulation during the pandemic. Besides, Cancelas-Ouvina (2021) sizes up memes defined as local, graphic and contingent with specifically social, affiliative and self-enhancing functions and illustrates how, despite the pandemic, panic-stricken Spain did not lose its sense of humour.

Through Critical Discourse Analysis, Kopytowska and Krakowiak (2020) combine linguistics, tourism and the implications of the Covid-19 pandemic to explore the negative comments posted for newspaper articles about tourism companies asking for financial support from the government of Poland. Chouinard and Normand (2020) observe how the pandemic is at the centre of disequilibrium regarding the linguistic status quo in Canada. The study shows a total ascendance of English over French during briefings about the pandemic. Gruzdeva (2020) warns that seeing the fatal effect of the virus on the elderly, it is likely to speed up language attrition, especially in the Amazon regions and even the global linguistic landscape in general.

Through Twitter analytics and qualitative content analysis, Slavik, Buttle, Sturrock, Darlington and Yiannakoulias (2021) examine tweeting practices during the early stages of the pandemic by Canadian public health agencies and decision-makers and the ways tweets could be improved to effectively communicate risk and maximise engagement on this platform. Findings suggest that most account types focused on disseminating information, except for regional and local health departments, which tended to promote more action from users. Wicke and Bolognesi (2021) use topic modelling to explore how discourse about Covid-19 is reported on social media through time. Essentially, the sentiment polarity of the language used changed from a relatively positive valence during the lockdown to a more negative valence with the reopening. The study demonstrates a linear increase in the average subjectivity of the tweets.

Covid-19 research abounds with literature on several linguistic landscapes. Osi (2021) examines the healthscapes in a rural Philippines community and argues that language and multimodal resources are used to impart transactional, territorial and institutional discourses. The discourses indicate that the organisation of public health services and the reception of its stakeholders is influenced by institutional order, the range of services offered and the intended audience of these signs. Wibowo (2021) explores the linguistic landscape of Indonesian airports with attention paid to the language choice used in formulating the protocol signs for preventing the transmission of Covid-19 at the airports. The study establishes that there is a profuse use of monolingual and bilingual top-down signs, monolingual and bilingual bottom-up signs. Besides, English is the primary language used as compared to Indonesian. The signs used tend to serve a dual function - instruction and assertion. Protassova (2021) reports on the linguistic landscape of Helsinki tourism businesses and indicates that the most significant changes occurred on social media, followed by texts inside the public spaces of the companies and texts outside. The least changes happened in staff spaces and internal communications of the companies. However, the results varied slightly depending on the company type. Shops and restaurants preferred to change their language use in physical spaces, such as texts inside and outside. Hotels and "other" types made more changes in their virtual presence, such as social media and homepages, corresponding with the environments where the companies face their clients for the first time – hotels and "other" types usually require a reservation online, while shops and restaurants mostly attract their clients with their facilities.

Negri, Giovanbattista, Barazzetti, Zamin, and Christian (2020) analyse two sets of computerised linguistic measures on writings during the pandemic to study the linguistic markers of emotion regulation and elaboration. The study asserts that online expressive writing has helped respondents get more in touch with the intense emotions they experienced following the upheavals. Besides, the study shows that expressive writing can be used in a psychological emergency as a powerful instrument to investigate and detect the complex psychodynamic processes underpinning distress and as a valuable intervention to reduce the negative impact of traumatic events.

Following an ethnographic approach to linguistic landscaping, Hopkyns and van den Hoven (2021) study Covid-19 signage in two Abu Dhabi lifework multilingual contexts - a beachside community and an industrial site. The study establishes the presence of existing inequalities in linguistically diverse contexts and the need to ensure access to information and linguistic inclusion during the Covid-19 period and beyond. Insyirah and Sudarwati (2021) shed light on the phenomenon of multilingualism in the linguistics landscape about the usage of language on the Covid-19 flyers in the Pasuruan District of Indonesia, the impression of society regarding these linguistic signs, and the preference of linguistic signs used on the Covid-19 flyers. The study reveals monolingual, bilingual, and multilingual signs on Covid-19 flyers, and the multilingualism phenomenon serves as an intelligible, educational, and effective campaign to check the spread of the virus.

Data Presentation and Analyses

As previously indicated, all the data for this study was culled from *http://www.unicef.org*. An overview of the data reveals several situations. In one of its fundamental missions of guaranteeing universal health coverage, pre-empting health hazards and sensitising the masses on related issues, the WHO has been appreciated with mixed feelings and recognition. The information regularly churned out by its experts has engendered a plethora of reactions from bloggers, which are subsumed as follows:

Table 6.1. Distribution of bloggers' reactions

Type of reaction	Content	Frequency	Percentage
Negative	anti-vaccines	96	32
	anti-WHO	78	26
	anti-government	28	09.33
Sub total		220	73.33
Positive	pro-vaccines	32	10.66
	pro-WHO	24	8
	pro-government	18	6
Sub total		80	26.66
Neutral		24	8
Grand total		300	100

These reactions are considered in turns.

Negative Reactions

The introduction of vaccines by different pharmaceutical companies and their use have sparked innumerable contradictions and reservations concerning their effectiveness, options related to the right and choice to vaccinate or not, the ages concerned, the true reasons behind them and other related questions engendered by the different conspiracy theories animating the debate. These constituted the different negative reactions which ranked highest with 220 responses at 73 percent. They naturally castigated the vaccines' use and effectiveness, registering the highest number of reactions in this category at 32 percent. They included examples, viz:

1. *More fucking depopulation poison*
2. *Hospitals and graveyards are full of vaccinated people. What is the point? Money!*
3. *We will see the long term effects of the toxins they are injecting into these people in a few years.*
4. *What about all the people who have died of the vax? Why are they not talking about this as well?*
5. *Sorry for asking oooooooooh! What's the point of this vaccine if someone could still be tested positive of the virus after taking the vaccine?*

Reference to these vaccines as some 'depopulation poison' (excerpt 1) and 'toxins' (excerpt 3) which have failed to inhibit massive deaths as indicated in (excerpts 2, 4 and 5) but instead have long-term effects on the vaccinated, shows the people's indignation about their ineffectiveness and disastrousness. The WHO, the institution responsible for universal health administration, has not been spared by the lampoon. This is evident in the following posts that accounted for 78 percent of the reactions:

6. *WHO is the last place I would check information.*
7. *WHO-ZIONIST KILLER*
8. *Head Organisation of Medical Terrorism*
9. *The UN is nobody's friend. Just a mass of self-enriching bureaucrats.*

As the ultimate institution that issues clearance for the vaccines that continue to affect the vaccinated negatively, it is therefore branded in the foregoing sneering terms. Similarly, governments implementing the WHO's policies share 9.33 percent of the blame as they are considered accomplices and are addressed as such.

10. *We don't trust you, we don't trust governments and it's getting to where we don't trust doctors.*
11. *I am vaccine hesitant and it is because the Chinese Communist Party Virus Vaccines are leading us to massive super spreader events, infections and deaths along with variants.*
12. *WHO is the trusted governing source ... Vanguard?? A bunch of billionaires*
13. *Anyone who supports mandatory jabs, obviously supports communist countries. Remember, my body, my choice.*

Thus, according to these bloggers, governments that are supportive of the WHO's initiatives are in no little way helping their citizens in terms of health and life assurance. As such, they lack trust (excerpts 11 and 13) and are likened to 'communist countries' and 'Communist Party Virus Vaccines' (excerpts 12) responsible for massive deaths.

Positive Reactions

Despite the desperation and pessimism inherent in the foregoing responses, reactions positively appreciative of the prevailing situation were equally registered and accounted for 26.66 percent of the responses. They favoured the use of the vaccines and encouraged 'anti-vaxers' to be more responsible and optimistic in their behaviour towards the vaccines. The following reactions are in place:

14. *Vaccine really helps. 15) Vaccine is important. 16) My son's in phase 3 of trials for Novavax.*
15. *Yes, everyone to be vaccinated for a covid-free world.*
16. *This is great news but the anti-vaxers won't hear it through their tinfoil helmets.*

17. *You stubborn and narrow-minded people, get vaccinated. We're fed up you delaying everything.*
18. *Yes, we must eliminate that virus to the end by injecting of vaccine. Always stay strong.*
19. *Everyone should get the vaccine. It is our responsibility along with our safety.*
20. *I can see the antivaxxer's heads exploding with it very soon. LL.*
21. *Thank you WHO for your services, and promoting community healthcare services for all.*
22. *Keep laughing all the way to the morgue antivaxxers. I won't miss you when dead from covid.*
23. *Lets go get vaccinated.*

The above posts castigate hesitancy, irresponsible behaviour, and future regret and encourage a positive attitude towards vaccination.

Neutral Stances

It is worthy of note that other bloggers demonstrated some indifference through neutral reactions that addressed related issues. Such reactions accounted for 24 percent of the data. They concerned spirituality, divine intervention, man's helplessness in the face of the prevailing predicament, practical tips, and vital information. They are evident in the following excerpts:

24. *What I really know and I'm definitely sure of is that Gods people worldwide were never instructed by their creator, God, in his word, to lay their lives/trust/dependence/reliance on any scientific means, creature or creation because they are temporary and lead no one to eternal life. God's people, beware of ungodly education and wealth.*
25. *Jesus is the only refuge from the storm that is coming. Take it seriously. This is your Christmas present. The following is just my opinion about what is going on right now. So, if you don't like what I'm saying right now, ignore it. It's just what I think about, what I see happening among us.*
26. *The vaccine isn't the answer, it's very clear, stop sinning and repent to God.*
27. *Do you have a vaccine for satanic, diabolic and demonic minds? True Christian from Jesus Christ teachings. You have freewill to truly love your God Jesus Christ of Nazareth.*
28. *What I learned today is self-sanitation. Eat plenty of fruits and vegetables, proper rest and listen to the word of God vaccine is just only an alternative.*
29. *We won't vaccinate because we believe in God not in medicine.*
30. *We all over the world need to stick together in this pandemic. We must forget*

> *our anger, hate, trustworthy and whatever we think which is putting us in danger that humans are going to go extinct. Please, go for your personal protection. Wash hands, wear masks as much as you can because that's the key. We will destroy this virus. Stay safe.*

These neutral stances are couched on spirituality (excerpts 26 - 29), the relevance of appropriate hygiene/ sanitation (28) and sensitisation (30), which tend to add a new perspective to the prevailing debate and presuppose the possibility of other natural and less cumbersome remedies.

The Linguistic and Pragma-stylistic Dimension

The above reactions tend to be expressive of myriad stances, reflective of different moods and attitudes and characterised by a profuse use of interesting linguistic and stylistic features worth examining.

Referencing

Biblical and historical allusions are rife in the literature. The urge to be more expressive, to be understood and to create communicative effects are at the centre of these usages. This is manifested in the following example:

31. *This is gigantically bigger than Anthony Fauci. Fauci is a minion, albeit a high level minion. But they are using him as a scapegoat to draw attention away from the bigger picture, that this is a globalist takeover of the world and genocide. This calls for a Nuremberg style trial. The problem is finding who is in on it to prosecute them and who is not in on it to conduct the trial.*

Anthony Stephen Fauci, American physician and immunologist, director of the National Institute of Allergy and Infectious Diseases and Chief Medical Advisor to the American President Joe Biden, is considered here as servile and at the disposal of the Republicans. Undoubtedly, as an authority in the domain, his declarations on the subject are gospel realities and should be heeded unquestioned. Here, he is projected at the forefront of the 'globalist takeover of the world and genocide.' Historically, alluding to the 'Nuremberg style trial' indicates the eventual fate of all those purportedly involved in the 'globalist takeover of the world and genocide.' To this user, they merit the same fate (instant death) reserved to all Adolf Hitler's warlords judged guilty of Second World War crimes and executed. Here, through preconizing the instant execution of the perpetrators of the vaccination scheme, the user effectively expresses their utter indignation about the situation and those responsible for it. Similarly, Biden is likened to the biblical Noah, who, at God's command, saved humankind and other species from the punitive God-sent flood.

Expectedly, it is one of the principal prerogatives of the president to inform, sensitise, caution and advise citizens, especially during such precarious situations. According to this user, the president fails in the supreme mission of warning the most vulnerable people about the precarious nature of vaccines. Besides, he is accused of not insisting on their use of boosters seeing their effectiveness in fortifying the immune system, thus, checking contamination rates. Just like those in the biblical story who perished in the flood because they failed to heed Noah's advice, the post forewarns about the eventual decimation of vaccinated people. This allusion effectively draws attention to the eventual massive effect of the vaccines if people continue to be vaccinated.

32. *He President Biden has the job of telling and warning about vaccines, to stop viruses and getting boosters but like Noah in the Bible, he doesn't reach the people most vulnerable but do not listen. They will perish just like people in the Bible that Noah warned of the flood coming.*

33. *When I hear of 'India', all I think is hygiene.*

In (32) and (33), the allusion to the biblical Noah and the flood and India respectively castigates and pre-empts massive destruction or a huge calamity, just like in the time of Noah in the bible and the fact that the unhygienic conditions that prevail in India (39) are not propitious for the production of a reliable vaccine.

Explicit Denigration

As the world's most authoritative health institution that has as some of its mission the education, prevention, intervention and pre-empting of health disasters such as pandemics, the WHO has and continues to be overburdened by strong criticisms on account of its failure to accomplish some of the objectives and above all, in perpetrating acts considered to be anti-people. To many, it is the ultimate 'propaganda machine' at the service of pharmaceutical firms producing the vaccines. This is true as the WHO's clearance is a *sine qua non* for using the vaccine on people. The following denigrating concerns and even outright invectives are rife in the different reactions recorded:

34. *Stop cheap propaganda. It's our taxes that pay WHO. Defund WHO!*
35. *Propaganda machine at work.*
36. *Spreading lies and death again, it is criminal you know.*
37. *Don't spread the lies! WHO is WHO?*

38. *Head Organization of Medical Terrorism.*
39. *You have literally lost the plot. World Sick Organisation is an appropriate name.*

In the foregoing reactions, this reputable and 'educated' organisation seems to have lost its reliability and authoritative status. It is referred to as a 'propaganda machine' (34, 35), reputed in lies telling (36, 37), untrustworthy and linked to terrorism (39). It is equally responsible for the death of millions of people. A clarion call is emitted for the organisation to put an immediate end to vaccine mandates because not only are they ineffective, but forcing the people to vaccinate is tantamount to an outright violation of their right to choose. Other illuminating posts abound:

40. *We can't trust the WHO.*
41. *WHO isn't trying to save lives but to start a civil war.*
42. *The UN is nobody's friend. Just a mass of self-enriching bureaucrats.*

Apart from losing their trustworthiness (40), they are nobody's friend (42), 'a mass of self-enriching bureaucrats' (42) who constitute a profit-making machine. In failing in its ultimate mission of providing health assurance and pre-empting hazards, they are construed as 'trying to start a civil war' (41) by whipping up negative emotions, disgruntlement and contempt. Besides, just like the WHO, the UN is accused of financial (mis)appropriation. These reactions effectively represent the collective predicament of a people unfortunately held hostage by the very institutions that are supposed to guarantee their health.

Foreshadowing

There are reactions indicative of a fear of the unknown, uncertainty and imminent lack of assurance; unfortunately, the very issues vaccines are supposed to provide guarantees for. As such, in responses such as the following, more apprehension is kindled.

43. *We will see the long term effects of the toxins they are injecting into these people in a few years.*
44. *The long-term side effects are unknown.*
45. *We don't trust you, we don't trust governments and it's getting to where we don't trust doctors.*
46. *Sounds like a new variant will emerge.*
47. *As cooler weather hits the south, we will see our numbers go up.*

In the midst of uncertainty and the dearth of information, bloggers take recourse in pessimistic anticipation. They respectively anticipate the long-term negative effects of the vaccines (43, 44), the untrustworthiness of medical personnel (45), the inevitability of new variants (46) and a surge in causality rates as cold weather sets in (47). Coincidentally, these predictions were only made when some of them started being fulfilled. A case in point is the emergence of the omicron variant in South Africa in December 2021. These emotions of uncertainty and dread appear to be founded, taking into cognisance that clinical tests to measure the long-term adverse effects of the vaccines have not yet produced concordant results. As such, such unassuming speculations become unavoidable.

Sarcasm

Attempts to discredit the idea of vaccinating have been through evoking thought-provoking, doubtful ironical situations that leave the impression that all is not well.

48. *Hospitals and graveyards are full of vaccinated people. What is the point? Money!*
49. *Sorry for asking oooooooooh! What's the point of this vaccine if someone could still be tested positive of the virus after taking the vaccine?*

The foregoing reactions point to the ironic situation where even those vaccinated eventually become victims of the vaccines (49), yet they insist on being vaccinated. The vaccines are not as effective as projected in the propaganda or have a deadly effect, with graveyards 'full of vaccinated people' (48). The intention is not, therefore, to save humanity but to generate income. This claim seems to be corroborated in the next view.

50. *Real pandemic doesn't need 24/7 advertising ... pan-democrat has been over for some time.*

This blogger claims that adverts on vaccines have overshadowed the situation about the pandemic at the expense of sensitisation. Here, priority is given to the different contending vaccines in the market rather than sensitising the masses about how to check the virus's rapid spread. The greatest irony remains that health professionals who are supposed to preach by example are also caught in the web of mistrust and apprehension, as seen in (51).

51. *What is as big as a travesty is that we still have health professionals in the western world who still refuse to be vaccinated even though it is available to them and they are still working in a health care environment!*

Their categorical refusal to be jabbed only heightens the already high levels of suspicion. This casts considerable doubt on the effectiveness and acceptability of the vaccines.

Dark Metaphors

In strong metaphorical terms, bloggers castigate all those concerned about vaccination propaganda. This is evident in the posts below.

52. *Deathdealers*

53. *Smoke and mirrors, it's all about money and power, these people are phony silent killers.*

As earlier indicated, if people are vaccinated and end up dying, it presupposes that the vaccines are either ineffective or deadly. As such, stakeholders in the vaccination scheme are, therefore 'deathdealers' (52) and 'phony silent killers' (53) simply preoccupied by 'money and power' rather than saving humankind. According to the next blogger in (54), in their machination, they use a 'depopulation poison.'

54. *More fucking depopulation poison.*

Metaphorically, referring to the vaccines as some poison meant to depopulate the world shows the extent to which they are considered dangerous and therefore instil more fear than assurance. The metaphor of the guinea pig (55) is indicative of the dehumanising, subclinical and unethical nature of medical practice with humans used for clinical tests instead of animals.

55. *I won't be the guinea pig.*

56. *Does this one come with a microchip too? I need one that can get HB + better than the current hardware.*

Excerpt (56) is in concordance with the conspiracy theory that vaccines (metaphorically referred here to 'the current hardware planted in my brain') contain microchips meant to cull and transmit personal information to be used to control human activities and behaviour.

Rhetoric

Many issues related to the origins, forms, types, mutation, prevention, treatment, effectiveness of vaccines, number of jabs, etc., have been compounded by innumerable conspiracy theories geared towards discrediting the WHO and the different stakeholders in the vaccination programme. These polemics have been expressed rhetorically as if to find answers to these roaming questions. Some excerpts are examined in turn.

57. *Don't spread the lies! WHO is WHO?*

The above reaction questions the world's leading health institution's authority in guaranteeing universal health and pre-empting health hazards. The reaction is indicative of the failure of the organisation to live up to the expectations of its creed regarding the coronavirus pandemic. In posts (58 and 59), the effectiveness of the vaccines is questioned through rhetoric indicative of the people's sense of indignation especially concerning the number of vaccinated people who continue to die.

58. *What about all the people who have died of the vax? Why are they not talking about this as well?*
59. *Sorry for asking oooooooooh! What's the point of this vaccine if someone could still be tested positive of the virus after taking the vaccine?*

There is misinformation and attention diversion with the avoidance of topics related to the condition of those who have either tested positive or have lost their lives after taking the vaccines. According to the above responses, stock should be taken of the vaccine casualties instead of insisting on massive unproductive vaccinations, and an attempt should be made to figure out what exactly is wrong with the vaccines. Still, another vaccine adept in example (60) finds the problem not at the level of the vaccines but with the mindset of those to be vaccinated.

60. *Do you have a vaccine for satanic, diabolic and demonic minds? True Christian from Jesus Christ teachings.*

Mindsets that have already been hardened by the 'satanic', 'diabolic' and 'demonic' habits they have imbibed need something other than a vaccine. This rhetoric effectively alludes to the difficulty in convincing an anti-vaccine adept to be vaccinated. From a different perspective, the reaction in example (61) questions the environmental impact of the syringes as one of the vaccine fallouts.

61. *Has anyone calculated how much plastic has been produced for syringes, the carbon burden to the planet we added?*

Accordingly, vaccines constitute a serious environmental hazard by their massive production, and when syringes are destroyed, especially through incineration, the carbon effect on the planet cannot be underestimated.

Anecdotes

Personal experiences recounting how people grapple with the side effects of vaccines have been recorded across the globe. This is evident in the ones that follow.

62. *Hi, I'm from South Africa and I got vaccinated on the 1st of December and I'm 17 weeks pregnant. Do you think my baby will be safe? I was sleeping the whole day yesterday as my back, hand and neck are painful. I cannot move around but I could feel my baby was playing and moving around. I'm worried about her being affected by it maybe birth defects is it 100% safe.*
63. *Hi guys, I need advice, since my uncle got his jab twice he is crippled and can't walk. What can I do? Maybe sue the state for negligence?*

64. *Murderers!! ... a relative died of it. And dozens and dozens of friends are jab injured/have had terrible adverse effects.*

The reactions in (62), (63) and (64) indirectly index the dangerous effects of the vaccines, which, for example, are unfortunately responsible for the crippling of an uncle (63). Similarly, it questions the number of vaccines to be taken. Even with two jabs, the uncle still ends up a disabled person. In the face of this unfortunate health mishap, the government is equally discredited for failing to ascertain the effect-free nature of these vaccines before they are administered.

Rebranding

In a bid to express their indignation and frustration with the WHO, it is rebranded in the following blatant negative terms:

65. *Whatever!!!! I have only one perception towards WHO - World Hallucinated Oppression*
66. *Yeah, Misinformation from the biggest BS artists. Nothing but a bunch of Paid Chinese Shills.*
67. *WHO is the trusted governing source ... Vanguard?? A bunch of billionaires*
68. *WHO-ZIONIST KILLER*
69. *Head Organisation of Medical Terrorism*

Because the organisation authorises vaccines considered harmful and even deadly, these bloggers see it as a 'killer' (68), 'a bunch of billionaires' (67), 'Paid Chinese Shills' (66) who are regrettably responsible for 'Medical terorrism' (69) and 'Hallucinated Oppression' (65).

Slanguage and Truncations

Responses abound characterised by a plethora of colloquialisms indicative of different mindsets and moods. This is evident in the examples below:

70. *This is the funniest ad on facebook I've ever seen, lol!!!*
71. *OMG people, this is so laughable at this point*
72. *Where are the fact checkers on this?????? Children must not be vaxxed, are you serious????*
73. *Wanna talk about deaths from the vaccine????*
74. *Why are the vaxxed so scarred? Aren't they safe after the booster? Why are they so scared?*
75. *Geezuz! How many vaccine brands are there? It's like buying biscuits people.*
76. *Gosh!! I wonder why people are so hesitant.*

The use of expressions such as 'lol' (Laugh out loud) (70), 'OMG' (Oh My God!) for surprised disapproval (71), 'vaxxed' (72, 74) for vaccinated, 'wanna' for want to (73), 'Geezuz' (75), 'Gosh' (76) to indicate disapproval, for Jesus; 'lol' is for mockery and cynicism, and not only explicated by the context of expression (virtual space where time, speed and poetic licence play important roles) but the bloggers' urge to quickly express emotions of dissatisfaction, disapproval and contempt.

Magnification
Indignation and mistrust are equally expressed in strong exaggerated terms as the following cases intimate.
77. *How can we trust you people when you're hiding all data? I'll wait till 2076 and decide then.*
78. *Vaccine #20 within 1 year?*
79. *After the 6th, 7th or 8th booster, might be you will be protected.*

Judging from the user's physical appearance, it is easier for the blogger in excerpt (77) to live up to 2076 before deciding whether to vaccinate. This is an utter disapproval and rejection of the vaccine. In (78), the user's reference to the production of the 20th vaccine just in a single year is an outrageous condemnation of the ease and speed with which vaccines are produced. It takes several years of clinical tests to emerge with an effective vaccine. This is corroborated in example (79), which intimates that from the 8th booster, the vaccines are effective. All three posts are pointers to the ineffectiveness of the vaccines.

Theorisation
This is akin to recourse to various reasons in the guise of theories aimed at justifying specific acts and luring others into believing and adopting similar stances. This is evident in the following posts:
80. *This vaccine is an intentional act of man, this isn't happening to you, this is being done to you. mRNA technology. Gene therapy. Biotech. Nothing to do with your health. Ya all been deceived. Wake up! Ya brain will be connected to the 5G grid You'll be a controlled zombie. That's whoever survives the reset.*
81. *Covid is a deceptive propaganda and covid vaccines are equal to the mRNA poisons and blood clots from AstraZeneca, for the sake of decreasing the population of the earth for the sake of fake climate change.*

Accordingly, all the different technologies used to produce these vaccines are dismissed as 'deceptive propaganda' (81) that has 'Nothing to do with your health' (80). Besides, the vaccine transforms you into a zombie that will be controlled via the 5G grid (80). Otherwise, its deadly effect is in tandem with the depopulation program because of 'a fake climate change' (81). The precarious situation of the virus and its dismal consequences are not a natural phenomenon but an intentional dehumanisation programme orchestrated by humans on fellow humankind. Not only do these "conspiracy theories" justify vaccine hesitancy, but they also ignite panic, mistrust and indignation.

Syllogising

In syllogising, users effectively express deep emotions based on their appreciation of the prevailing situation. The cases below are vivid illustrations of the lack of trust in medical science but full of faith in God the protector and healer.

82. *UN and WHO have same logo.*
83. *Stop the child abuse! 8% of polio cases were caused by the polio vaccine.*

Because the WHO has been at the centre of vaccine schemes that have considerably drained its reputation, it is therefore no longer reliable. Because it shares a similar logo with the UN, it makes the UN as guilty and untrustworthy as the WHO (82, 83). Similarly, post (84) deduces that if the polio vaccine was responsible for the polio pandemic, the present pandemic should be explicated by the different vaccines used. These syllogisms are effectively expressive of disgruntlement and outright rejection.

Duplication for Emphasis

Repetitions like the ones contained in the following excerpts are in place.

84. *Strong strong strong but I still hear people die die die die, so why WHO, I'm asking.*
85. *Tell you lies, tell me sweet little lies, tell lies Fleetwood Mac was right.*
86. *Vaccine injuries and deaths, cover-ups, no liability, no information on vaccine trials, no long term safety data, no honesty and they still tell us it's safe.*

The repetition of 'lies' in (86) reflects the untrustworthy nature of the WHO and how disgruntled the bloggers are. For instance, they lie about how 'strong strong strong' (85) the vaccines are, yet people continue to 'die die die' (85). Besides, when there is 'no liability', 'no information' and 'no long term safety data' (94), this only helps to further blur the situation and heighten doubt.

Loans and Loan Blends

Usage is equally characterised by linguistic borrowing as seen in the example below.

87. *Get out of here! Don't listen to this scheisse.*

The choice to use the German expression 'scheisse' (shit) is explicated by the nasty effect it creates when pronounced.

Epistolary Device

For fear of being intercepted, misunderstood or misquoted, the bloggers address mocking correspondences to the WHO as indicated in example (89) as follows:

88. *Hello WHO,*
89. *Its been long since I heard from you. How's the devil's contract with you? It seems your desperation is still showing.*

In this way, sentiments of distrust and rejection are directly expressed.

Aphorisms

In beautiful proverbial terms such as the one that follows, the fate of the WHO is synthesised.

90. *When an elephant is in trouble, even a frog will kill it.*

The mighty elephant, symbolic of the WHO, is troubled by propaganda, lies telling, indecision and wrong decisions, corruption, etc., which constitute the ailments that weaken its status. The proverb pre-empts the organisation's demise when it is eventually unable to live up to the expectations of its credo.

Novel Coinages

Responses abound with the profuse use of novel expressions as bloggers express their different stances on vaccine-related issues. Responses mention the different varieties of vaccines produced, many of which constitute neologisms. Thus far, national regulatory authorities recognised by the WHO have granted emergency use authorisations for the following Covid-19 vaccines:

91. *Moderna, Janssen, CoronaVac, Covaxin, Novavax. Sputnik V, Sputnik Light, Sinopharm WIBP, Convidecia, Sanofi–GSK, SCB-2019, Valneva, Covishield, BBIBP-CorV, QazCovid-in, Soberana 02, Zifivax, EpiVacCorona, Abdala, Abdala, Minhai, CoviVac, COVIran Barekat, Medigen, ZyCoV-D, FAKHRAVAC, COVAX-19, Razi Cov Pars, Turkovac, Sinopharm CNBG, Corbevax, Soberana Plus, Pfizer–BioNTech, Oxford–AstraZeneca, Sinopharm BIBP.*

For reasons of easy reference, these vaccines are branded differently, taking into cognisance the technology used, the place of production, the purpose and several other determining characteristics. Besides, abbreviating, clipping, and blending are the processes mainly used. In addition, other novel forms characterise usage as indicated in the following posts:

92. *What about all the people who have died from the vax? Why are we not talking about this as well?*
93. *I can see the antivaxxers heads exploding very shortly. LoL.*
94. *Deathdealers!*
95. *Omicron is a lighter variant and more contagious as a lot more people will get sick and heal with a natural immunity, we will win covid.*
96. *Anti-vax friends: Hi Laura. I feel sorry for you. Don't you trust your immune system? You don't have to be a slave. Don't you know the pharma companies are minting money out of this PLANdemic.*
97. *WHO quacksine marketing.*
98. *Stop! Stop! This Menticide!*

In the foregoing, *vax* (92) refers to vaccine; *antivaxxers/anti-vaxers* (93) are those against vaccines; *deathdealers* (94) are those promoting deadly vaccines; *omicron* (95) is a new variant that emerged in South Africa; *PLANdemic* (96) is a blend of planned pandemic; *quacksine* (97) refers to non-experts involved in a bad business; *menticide* (98) is a blend of mental and suicide, referring to the massive disinformation campaigns. Apart from helping express feelings of disdain, they significantly enrich the lexical economy of the language.

Conclusion

Pandemic situations are known to ignite fear which is a subjective emotion that can engender idiosyncrasies. It has been established that people's fear of the coronavirus relates to different topics such as contamination risks, fears about economic consequences, coronavirus-related xenophobia, compulsive checking and reassurance seeking, and traumatic stress symptoms. These emotions often reveal stakeholders' helplessness, especially when the situation is not under control. As such, subjective idiosyncrasies reminiscent of individual and collective reactions and predicaments become inevitable. In typical situations, shades of stances are expected to be divergent as personal experiences during such situations differ from person to person. As the world moves through the different phases of the pandemic with more aggressive infections sweeping many areas, considerable efforts to check it cannot be underestimated. This notwithstanding, an appreciation of the strides towards checking the continuous spread of the virus has met with contending attitudes. Whereas responses indicative of apprehension, distrust and complete rejection, especially of the vaccines proposed and the institution in charge of providing universal health guarantees, are rife, many others still see in the efforts put in, reason and hope.

A noticeable implication of the situation remains the fact that although the negative reactions are revelatory of humankind as egocentric, they can be construed as the galvanising force behind the advances in medical technology and the eventual proliferation of vaccines, all in a bid to salvage humanity from the prevailing scourge. On the other hand, reactions in the guise of positive appreciation and encouragement rekindle necessary hope in the face of adversity. For neutral stances to be registered as part of the reactions is in consonance with societal equilibration. As such, the situation of the pandemic raises awareness about the individual and collective predicament of humankind virtually at loggerheads in the face of a precarity.

This study asserts that eccentricities emanating from the appreciation of a specific reality could be revelatory of language behaviour and behaviour towards language. In response to the situation, bloggers demonstrate profuse and effective use of linguistic and stylistic devices through which emotions are expressed. Like rudimentary weapons in the hands of protesters, these devices vividly portray language as an invaluable instrument in the communication of thought, expressing deep emotions and lashing out against related misdemeanours.

Abstract

Today, with pandemic literature overwhelmingly exposing the human predicament, the role of the scientific community in restoring hope in despair cannot be underestimated. Within the context of a plethora of conspiracy theories, the novel vaccines aimed at checking the ravaging Covid-19 pandemic have broadly been acclaimed and recommended as a prompt remedy. Despite this laudable scientific breakthrough, reservations from mavericks and purists continue to cast doubt, both on the suitability and efficacy of the vaccines and the intentions of the benefactors. This chapter hinges on the Pragma-stylistic Approach, which builds on Austin's (1962) Speech Act Theory and explores the different attitudinal shades that characterise vaccine opinions. The data set for this study consists of microblog reactions that ensued from posts by the WHO authorities on vaccines. Based on a total of 126 excerpts culled from the microblogs, the study demonstrates that reactions were either positive, negative or neutral and were shrouded in a myriad of relatively productive linguistic and stylistic resources inter alia, sarcasm, anecdotes, rebranding, hyperbole, syllogisms, metaphors and allusions, through which users successfully expressed mixed feelings of assurance, hope, doubt, fear and mistrust.

Keywords: (mis)apprehension, (dis)distrust, assurance, pragma-stylistic dimension, Covid-19

References

Al-Salman, S. & Haider, A. S. (2021). Covid-19 trending neologisms and word formation processes in English. *Russian Journal of Linguistics, 25*(1), 24–42.

Austin, J. (1962), *How to Do Things with Words*. Cambridge: Cambridge University Press.

Berg, S., O'Hara, K., Shortt, M., Thune, H., Brønnick, K., Lungu, D., Røislien, J. & Wiig, S. (2021). Health authorities' health risk communication with the public during pandemics: A rapid scoping review. *BMC Public Health, 21*(1401), 1-23.

Cancelas-Ouviña L. P. (2021) Humor in times of Covid-19 in Spain: Viewing coronavirus through memes disseminated via WhatsApp. *Frontiers in Psychology, 12*, 1-12.

Chlopicki, W. & Brzozowska, D. (2021). Sophisticated humor against Covid – the Polish case. *Humor: International Journal of Humor Research, 34*(2), 202-227.

Chouinard, S. & Normand, M. (2020). Talk Covid to me: Language rights and Canadian government responses to the pandemic. *Canadian Journal of Political Science, 53*(2), 259–264.

Goddard, C. & Wierzbicka, A. (2021). Semantics in the time of coronavirus: "Virus", "bacteria", "germs", "disease", and related concepts. *Russian Journal of Linguistics, 25*(1), 7–23.

Harding, C., Aloysius, A., Bell, N., Edney, S., Gordon, Z., Lewis, H., Sweeting, M. & Murphy, R. (2020). Reflections on Covid-19 and the potential impact on preterm infant feeding and speech, language and communication development. *Journal of Neonatal Nursing*, 1–3.

Hopkyns, S. & van den Hoven, M. (2021). Linguistic diversity and inclusion in Abu Dhabi's linguistic landscape during the Covid-19 period. *Multilingua*, 1-32.

Hua, T., Woods, P., Azman, H., Abdullah, I., Hashim, R., Rahim, H., Idrus, M., Said, N., Lew, R., & Kosem, I. (2020). Covid-19 insights and linguistic methods. *3L: The Southeast Asian Journal of English Language Studies, 26*(2), 1-23.

Insyirah, A. & Sudarwati, E. (2021). Are you Covidient or Covidiot? A linguistic landscape study on COVID-19 flyer in Pasuruan District. *JELTL (Journal of English Language Teaching and Linguistics), 6*(2), 319-341.

Kopytowska, M. & Krakowiak, R. (2020). Online incivility in times of Covid-19: Social disunity and misperceptions of tourism industry in Poland. *Russian Journal of Linguistics, 24*(4), 743–773.

Leech, G. (1981), *Semantics* (2nd ed.). Middlesex: Penguin Books.

Leyva-Moraga, F., Leyva-Moraga, E., Leyva-Moraga, F., Juanz-González, A., Barreras-Espinoza, J., Soualhi, A., Ocejo-Gallegos, J., Urquijo, M. & Ibarra-Celaya, J. (2020). Effective surgical communication during the Covid-19 pandemic: Sign language. *British Journal of Surgery, 107*(10), 243-244.

Mertens, G., Gerritsen, L., Duijndam, S., Salemink, E., & Engelhard, I. (2020). Fear of the coronavirus (Covid-19): Predictors in an online study. *Journal of Anxiety Disorders*, 1-34.

Mey, J. (2009). *Concise encyclopedia of pragmatics*. Oxford: Elsevier Science and Technology.

Mustajoki, A., Zorikhina Nilsson, N., Guzman Tirado, R., Tous-Rovirosa, A., Dergacheva, D., Vepreva, I. & Itskovich, T. (2020). Covid-19: A disaster in the linguistic dimension of different countries. *Quaestio Rossica, 8*(4), 1369–1390.

Negri, A. Giovanbattista, A., Barazzetti, A., Zamin, C. & Christian, C. (2020). Linguistic markers of the emotion elaboration surrounding the confinement period in the Italian epicenter of Covid-19 outbreak. *Frontiers in Psychology, 11*, 1-14.

Osi, S. C. (2021). A linguistic study of multilingual private signs in Puregold QI Central in Quezon City, Philippines.

Piekkari, R., Tietze, S., Angouri, J., Meyer, R. & Vaara, E. (2021). Can you speak Covid-19? Languages and social inequality in management studies. *Journal of Management Studies, 58*(2), 587–591.

Olah, A. R. & Hempelmann, C. F. (2021). Humor in the age of coronavirus: A recapitulation and a call to action. *Humor,* 34(2), 329–338.

Protassova, M. M. (2021). Linguistic reactions to Covid-19: The case of tourism services in Helsinki in summer 2020. Master's Dissertation. University of Helsinki.

Reed, N. S., Ferrante, L. E. & Oh, E. S. (2020). Addressing hearing loss to improve communication during the Covid-19 pandemic. *Journal of the American Geriatrics Society (JAGS), 68* (9), 1924–1926.

Sebba-Elran, T. (2021). A pandemic of jokes? The Israeli Covid meme and the construction of a collective response to risk. *Humor: International Journal of Humor Research, 34*(2), 229-257.

Slavik, C., Buttle, C., Sturrock, S., Darlington, & C., Yiannakoulias, N. (2021). Examining tweet content and engagement of Canadian public health agencies and decision makers during Covid-19: Mixed methods analysis. *Journal of Medical Internet Research, 23*(3), 1-18.

Strick, M. (2021). Funny and meaningful: Media messages that are humorous and moving provide optimal consolation in corona times. *Humor: International Journal of Humor Research, 34*(2). 155-176.

Wibowo, M. P. & Indrayani, L. M. (2021). Language choice at the airport within the covid-19 pandemic. *English Journal Literacy UTama, 6*(1), 423-431.

Wicke, P. & Bolognesi, M. M. (2020). Framing COVID-19: How we conceptualize and discuss the pandemic on Twitter. *PLoS ONE, 15*(9), 1-24.

SEVEN

Language Shift amongst Refugee Children in Koza

JAMES N. TASAH

Cameroon is home to many languages, and consequently, there is a staggeringly large number of different contact situations, particularly those triggered by the Boko Haram insurgence in Nigeria and the Far North region of Cameroon. Uncovering the patterns of contact obtained in the past is difficult, given the relatively poor level of documentation. The speakers of many of these languages gradually shifted to the more dominant languages at the higher level, thus progressively losing their ethnic identity. This study probes into one of the linguistic phenomena of language shift as an outcome of the migration of some refugee children in Koza to find out if their language is still vital or is gradually shifting during their stay in the host community.

Background to the study

Migrants and the communities in which they reside form an integral and vital relationship in the migration cycle. This symbiotic relationship forms around "psychological, and ecological processes of adaptation between migrants among themselves and the receiving community affect the degree of inclusion including their sense of belonging" (Hutchison, Abrams and Christian, 2007).

Settlement in a new community, permanently or temporarily, for socio-economic or political reasons may lead migrants to adapt progressively to the community's way of life and languages. The Boko Haram crisis that started in Nigeria by 2014 resulted in the migration of some people who moved away from their localities in search of safer communities across linguistic borders to settle and those who migrated to Koza were supposed to socialise and integrate the speakers of the host community socioeconomically and sociolinguistically. In the process of their socialisation and sociolinguistic integration, some of their children seemed to have been shifting progressively from their minority languages to the dominant languages spoken in Koza. Some of those who migrated to Koza in the Mayo Sava Division experienced language re-socialisation, and the degree of re-socialisation normally determines the degree of sociolinguistic and socioeconomic integration into the host community. An essential determinant of the nature of re-socialization is the migrants' attitudes towards self, the target language and the people who speak it (Richard-Amato, 1998, p. 58). Although the concept of language shift (LS) at the population level can be traced back to Fishman (1964), it is Fishman (1991) that made it particularly relevant to the discourse on Language Endangerment and Loss (LEL), as also underscored by Ostler (2011) and Pauwels (2016). Language shift usually occurs when speakers of a given language abandon their language, either willingly or under pressure, in favour of another, which then takes over as their means of communication and socialisation, as in the case of refugees in Koza. This study examines language use among Nigerian refugee children to ascertain whether their MT is thriving or if there is a potential shift to the languages spoken in Koza. To address the problem, 58 pupils and students were surveyed using a questionnaire that investigated their language use patterns.

The term "language shift" emerged in the 1960s when sociolinguistics first gained prominence as a field of study in Applied Linguistics (Fishman, 1964; 1994). However, despite its popularity and prominence in sociolinguistic literature, there is no fixed definition or conceptualisation. Bodomo and Dzahene-Quarshie (2009 p. 2) have broadly defined "language shift" as "a process in which successive generations of speakers, both at individual and at community levels, gradually lose proficiency in their mother-tongues or the language of their speech community in favour of other languages." This process may ultimately lead to language loss among individuals or even language death for an entire community.

The process of language shift from one language to another is widespread in Africa, where languages are not only in constant contact but also differ in size, status, prestige and function (Brenzinger, 1992; Smieja, 1996). The indicators of critical language endangerment include the development of negative attitudes towards one's language, ambivalent language loyalty, and association of mother tongue with low economic and social status, language transmission to children, reduction of domains of use, diminishing number of speakers, and limited stylistic variation, structural erosion and simplification, and lexical reduction (Batibo, 2005, p. 65). Language shift in Koza is enhanced by the Nigerian refugee children who need to be socio-economically integrated into the life of the host community.

When moving from a rural area where several languages may be used in essentially complementary domains by individuals (at home versus the marketplace) to a major urban centre (because of better job prospects in the latter), this migration usually results in a modification of social networks and corresponding language behaviour on a day-to-day basis. Vigouroux and Cécile (2008) note that discourse on migration has often been constructed along several dichotomies, including (i) duration of stay in the host country (permanent versus temporary residents), (ii) geographic roles (sending versus receiving countries), (iii) direction (migrant's point out departure versus point of arrival), (iv) types of migration (forced versus free migrants), and (v) individual versus family-type. Such dichotomies are often unsatisfactory partly because they tend to project human migrations as organised and highly structured systems. Hoffmann (1991, p. 186) argues that "when a community does not maintain its language, but gradually adopts another one, we talk about LS while language maintenance refers to a situation where members of a community try to keep the language(s) they have always used." LS, i.e., abandoning one's language in favour of another, may be voluntary or due to pressure (Batibo, 2005, p. 87). Generally, LS in most cases is induced by forces that may result in the death of a language in response to various social, cultural, economic, and even military pressures on a community (Nettle & Romaine, 2000, p. 7). Every time a language stops performing a particular function, it will lose some ground to another that takes its place. As in other cases of LS worldwide, LS in Koza occurs due to contact through the migration of the refugees.

The migration of respondents into Koza exposed them to linguistic needs that resulted in their economic dependence, favouring the use of a common lingua franca. This motivated most of them to learn the community's languages. Migrations are of two types: a minority language community may move into an area settled by a majority group, or a large majority language group may move into an area where a minority language is spoken. The result in both cases is the doom of the minority language; in either case, the type of language contact is superordinate. That is, a dominant language is imposing itself on a minority language (Batibo, 2005a).

Language Profile or Sociolinguistic Situation of Koza

Koza is found in the Mayo Tsanaga Division of the Far North Region. It is a multilingual area where Mafa, Fulfulde and French are spoken. Mafa is the indigenous language widely spoken in the locality alongside Fulfulde, which is used as the lingua franca. French is one of the official languages used as a medium of instruction in education and administration. The linguistic situation of the community enhances not only the indigenes to be bilingual in Mafa and Fulfulde but also the non-natives to be bilingual or multilingual in their respective MTs and any of the languages spoken in the locality.

Review of Literature and Theoretical Framework

Several studies have been carried out on how language shift or maintenance occurs in contact conflicting situations in various communities across the globe. In many of the research carried out on language shift, factors like migration, industrialisation, ethnicity, urbanisation, prestige, changes in the way of life of a group, changes in the power relationship between the groups, and stigmatised attitudes toward the minority group values and language have all been identified as promoters of language shift (see also Fishman,1964; Clampitt-Dunlap,1995). Thomason (2001, p. 58) also indicates that apart from migration, the issues of politics, economic, and social changes can also result in language shift. Interestingly, most of the factors mentioned above do not just promote language shift but also interfere with and slow down or prevent the shift in its totality. He also notes that language contact often involves face-to-face interactions among speakers in a particular geographical locality. Sometimes, speakers of two or more languages live together in a single community. This is the case with some Nigerian refugees in Koza. Most often, in language contact situations involving speakers of diverse languages, intense pressure from a dominant group could lead to multilingualism. In this global dispensation, Mufwene (2001, p. 154) notes that the more a population is integrated into another that controls its socioeconomic system, the more likely it is to lose its language. As the new space requires different communication materials, migrants' and autochthones' language requirements are organised and evaluated according to the market value concerning spatial dimensions in their new environment (Vigouroux, 2008, p. 241). The power dynamics of languages are related to the value of the languages within the market. Other studies (Tabouret-Keller, 1968, 1972; Dorian, 1980; Timm, 1980) have shown that migration is another cause of language shift. When members of a small group migrate to an area where their language no longer serves them, they will shift to the socially and economically viable language of the host community. It is also possible that migration may involve large groups. The local population may shift if they are swamped with a new language by the migrants. This is particularly common in situations where the local population is militarily defeated by the migrating group. Tasah (2021) also analyses the domains of language use and choice of the refugee children in Koza based on his argument that their indigenous language may be threatened as they shift to the host community language in Koza. He uses Fishman's (1968) domain analysis following the different domains in which respondents' languages choices within the community, and his findings revealed that the respondents relatively maintain their mother tongues but have primarily succeeded in integrating the host community's activities and may likely lose their indigenous language and identities progressively in the process of continuous stay and integration of the Koza community.

Regarding the framework, it is essential to indicate that language shift gradually proceeds from one domain to another. When two languages of unequal socio-political or economic strength come into contact, such as that of the refugees' children from Nigeria in Koza, a pressure–resistance relationship will arise, as demonstrated in Figure 7.1 below.

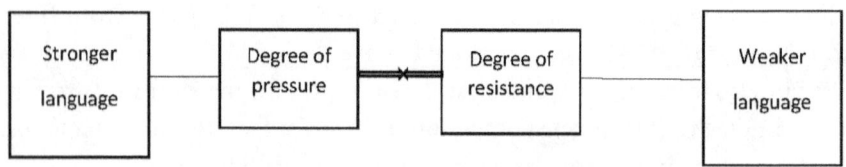

Figure 7.1. Pressure and resistance in language endangerment

As presented in Figure 7.1 above, such a situation which is similar to the context of this study may lead to language endangerment because when there is a net loss of resistance on the part of the weaker language (that of the refugees' children). Since the weaker language may be overpowered based on the duration of time the refugees' children may spend in Koza, the first indicators of endangerment and the beginning of the process towards endangerment may start to appear. The first indicator involves a highly bilingual situation in which speakers of the weaker language community speak both their MT and the stronger languages, such as Mafa and French. At first, the stronger language(s) is used mainly in secondary domains, particularly in inter-ethnic communication. Gradually, however, its use may expand into some of the primary domains where the speakers of the weaker language start using it as their means of communication in other domains, even in the family. At the same time, there may be a growing parental indifference to how well children acquire the MT as they may no longer be strict about how perfectly they are acquiring the language or if it is acquired at all. The children learn the MT less and less perfectly and may acquire only fragments, giving more attention to the stronger language(s), which becomes increasingly dominant in their lives. As a result, the weaker language may be used less frequently, and its stylistic and structural complexities may start to erode or simplify.

Once the domain of home is affected, a language becomes endangered. The theoretical concept of "domain" refers to clusters of types of interaction relevant to different fields of use. Some areas are notorious for exchanging refugees, depending on where a conflict arises or is sustained. When migrants leave their communities, like the Nigerian refugees in Koza, their language is supposed to be part and parcel of their lives, but it may be progressively endangered as some of them preferred to stay longer in Koza. These clusters of interaction types require one specific language as the default choice. Fishman (1966, pp. 424–458) maintains that domains are constituted according to three essential components: "role relation between participants," "topic of interaction," and "place of interaction." Since the number and character of domains differ according to the language and ecological environment of the communities in question, no fixed inventory of domains exists. Instead, scholars studying the language choices of specific communities indicate that their languages and cultures are supposed to be inseparable from them, even in the host community. However, some migrants gradually adjusted their language repertoires, styles and cultures to fit into their new environment because the host community was not an empty space. Surrounded by bilingual or multilingual speakers of one or more languages of different styles and cultures, the refugees had to interact with the indigenes from Koza daily for different purposes. Mufwene (2002, p. 19) argues that "shifting to a particular language is [definitely] associated with particular benefits to be derived from its usage, especially economic benefits." Otherwise, speakers would prefer to stick to their traditional languages, which they have always spoken, although they may learn another language for interaction with outsiders. In Koza, where three languages are spoken, the respondents can understand and respond to a certain extent relatively in Mafa, Fulfulde or French, depending on the length of time already spent in Koza. One language may also be more appropriate than the other in some domains. Usually, it is the prestigious language, or the one the respondent(s) is more exposed to daily that he or she may learn to interact with the indigenes. Language shift usually occurs in a diglossic situation when the more privileged language or language of higher status (H) exerts pressure on the less privileged or low-status language (L). In the context of this study, the Nigerian refugee children whose parents migrated to Koza are shifting gradually to the languages spoken in the host community, not only for their integration but also for survival. It is a sociolinguistic phenomenon examining how informants select different languages in different contexts. The choice of languages might be unconscious, but any speaker's choice depends on the subject matter, the respondents' relationship with the interlocutor, the mode of communication, the context of discourse and other variables (Batibo, 2005, p. 43). In this vein, the migration of the refugees to Koza brought about the constant contact between their language and those spoken in Koza, and this gave rise to language competition, overlap and has in turn certainly created complex dominance patterns and linguistic marginalisation.

Methodology

Selection of Participants

Since this study is concerned with the Nigerian refugee students who live in Koza, data were obtained mainly from those identified in the selected schools in the area. The selection of the respondents was based on the assumption that pupils and students represented the language situation of most of the refugees in the host community. The subjects were also selected based on their relative multilingual ability and knowledge of other languages. The only requirement was that they were refugee children attending school in Koza. The data for this study were collected through a questionnaire which investigated 58 respondents' language repertoire, use in the family, at school and in daily communication in the community for their social integration in the locality of Koza and their possibility of returning to their original home country, etc.

Description of participants

The subjects in this study comprised 58 Nigerian refugee children who live in Koza between the ages of 12 to 20 years. While 29.3% attended primary school, 36.20 % were in secondary school, and 34.48 % were in high school. This information is presented in Table 7.1.

The Survey items

Surveyed items were mainly questionnaires carefully designed to elicit respondents' patterns of language use in different domains in Koza. It was explicitly intended to obtain information about the respondents' educational institution, languages used at home, knowledge of the language spoken in the area, the degree of comfort with the community's languages, adaptation to the linguistic and cultural traditions of Koza and their plan to return to their original country. The questionnaires were distributed to all willing participants along with necessary instructions.

Administration of Questionnaires

The questionnaires were only administered to the target refugee pupils and students in the schools they attended in Koza. Although brief instructions were provided in the questionnaire, additional explanation was given to those who needed assistance in filling out the questionnaires.

Data analyses

The study employed descriptive statistical methods. The simple percentages and frequency tables were used for descriptive inferences. The data collected from the questionnaire items were analysed using statistics, and the results are presented below, with a few tables provided for illustration. Before analysing the data obtained from the respondents, it is vital to provide information on the number of participants, as seen in Table 7.1 below.

Table 7.1. Number of respondents from the selected schools in Koza

Institution	Respondents	Percentage
Primary	17	29.3
Secondary	21	36.20
High School	20	34.48
Total	58	100

As presented in the table, 17 (29.3%) of the respondents were from primary school, 21 (36.20%) were from secondary while 20 (34.48%) were from high school. Generally, in situations of language contact like the case of Koza, the MT and other languages spoken in that community are allocated specific functions; one would expect the respondents' MT to dominate the home domain since the children are supposed to communicate with their parents in their respective MTs as close associates from the same ethnic group. The results of respondents' language use at home are presented in Table 7.2.

Table 7.2 shows that the majority, 37 (63.8%) of the respondents still communicate with their parents in their MT, but 4 (6.9%) claimed to communicate with their parents in French, 4 (6.9%) indicated Fulfulde, 22 (22.4%) used Mafa which is an indication that some of the respondents had already learnt the languages spoken in Koza with their parents as in Table 7.3.

Table 7.2. Language use with parents at Home

	Languages	French	Fulfulde	Mafa	Mother Tongue	Total
	Respondents	1	0	0	1	2
	%	1,7%	0,0%	0,0%	1,7%	3,4%
	Respondents	0	2	4	9	15
	%	0,0%	3,4%	6,9%	15,5%	25,9%
	Respondents	2	2	6	17	27
	%	3,4%	3,4%	10,3%	29,3%	46,6%
	Respondents	1	0	3	10	14
	%	1,7%	0,0%	5,2%	17,2%	24,1%
Total	Respondents	4	4	13	37	58
	%	6,9%	6,9%	22,4%	63,8%	100%

Table 7.3. Language used with Neighbours

Languages			French	Fulfulde	Mother Tongue	Mafa	Total
Duration in the host community	2 years	Respondents	0	1	0	1	2
		%	0,0%	1,7%	0,0%	1,7%	3,4%
	3 years	Respondents	2	5	1	7	15
		%	3,4%	8,6%	1,7%	12,1%	25,9%
	4 years	Respondents	0	15	0	12	27
		%	0,0%	25,9%	0,0%	20,7%	46,6%
	More the 5 years	Respondents	0	7	0	7	14
		%	0,0%	12,1%	0,0%	12,1%	24,1%
Total %		Respondents	2	28	1	27	58
			3,4%	48,3%	1,7%	46,6%	100%

The results in this table show that the majority, 28 (48.3%) of the respondents used Fulfulde and 27 (46.6%) used Mafa with neighbours, while only 2 (3.4%) used French. Some respondents' ability to communicate with their neighbours in Fulfulde and Mafa within a relatively short period spent in Koza indicates the extent to which the refugee children have learnt the languages spoken in the host community.

In addition, only 2 (3.4%) of the respondents spent two years in Koza, 15 (25.9%) had been staying in Koza for three years, 27 (46.6%) spent more than four years while 14 (24.1%) had spent more than five years. The respondents' level of understanding and communicating in the host community's languages was also due to their exposure and length of interaction in Koza. The results are presented in Table 7.4 concerning the respondents' knowledge of the host community's languages.

Table 7.4. Respondents' knowledge of languages spoken in Koza

Respondents	Very good	Good	Average	Fair	Total
Respondents	1	1	0	0	2
%	1,7%	1,7%	0,0%	0,0%	3,4%
Respondents	5	9	1	0	15
%	8,6%	15,5%	1,7%	0,0%	25,9%
Respondents	5	21	1	0	27
%	8,6%	36,2%	1,7%	0,0%	46,6%
Respondents	7	5	1	1	14
%	12,1%	8,6%	1,7%	1,7%	24,1%
Respondents	18	36	3	1	58
%	31,0%	62,1%	5,2%	1,7%	100%

As presented in the table, 18 (31%) of the respondents claimed to have an excellent knowledge of the respective languages of Koza, 36 (62%) had a good knowledge, 3 (5.2%) had an average knowledge, while only 1 (1.7%) had a fair knowledge. These results indicate that most respondents knew the host community's languages. If the participants could understand and speak the languages spoken in Koza with different levels of competencies, it implies that they were pretty comfortable in the area and Table 7.5 below presents the extent of their comfort concerning the linguistic situation of Koza.

Table 7.5 shows that 14 (24%) of the respondents claimed to be very comfortable, 10 (17.2%) were less comfortable, and 34 (58%) were comfortable with the languages spoken in Koza. These results are in line with those of Table 7.4, where most of the respondents were relatively knowledgeable in the languages of Koza. Although some challenges must be faced when people find themselves in new environments, the degree of the respondents' comfort in Koza was an indication that some had adapted themselves to the linguistic and cultural traditions of the community, as shown in Table 7.6.

Table 7.5. Respondents' degree of Comfort with the host community's languages

Respondents		Very comfortable	Less comfortable	Comfortable	Total
	Respondents	0	0	2	2
	%	0,0%	0,0%	3,4%	3,4%
	Respondents	6	1	8	15
	%	10,3%	1,7%	13,8%	25,9%
	Respondents	5	4	18	27
	%	8,6%	6,9%	31,0%	46,6%
	Respondents	3	5	6	14
	%	5,2%	8,6%	10,3%	24,1%
Total	Respondents	14	10	34	58
	%	24,1%	17,2%	58,6%	100%

Table 7.6. Respondents' Adaption into the linguistic and cultural traditions of Koza

Respondents		Yes	No	Total
Respondents		1	1	2
%		1,7%	1,7%	3,4%
Respondents		10	5	15
%		17,2%	8,6%	25,9%
Respondents		15	12	27
%		25,9%	20,7%	46,6%
Respondents		10	4	14
%		17,2%	6,9%	24,1%
Total	Respondents	36	22	58
	%	62,1%	37,9%	100%

As seen from the table, the majority, 36 (62.1%) of the respondents adapted to the linguistic and cultural traditions of Koza, while others, 22 (37.9%) did not. The relative adaptation of most of the respondents to the linguistic and cultural traditions of Koza was a demonstration that they were already learning the host community's languages and their ways of life. The respondents' degree of adaptation to the linguistic and socio-economic context of the area is also confirmed by the ability of the majority to communicate with their classmates in French, as presented in Table 7.7.

Table 7.7. Language use in communicating with classmates in school

Languages			French	English	Ful-fulde	Mother Tongue	Mafa	Total
Minority languages	Kanuri	Respondents	8	2	2	0	0	12
		%	13,8%	3,4%	3,4%	0,0%	0,0%	20,7%
	Mandara	Respondents	13	1	1	1	0	16
		%	22,4%	1,7%	1,7%	1,7%	0,0%	27,6%
	Hausa	Respondents	8	3	1	0	2	14
		%	13,8%	5,2%	1,7%	0,0%	3,4%	24,1%
	Mafa	Respondents	12	0	0	0	2	14
		%	20,7%	0,0%	0,0%	0,0%	3,4%	24,1%
	Fufulde	Respondents	2	0	0	0	0	2
		%	3,4%	0,0%	0,0%	0,0%	0,0%	3,4%
Total %		Respondents	43	6	4	1	4	58
			74,1%	10,3%	6,9%	1,7%	6,9%	100%

This table shows that the majority, 43 (74.1%) of the respondents communicated with their classmates in French, mainly because French is the medium of instruction in education. Concerning minority languages, 4 (6.9%) interacted in Fulfulde and Mafa, respectively. The dominance of French language use among the respondents and their mates and Fulfulde as well as Mafa to a small extent, indicates that the respondents were striving to integrate the indigenous community of Koza as a determinant for their sociolinguistic and socioeconomic integration. Regarding respondents' plans to return to their country of origin, the results analysed are presented in Table 7.8.

This table shows that most of the respondents' parents, 38 (65.5%), did not plan to return, while only 20 (37.9%) preferred to return to their original country. If the majority of the participants did not want to go back to their home country, it is another confirmation that they were accepted and loved by the host community and that they could understand and speak at least one of the three languages spoken in Koza.

Table 7.8. Respondents' parents plan to return to their original country

Respondents	Yes	No	Total
Respondents	1	1	2
%	1,7%	1,7%	3,4%
Respondents	6	9	15
%	10,3%	15,5%	25,9%
Respondents	9	18	27
%	15,5%	31,0%	46,6%
Respondents	4	10	14
%	6,9%	17,2%	24,1%
Respondents	20	38	58
%	34,5%	65,5%	100%

Discussion of Findings

It is evident from the analyses that language shift is gradually taking place in Koza as 4 (6.9%) of the respondents claimed to communicate with their parents in French, while 4 (6.9%) were speaking Fulfulde, and 22 (22.4%) used Mafa at home. Some respondents' ability to communicate with their parents in any language apart from their MT is prima facie evidence that language shift was already in process. The results also suggest that intergenerational transmission of MT is gradually being disrupted in some of the homes, thereby putting the refugees' MT at risk of displacement if more children communicate with their parents in the languages spoken in Koza. However, it is essential to point out that most migrant families (63.8%) still interacted with their children in the MT. It is essential to point out that without safeguards for language use at home, sufficient to ensure transmission, attempts to prop the language outside the home will be like blowing air into a punctured tire. Achieving a steady state based on the incoming air will be impossible due to the continual losses resulting from the unpatched puncture (Nettle & Romaine, 2000, p. 178). In addition, Nettle and Romaine (2000) explain that without transmission, there can be no long-term maintenance and that when a language is no longer being passed on at home, efforts to promote it outside that domain in church or school, for instance, will typically end up being symbolic and ceremonial. This can be the fate of the respondents' MT if it is not used effectively in their respective families and if they stay longer in Koza.

Language shift was certainly already visible not only as most of the respondents 28 (48.3%) could communicate with their neighbours in Fulfulde and 27

(46.6%) in Mafa, but also based on the fact that 36 (62%) of the respondents claimed to have good knowledge in the languages spoken in Koza. Considering that 14 (24%) of the respondents felt very comfortable while 34 (58.6%) were comfortable in the languages spoken in Koza following the analysis of data, there is a possibility that the respondents' MT could be endangered if they stay longer in the host community as was the wish of most of the participants' parents 38 (65.5%) who did not want to return to their homeland. If most respondents preferred Koza to their homeland, it is also a confirmation that they were already knowledgeable in the host community's languages and had been integrated linguistically and socioeconomically. The respondents' gradual shift to the use of the languages in Koza could result in the progressive weakening of their MT and its eventual endangerment if the phenomenon of Boko Haram persists. Language shift is, therefore, irreversible in Koza since some respondents are already knowledgeable in the languages spoken in Koza to the detriment of their MT as they felt integrated into the host community both linguistically and socioeconomically.

Conclusion

Generally, there is a high tendency for the speakers of a minority language who migrate to a new locality to shift to the community's languages for survival, mainly if they stay longer in that locality. This study sought to ascertain whether there was any tendency for language shift among Nigerian refugee children in Koza in the Far North Region. The results revealed some symptoms of language shift which predict that the respondents' MT may lose ground to those spoken in Koza if there is no practical use of the respondents' MT at home. The results analysed indicate that the respondents are shifting to the languages spoken in the host community at the expense of their languages, and this may lead to the endangerment and death of their MT in future. However, the respondents' shift to other languages in Koza may not automatically result in the endangerment and death of their MT if there is a strong language loyalty among the speakers and its perfect transmission in their families.

Abstract

In migratory contexts, migrants' language repertoires and cultural identities are often challenged as they face new socioeconomic environments and sociolinguistic needs to enhance their position in the host community. Migration as a result of the Boko Haram insurgence and the ensuing refugeeism in the Far North Region produced social and linguistic changes as some Nigerian migrants who settled in Koza had to establish a sense of belonging in the host community by adapting not only to the language(s) but also to the local cultures while remaining loyal to their Mother Tongues (MT). It is both a product of globalisation itself, and the presence of migrants in a new locality usually triggers complex linguistic and socioeconomic issues that may lead to language shift. Migration has long caught linguists' attention as an ideal domain for investigating language dynamics that can shed light on language shift and change. This chapter analyses the language use patterns of Nigerian refugee children in Koza to determine whether their MT is being maintained or they are progressively shifting to the host community's languages as they struggle to integrate linguistically and socioeconomically. It uses Batibo's (2005) pressure and resistance relationship that can result in language shift and endangerment. Data were obtained through questionnaire administration. The findings generally show that the respondents may gradually lose proficiency in their MT in favour of other languages spoken in the area in their attempt to adapt to the linguistic and socio-economic activities of the host community, and most 38 (65.5%) of them preferred to stay longer in Koza.

Key Words: Shift, endangerment, language loss, conflict, ethnicity

References

Batibo, H. M. (2005). *Language Decline and Death in Africa: Courses, Consequences and Challenges*. Clevedon: Multilingual Matters.

Brenzinger. (1992). *Language death: Factual and theoretical explorations with particular reference to East Africa*. Berlin: Mouton de Gruyter.

Bodomo, A., J. Anderson, & J. Dzahene-Quarshie. (2009). "A Kente of Many Colours: Multilingualism as a Complex Ecology of Language Shift in Ghana." *Journal of Sociolinguistic Studies* Special Issue on Language Shift 3 (p.2) https://journals.equinoxpub.com/SS/article/view/6339 [archive].

Clampitt-Dunlap, S. (1995). *Nationalism, Native Language Maintenance and the spread of English: A Comparative study of the cases of Guam, the Philippines and Puerto Rico*, PhD Thesis. University of Puerto Rico.

Dorian, N. (1980). Language shift in community and individual: the phenomenon of the laggard semi-speaker. *International journal of the sociology of language*, 25, 85–94.

Fishman, J. (1972). *The sociology of language: an interdisciplinary social science approach to language in society*. Rowley, MA: Newbury House.

Fishman, J.A. (1991). *Reversing Language Shift: Theoretical and Empirical Foundations of Assistance to Threatened Language*. Clevedon: Multilingual Matters.

Fishman, J. A. (1964). Language maintenance and language shift as a field of inquiry: A definition of the field and suggestions for its further development. *Linguistics*

9, 32–70.

Hoffmann, C. (1991). *An introduction to bilingualism*. London: Longman.

Haruna, A. (2009). Language shift in northern Nigeria: The precarious situation of the minority languages of the region. A paper read at the 6th World Congress of African Linguistics, University of Cologne, Germany, August 17-21.

Hutchison, P., Abrams, D. & Christian, J. (2007). The social psychology of exclusion. In D. Abrams, J. Christian & D. Gordon (eds), *Multidisciplinary handbook of social exclusion research*. New York: John Wiley & Sons, Ltd.

Mufwene, S. (2001). *The ecology of language evolution*. Cambridge: Cambridge University Press.

Mufwene, S. (2002). Colonisation, globalisation, and the Future of Languages in the Twenty-first Century. *International Journal on Multilingual Societies, 4*(2) 162–193.

Nettle, Daniel and Romaine, S. (20000. *Vanishing Voices: The Extinction of the World's Languages*. New York: Oxford University Press.

Ostler, N. (2011). "Language Maintenance, Shift, and Endangerment." *In The Cambridge Handbook of Sociolinguistics*, edited by Rajend Mesthrie (pp. 315–334). Cambridge: Cambridge University Press.

Pauwels, A. (2016). *Language Maintenance and Shift*. Cambridge: Cambridge University Press.

Richard-Amato, P. A. (1998). *Making it happen: Interaction in the second language classroom from theory to practice*. White Plains, New York: Longman.

Tabouret-Keller, A. (1968). Sociological factors of language maintenance and language shift: a methodological approach based on European and African examples. In J. Fishman, C. Ferguson, & J. Das Gupta (eds.), *Language Problems of Developing Nations* (107-18). New York: John Wiley & Sons.

Tasah N. J. (2021). Patterns of language choice in contact situations between Nigerian Secondary School refugee children in Koza. *International Journal of Research in Humanities and Social Studies, 8*(1), 36–40.

Timm, L. (980). Bilingualism, diglossia and language shift in Brittany. *International Journal of the Sociology of Language, 25,* 29-42.

Thomason, S.G. (2001). *Language contact: An introduction*. Washington, D.C.: Georgetown University Press.

Vigouroux, B. and Cécile (2008). From Africa: Globalization, Colonization, migration and language Vitality. In *Globalization and Language Vitality: Perspectives from Africa*, (pp. 229–254). London: Continuum.

EIGHT

Addressing Global Challenges from a Linguistic Perspective

JULIUS NGUAFAC & GILBERT TAGNE SAFOTSO

In the early years of the twenty-first century, the world has been affected by many challenges. Since the Great Depression of 1929-32 (due to the worldwide economic depression which began in the USA) and the Second World War, humankind has never been so unhappy. The quick reconstruction of the global economy after the war and its rapid growth led to excesses in goods consumption. This forced the food and equipment industries, as well as the car industries, to put excessive pressure on land, forest and natural minerals around the world. For example, food industries through excessive exploitation of land have destroyed the soil across the planet; manufacturing industries have depleted the forests, car industries and other technological industries have led to the depletion of many minerals (Yellishetty et al., 2011; Mitra, 2019). Thus, the global challenges that man has created, coupled with natural disasters, are now numerous worldwide. This study which works from an interactionist perspective aims to survey some of those challenges and propose possible linguistic solutions. It first reviews some related literature, examines some major challenges afflicting the world, and finally proposes some solutions to them.

Literature Review

It is hard to define the term global challenges as there is no exact definition. Gelsdorf (2010) sees global challenges as any significant trend, shock or development that has the potential for severe global impacts. Ludwig, Blok, Garnier, Macnaghten & Pols (2021) suggest that global challenges such as climate change, food security or public health have become dominant research and innovation policy concerns. They argue that the appeal to global challenges can give rise to a solution strategy that presents the responses of dominant actors.

To George, Howard, Joshi & Tihanyi (2016), global challenges are becoming more complex and sophisticated and demand a multidisciplinary and interdisciplinary approach. Therefore, research management can make valuable contributions to understanding and tackling global grand challenges. Karaduman (2014) lists some global challenges and proposes some solutions to them. He opines that cooperation is the most important solution and that humanity should be the caretaker of the challenges with collaboration from states and non-state actors.

Gelsdorf (2010) holds that global challenges are already exacerbating vulnerability and increasing humanitarian needs. He remarks that the outskirts of Harare, Mogadishu and Port-au-Prince have already experienced rapid urbanisation and that climate-related disasters, environmental degradation and the high price of fuel can dangerously combine to undermine the economy severely, food security and the health of communities. He also maintains that countries, regions and even the global community may lack the capacity, financial resources and governance systems to respond to multiple and competing challenges. Kaul, Conceicao, Le Goulven & Mendoza (2003) point out that global challenges call for cooperation to create a public good or protect the global commons. For example, a stable climate is a global public good. It can be endangered by the global warming that comes from the emission of greenhouse gases due to the group actions of many individuals and society. McMichael, Haines, Sloof & Kowats (1996) note that many global challenges are interrelated across regions and disciplines. Global climate change is believed to directly and indirectly, impact human health, including malaria, yellow fever and hantavirus. Before proposing solutions, it is essential to list the major global challenges today.

Significant Contemporary global challenges

Among the numerous challenges afflicting the world today, Hutt (2016) lists the following:

Food security: By 2050, the world will have to feed 9 billion people. So, the demand for food will be 60 percent greater than today.

Inclusive growth: The present social, political and economic systems are exacerbating inequality rather than reducing them. For example, the many wars in Africa, Asia and Eastern Europe are causing unprecedented migration and displacement of people.

Future of work employment: In 2016, the International Labour Organisation estimated that more than 61 million jobs had been lost since the start of the global economic crisis in 2008, leaving more than 200 million people jobless globally. This situation, which in 2016 was already dire, is now aggravated by the

Covid-19 pandemic. The International Labour Organisation estimates that the working hours lost in 2020 compared to pre-pandemic levels were equivalent to 225 million full-time jobs, leading to 3.7 trillion US dollars in lost labour income.

Future of global finance: Two billion people cannot access high-quality, affordable financial services. Additionally, 200 million small and medium-sized enterprises worldwide cannot access formal financial services.

Future of the Internet: By 2025, it is expected that 10 percent of people worldwide will be wearing clothes connected to the Internet, and the first implantable mobile phone will be sold.

Future of gender equality: According to the Global Gender Gap Report, at the current rate, it will take another 118 years to achieve gender equality.

Other world challenges

In addition to the challenges Hutt (2016) listed above, many others are plaguing the world, including urbanisation and food security, migration, ocean conservation, water crisis, girl child education, and all sorts of disasters. Ibrahim, Uba-Eze, Oyewole & Omuk (2009) note that urban areas are hit with the problem of increasing population and, consequently, an inadequate supply of food items. The Food and Agricultural Organization (FAO) in 2012 estimated that the global population is expected to reach over 9 billion by 2050. As such, there will be a continuous demand for food production and buffer stuck. With an urban growth rate of 5 percent per annum, over 300 million new residents are expected to be added to urban areas in the African subcontinent between 2000 and 2030 (Kessides, 2005). Urban dwellers and households are generally food buyers who depend on their income for food security. They spend a large proportion of their household budget on food.

Africa is often regarded as a continent of mass displacement and migration caused by poverty and violent conflicts. The portrayal of Africa as a continent on the move is linked to stereotypical ideas of Africa as a continent of poverty and conflict. Clandestine migration from Africa to Europe and America has been a severe cause for concern in recent years. This irregular migration from sub-Saharan Africa and the Maghreb has also been associated with international crime, trafficking and terrorism (Castles et al., 2014). According to the United Nations Office on Drugs and Crime (UNODC), the system of migrant smuggling has become nothing more than a mechanism for robbing and murdering some of the world's poorest people (UNODC, 2006).

The earth is mainly covered with water, and people depend on the ocean to maintain the rainwater systems. Many populations rely on it for food and income. The oceans also absorb carbon dioxide and produce more than half of the oxygen on earth. Despite their importance, they are under threat. Overfishing and unsustainable fishing practices are causing the endangerment and extinction of many marine species. Industrial fishing takes a lot of fish out of renewable capital, like withdrawing more money from a bank account than the savings can generate annually. Overfishing can be seen as direct pressure and a significant risk to the marine environment and ocean health, drastically reducing fish biomass (Halpern et al., Lowndes, Rockwood, Selig, Selkoe, & Walbridge, 2015).

The water crisis is often used to describe the lack of access to water worldwide and the resulting consequences. The development of civilisation would not have been possible without the earth's water coverage, as it has provided a means for transportation and power sources (Atteberry, 2010). However, pollution has rendered some waters unsafe for consumption. It is estimated that 4% of all deaths could be attributed to water-related diseases (Pruss et al., 2002). According to the CDC (Centers for Disease Control and Prevention), approximately 11 percent of child deaths worldwide are attributed to diarrhoea diseases. Of these cases, 88 percent are caused by unsafe water or improper sanitation (CDC, 2013).

In many Arab and some African countries, young girls are sent to early marriage, denying them their fundamental right to education. The BBC News (2006) reported that the African patriarchal societal viewpoint favours boys over girls because boys maintain the family lineage. Another reason for the deprivation of the girl child's education in Africa is that some of their mothers were not educated. Mwangi (2004) remarks that poverty, diseases and harmful cultural practices continue to deny the girl child the right to education. The low literacy level of girls is one of the world's challenges, particularly in Africa.

Hutt (2016) mentions ecological collapse, nuclear holocaust, pandemics, molecular nanotechnology, and long-term investment as other global challenges. Of all the problems listed above, the Coronavirus and climate change are the most urgent. According to the World Health Organisation, as of 7th November 2021, more than 249 million cases and 5.05 million deaths were recorded, making the coronavirus the deadliest pandemic in history.

Since 2015, with COP 21 Summit held in Paris on 12 December 2015, the fight against climate change has always been the order of the day, with little agreement among the world's leaders on reducing pollution and deforestation. For example, the US, one of the world's largest polluters, left that movement on 1st June 2017. At COP 26 in Glasgow recently, only 23 new countries promised to abandon their coal industries between 2025 and 2040. However, this should be taken with much caution because, at the same time, huge amounts of money continue to be invested in fossil energy such as oil. The demonstrations clearly express the disappointment of many people worldwide about the issue. Although few world leaders sincerely believe in the proposed solutions, some are achievable, as discussed below.

Some possible solutions

This section discusses language and dialogue as possible solutions to several global challenges.

Use of appropriate language

Used adequately, language can be one of the valuable instruments in the search for solutions. It can help in addressing some of the challenges highlighted above. Concerning food security, for example, in Cameroon and Africa, many farmers are illiterate and ignorant. A good use of home languages by agricultural technicians to translate some new agricultural techniques can help farmers understand what to do on their farms and what not to do. Many African farmers spend much energy doing wrong things on their farms due to the lack of information. Some agricultural technicians are sent to areas where they do not understand the local language. Those technicians can explain to farmers the risk of deforestation on their various lands in their indigenous languages. If this is done in a language that farmers understand, they will adopt new farming techniques, and some change can occur.

Globally, there is a severe lack of job opportunities in the world. The ILO (International Labour Organisation) Report (2022) indicates that all regions face severe risk to their labour market recovery due to the ongoing impact of the Covid-19 pandemic. As the report continues, "overall, key labour market indicators in all regions–Africa, the Americas, the Arab States, Asia and the Pacific, Europe and Central Asia -have yet to return to pre-pandemic levels. For all regions projections to 2023 will remain elusive" (ILO Report, 2022, p. 13). The World Bank Report (2021) points out that "Covid-19 impacts could leave an entire generation behind, and that 'the Covid-19 Generation' includes recent graduates, first-time job seekers, and workers who have lost their jobs due to the pandemic. They are likely to be scarred from this crisis the longer they are out for work or unemployed" (World Bank Report, 2021, p.13). Thus, the younger generation of Africans should be advised to be job creators and not job seekers as has been the case until now. However, the current educational programmes do not enable this. New programmes need to be designed in clear language and with explicit curricula and objectives (see Safotso, 2020). This can effectively work only if all the stakeholders work hand in hand through nationwide discussions on the issue. While waiting for this to happen, young Africans trained in the bureaucratic way of looking for jobs should know how to compete. The few available opportunities on the job market are highly competitive. However, in Africa, many young school graduates do not know how to adequately write a job application, a curriculum vitae or a personal statement, which are the basic requirements to get any serious job. These elements should be included in all language programmes of African universities and taught by experts in the domains. Their knowledge can be a way out for job seekers.

Flauhaux & de Hass (2016) point out that Africa is often seen as a continent of mass migration and displacement caused by poverty, violent conflict and environmental stress. Such perceptions are based on stereotypes rather than informed empirical research. It would be necessary to conduct large-scale studies to determine the number of Africans who migrate to Europe. The stereotypical language or perception will thus be wiped away. Suitable language should be used to address migration issues. If this could be done through vast campaigns across Africa, it would permit those willing to embark on a migration trip to understand the realities of the myth of Europe and America, often seen as an El Dorado.

About scamming, social media users must know some of the tactics that forgers use to get to them. One of these tactics is the language used. Many scammers use flattering, sweet and convincing language to trap their victims. In Cameroon, some scammers send messages to people to tell them they have been selected as winners of a competition in which they did not take part or assure them that they are money multipliers. When naive people send their pin code or money to them to be multiplied, it is swept out and the account blocked. Being updated on the new scamming methods can help. Other scammers create fake profile pictures on Facebook with beautiful women's faces. Men who are looking for attractive women easily fall into their trap. It is thus essential that society be educated on their various tricks.

Use of sincere dialogue

In politics, citizens in developing countries are used to lies and violence (Höglund & Jarstad, 2010; Ezeibe, 2020). Ezeibe points out that an entrenched culture of hate speech is an off-neglected major driver of election violence in Nigeria and remarks that the implementation of anti-hate speech laws presents an opportunity for protecting the rights of minority groups, promoting inclusion and preventing election violence in Nigeria and beyond. Pant (2020) reports that hate speech against particular linguistic groups (commonly interlinking) has often been deliberately employed for political ends in Cameroon. "In September 2017, the prominent TV journalist Ernest Obama publicly encouraged the government to take violent measures against Anglophone protestors" (Pant, 2020, p. 1). In Africa and Cameroon in particular, politicians make so many unfulfilled political promises. Some wars and uprisings are due to political deadlock. However, as with many Western countries, trust in politicians can lead to peace, hard work and development. The National Dialogue, held in Yaounde from 30 September to 4 October 2019, and whose outcome later exacerbated the rebellion in the North West and South West Regions, is an example of political failure. The Peace Security Report (2020) on Cameroon indicates that key separatist leaders refused to attend the dialogue since their demands were unmet. Among others, they demanded that the dialogue should hold in a neutral place and in the presence of an international mediator, which the government obstinately refused. As the report projects, "the worst case scenario would be for the Anglophone crisis to escalate into a protracted civil war and/or eventually lead to secession of the Anglophone regions from the rest of the country" (p. 14). If in Africa in general and Cameroon in particular, politicians could tell the truth to their people and discuss all the sensitive social and political issues with them through a language of sincerity and dialogue, confidence and development will begin. In the present state of lies, verbal confrontation and wars, achieving change is quite difficult.

Our everyday life is inundated with various disasters, which have enormous consequences on the community. The media are generally at the centre of reporting them. Very often, depending on their editorial policies, some media tend to reassure the victims or exaggerate the gravity of the situation. However, the kind of language used is essential in those types of situations. The objectivity in reporting the number of casualties can help assist the victims. For example, using soft, comforting or healing language in reporting the events can console those affected. A sincere dialogue with the victims can also help determine their urgent needs. In Cameroon, for example, after certain disasters like the Lake Nyos explosion in 1986, much controversy has often been observed regarding the urgent needs of the victims. After the Lake Nyos disaster, in general, the management of that crisis was poor as the government was facing that type of situation for the first time: "material for burying the dead such as spades, gloves and boots arrived 11 days late, while other utensils in great need for carrying, treating and distributing water and drugs to treat water-borne diseases fell short of demands" (Bang, 2009, p. 121).

The controversy surrounding the coronavirus pandemic is a typical example of what divides the world in some situations. Since the outbreak of the disease in 2019 in China, much information and counter-information have been given on it, even by the WHO (World Health Organisation), which is supposed to hold the absolute truth in that domain. The various demonstrations observed worldwide by the anti-vaxxers testify to the degree of doubt about what the world leaders say about it. In France, for example, they are already envisaging a fourth dose of the vaccine, whereas, in previous speeches, the officials said that a single dose would save any vaccinated person from all the trouble. In Cameroon, the situation is almost the same. Few people trust what the government says about the pandemic, and those who accept to receive the vaccine are rare. However, sincere dialogue with the various communities and all the actors involved in the fight against the disease and clear information on the situation can reassure the population.

Conclusion

To conclude, language and dialogue can help solve some of the global issues the world faces today if used appropriately. People need to know the truth about the various global problems plaguing the world, such as food security, inclusive growth, Covid-19, employment, migration, water crisis, climate change, and pandemics. They need to be involved in the various talks on global issues to better understand their impact/effects on their lives. They want to be informed on issues that affect their lives by the government using reliable, verifiable information sources. This should be in a language full of truth and sincerity.

Abstract

Globally, humans have faced numerous problems like drought, floods, wars, etc. At the dawn of the twenty-first century, the world is experiencing unprecedented challenges that may worsen. Climate change, refugees, natural and man-made disasters, epidemics, food security, deforestation, and political disturbances are the most recurrent problems. Many solutions have been tried without success, leaving many problems intact. Important decisions are generally taken without enough discussions and the stakeholders' participation. Non-experts of the situation sometimes spend huge funds with no concrete solutions. From a theoretical perspective, this chapter draws examples from Cameroon and Africa to highlight the importance of language and dialogue in solving some global challenges.

Keywords: global challenges, language, discussions, wars, disasters, politics, education

References

Atteberry, J. (2010, January 2015). *Why is water vital to life?* Retrieved from http://science.howstuffworks.com/environmental/earth/geophysics/ water-vital-to-life.htm

Bang, H. N. (2009). *Natural Disaster Risk, Vulnerability and resettlement: Relocation Decisions following the Lake Nyos and Monoun Disasters in Cameroon.* PhD Thesis, University of East Anglia.

BBC News (2006). UN Appeal for Girls' Education World: Africa.26 Apr 2006 – 08 Oct 2006. Retrieved from http://www.news.bbc.co.uk

Castles, S. de Hass, H. & Miller, M. J. (2014). *The Age of Migration: International Population Movements in the Modern World.* Houndmills, Basingstoke, Hampshire: Palgrave Macmillan Higher Education.

CDC (2015) *Global Diarrhea Burden.* Retrieved from http://www.cdc.gov/healthywater/global/diarrhea-burden.html

CRED (2018). The emergency events database. Brussels, Belgium: Centre for research on the epidemiology of disaster. Retrieved from http://www.emdat.be/accessed.

Ezeibe, C. (2020). Hate Speech and Election Violence in Nigeria. *Journal of Asian and African Studies*, 56 (4), 919-935.

Höglund, K. & Jarstard, A. K. (2010). *Strategies to prevent and manage electoral violence: Considerations for policy.* Durham, South Africa: ACCORD.

Ludwig, D., Blok, M., Garnier, M., Machaghten, P. & Pols, A. (2021). What's Wrong with Global Challenges? *Journal of Responsible Innovation*, 9(1), 6-25.

FAO (2008). An Introduction to the Basic Concepts of Food Security. Food Security Information for Action: Practical Guides. *FAO Food Security Programme & European Commissions.*

Flahaux, M. L. & de Haas, H. (2020). African Migration: trends, patterns, drivers. *Comparative Migration Studies*, 4(1): 1–25.

Gelsdorf, K, *Global challenges and their Impact on International Humanitarian action;* 2010, https://docs.unocha.org/sites/dms/Documents/Global-Challenges-Policy-Brief-Jan 10. Pdf

George, G., Howard, J., Joshi, A. & Tihanyi, L. (2016). Understanding and tackling societal grand challenges through management research. *Academy of Management Journal*, 59 (6), 1880-95.

Halpern, B. S., Frazier, M., Potapenko, K.S, Koenig, K., Longo. Lowndes, J. S., Rockwood, R.C., Selig, E. R., Selkoe, K.A. & Walbridge, S. (2015). Spatial and temporal changes in cumulative human impacts on the world's ocean. *Nature Communication*, 6,1-7.

Hutt, R. (2016). What are the 10 biggest global challenges? *Vinod Koshy Annual Meeting.* Davos, p. 20-23 January 2016.

Ibrahim H., Uba-Eze, N. R., Oyewole, S. O. & Omuk, E. G. (2009). Food Security

Among Urban Households: A Case Study of Gwagwalada Area Council of the Federal Capital Territory Abuja, Nigeria. Pakistan *Journal of Nutrition 8* (6), 810–13.

ILO (2022). *World Employment and Social Outlook: Trends 2022*. Geneva: International Labour Office. Retrieved from https://creative commons.org//licences/by/4.0/

Karaduman, C, I. (2014). *Global Challenges for the World*. Obronnosc: Zeszyty Naukowe

Kaul, I. P., Conceicao, K. Le Goulven & R. Mendoza (2003). *Providing Global Public Goods-Managing Globalisation*. Oxford & New York: Oxford University Press.

Kessides, C. (2005). The Urban Transition in Sub-Sahara Africa: Implications for Economic Growth and Poverty Reduction, Urban Development Unit, Transport and Urban Development Department, The World Bank, Africa Region. Working Paper Series No. 97. Retrieved from http://www.worldbank.org/afr/wps/wp97/.pdf/18/11/08.

Kumaran, N. & Lugani, S. (2020) Protecting Businesses against Cyber Threats during COVID-19 and Beyond. *Google Cloud*. https://cloud.google.com/blog/products/identity-security/protecting-against-cyber-threats-during-Covid-19-and-beyond.

McMichael, A. J., Haines, J.A., Sloof, R. & Kowats, R. (Eds.) (1996). *Climate Change and Human Health*. Geneva: World Health Organization.

Mitra, S. (2019). Depletion, technology and productivity growth in the metallic minerals industries. *Mineral Economics*, 32(4), 30–37.

Mwangi, E. (2015). News and views from Africa. Retrieved from http://www.newsfromafrica/indeces/index-1707.html.

National Institute Statistics (NIS) (2016). Presentation of the First Result of the Fourth Cameroon Household Survey (ECAM 4) of 2014.

Pant, A. (2022). Fanning the Flames: Hate Speech and Elections in Cameroon.

Right, Preventing Mass Atrocities with Human Rights Report. Retrieved from https//www.rightforpeace.

Peace & Security Report (2020). *Cameroon Conflict Insight, Vol 1*. Addis: Institute for Peace and Security Studies. www.ipss-addis.org/pulications

Payne, R. J. (2012). *Global Issues*, 4th ed. London: Pearson Perspective.

Pruss, A., Kay, D., Fewtrell, L. & Bartram, J. (2019). Estimating the Burden of Disease from Water, Sanitation, and Hygiene at a Global Level. *Environment Health Prospect*, 110 (5), 537–42.

Safotso, G, T. (2020). Postcolonial Educational Failure in Africa: Some Proposals for the 21st Century. In Fondo, N. B. & Nkongho, M. B.(Eds.*)* *Interdisciplinarity and Transdisciplinarity-Maping the Episteme in Language and Literature* (pp. 92-107). Kansas: Miraclaire Publishing.

Seitz, J. L & Hite, K, A. (2012). *Global Issues,* 4th ed. Malden, M A: Willey & Sons.

Snaar, M. T. & Snaar, D. N. (Eds). *Introduction to global Issues,* 7th Edition. Boulder:

Lynne-Rienner Publishers.

UNESCO Institute of Statistics (2016). *Leaving no one behind: How far on the way to Universal Primary and Secondary Education?* Global Education Monitoring Report Advisory document: 27/Informational from 37. Retrieved from http://unesdoc. Unesco. org/ images/0024/002452/245238f.pdf

UNODC (2006). *Organized Crime and Irregular Migration from Africa to Europe.* United Nations Office on Drugs and Crime. Retrieved from https://www.unodc.org/pdf/research/Migration-Africa.pdf

Yaouba A. & Kamdem Kamgno, (2021). *Gender Inequity in the Northern Regions of Cameroon: Factors Research.* Retrieved from http://postcolonialist. com/civil-discourse/Inegalites-sexuelles-descolarisation-dans-les-regions-septentrionales-du-Cameroun-recherche-de-facteur/.

Yellishetty, M., Mudd, G. M. & Ranjith, P. G. (2011). The steel industry, abiotic resource depletion and life cycle assessment: a real or perceived issue? *Journal of Clearer Production*, 19 (1), 78–90.

World Bank Report (2021, May 2022). *Labour Markets.* From https://www.worldbank;org/en/topic/labour-markets

Part Two

Literature and Global Challenges

NINE

Freedom Fighters or Terrorists?
Terrorism in Helon Habila's Oil on Water

OPHILIA A. ABIANJI-MENANG

The term terrorism means different things to different people. Though it is an easily used label, it poses difficulties of definition, shifting from one naming to another. Among domestic and international governments, agencies, and non-governmental organisations (Wilson, 2022), the inherent ferocity, violence and intimation embedded in the action, especially against civilians by non-state armed groups in the pursuit of political, economic and social goals, ruffles what they represent. The French philosopher François-Noël Babeuf first used the term 'terrorist' to denounce Maximilien Robespierre's Jacobin regime as a dictatorship (Sultana, n.d.), implying acts of violence by a state against its citizens. Since the 20th century, the term has been most frequently applied to politically based uprisings intended to overthrow the established governance system and bring about a redistribution of income (Sandler & Hartley, 1995, cited in Sandler, 2014). In the 1970s, the terms "terrorism" and "terrorist" gained renewed currency due to various conflicts, including the Israeli-Palestinian conflict, the Northern Ireland conflict, the Basque conflict, and the operations of groups like the Red Army Faction. The topic gained further poignancy after the 1983 Beirut barracks bombings, the 2011 September 11 attacks and the 2002 Bali bombings (Sultana, n.d.).

Terrorism continues to be a contemporary global security challenge, Nigeria included. It challenges global security, threatens world peace, creates fear in victims globally, and hinders development in areas where its activities thrive. Terrorist activities and threats are the most talked-about security issues (Sandler, 2014). Governments are putting much effort into dealing with it. The Middle East is associated with modern-day terrorism, with Pakistan being considered its epicentre and "a safe haven for terrorist groups" (Sandler, 2014). Groups like Al-Qaeda, Taliban, Boko Haram, and Al-Shabaab, which the United Nations Security Council has designated as terrorist organisations, do not see themselves as terrorists but as liberators (UNODC, 2018). This raises the question of who defines and what criteria qualify a group as a terrorist. Defining terrorism and differentiating a freedom fighter from a terrorist is thus vital.

Borum (2004) defines terrorism as acts of violence intentionally perpetuated on civilians and non-combatants to further some ideological, religious or political objective. Enders and Sandler (2012), on their part, consider it as a premeditated use or threat of violence by individuals or subnational groups to obtain a political or social objective by intimidating a large audience beyond that of the immediate non-combatant victims (cited in Sandler, 2015). The term usually has as its principal focus non-state actors (Borum, 2004) and rules out state terror, where a government terrorises its own people (Sandler, 2014). The evolution of the concept of terrorism shows contemporary definitions of terrorism as biased and methodically excluding governments, even though the use of violence to achieve political ends is common to state and non-state groups. Many scholars and critics point out that states also commit terrorism against their citizens. Repressive regimes in postcolonial Africa, especially, terrorise their own citizens to maintain power. Because of this, it may go with the cliché that "one man's terrorist is another man's freedom fighter (Ganor, 2002). There are, besides, no legally binding definitions in all jurisdictions. This chapter, therefore, adopts Bockstette's (2008) definition of terrorism that brings out the psychological and tactical aspects lacking in other definitions of terrorism:

> Terrorism is defined as political violence in an asymmetrical conflict that is designed to induce terror and psychic fear (sometimes indiscriminate) through the violent victimisation and destruction of non-combatant targets (sometimes iconic symbols). Such are meant to send a message from an illegal clandestine organization. The purpose of the terrorist is to exploit the media in order to achieve maximum attainable publicity as an amplifying force multiplier in order to influence the target audience (s) in order to reach short and midterm political goals and /or desire long-term end states (Bockstette, 2008, p. 8).

Bockstette's perspective brings out elements of terrorism that resonate with this chapter: a) it is asymmetric warfare that employs guerrilla tactics, b) it involves the use of violence and seeks to create fear in victims and a broad audience, c) it relies on acts of terror, d) it uses the media and other forms of propaganda, and e) it attacks national symbols. These concepts will be examined from the prism of eco-terrorism, militant terrorism, and state/political violence. It is important to note that the form of terrorism depends on the country, political system and particular time in history. Thus, environmental abuse, coupled with the repressive regime of Sani Abacha gave rise to the ecological war in Irikefe.

Irikefe Island, the fictional world in *Oil on Water*, is the vortex of asymmetric warfare that employs guerrilla tactics to confront government forces. The story is that oil exploration at Irikefe Island gives rise to an "oil war" (Habila, 2010, p. 37) and the militancy on the Island (Abianji-Menang, 2021). The militant groups of Irikefe include the Black Belts of Justice, the Free Delta Army, and the AK-47 Freedom Fighters (Habila, 2010, pp. 34-35), opposing the environmental destruction of their land by multinational oil companies thanks to a complicit government. Led by Henshaw and "Professor," the militant group leaders, through the media, profess to be freedom fighters resisting environmental pollution. This militant terrorism in Irikefe Island evokes environmental abuse (ecoterrorism), land expropriation, lack of education, corruption, poverty, unemployment, and lack of development as motivation. They pick on environmental destruction through gas flares and oil spillage by oil exploration companies degrading their environment. Their acts of violence, such as kidnapping for ransom, vandalising pipelines, and hostage-taking, earn them the designation of militant terrorism. Their preoccupation with ecology puts them within the ambit of eco-terrorism, thereby justifying them as ecoterrorists and freedom fighters, all in the context of rising militancy.

Given the convoluted interconnection between the two labels, only threading can distinguish between "a freedom fighter" and "a terrorist." This is the focus here and within the context of postcolonial African literature, with *Oil on Water* as the focal text. The terms freedom fighter and terrorist need clear definitions for easy comprehension. For Ganor (2002), a freedom fighter is someone who fights for national liberation. Such are people actively involved in an armed rebellion rather than simply being activists, peacefully campaigning for freedom. Freedom fighters use physical force to cause a change in the political and social order. Any government facing violent acts from a resistant movement usually condemns and calls such acts terrorism, even if only military facilities or objects of their demand are targeted. Freedom fighters are thus often called rebels, insurgents, or terrorists, which are pejorative labels used mainly by governments to discredit groups fighting for change. Heskin (1985) highlights the fact that 'terrorism' is a pejorative term used to describe acts of violence with a political purpose perpetrated by groups without official status (cited in Horgan, 2019).

About who is a terrorist, Ganor (2002) postulates that it depends entirely on the subjective outlook of the definer. Wikan (2018), toggling the labels, explains that a terrorist in some instances may be considered a freedom fighter, that it takes "one man" to view the action, freedom fighting, for it to become such - and that "man" can very well be the terrorist. The aims of terrorist and guerrilla warfare may be identical, but they differ in their operational targets. Guerrilla fighters, according to their motivational goals or ideologies, target objects of their fight, such as military facilities, whereas terrorists deliberately target civilians (Ganor, 2002), which is a criminal act. Ideology plays a significant role in the selection of the terrorist's target. For ideology is the prism through which people and institutions are judged guilty and considered legitimate targets justifying their attack (Drake, 1998).

The target of militant operations in *Oil on Water* are pipelines, oil workers, expatriates, and military stations. These qualify them as freedom fighters. Professor declares, "By this time tomorrow, one of the major oil deposits will be burning. We will make it hot for the government and the oil company that they will be forced to pull out" (Habila, 2010, p. 231). Government propagandists call them "rebels," "kidnappers," "barbarians," terrorists" (Habila, 2010, p. 156), but the local communities identify with them and consider them freedom fighters. As the narrator declares, "It is no secret these islands and villagers are under his (Professor's) protection" (Habila, 2010, p. 136).

Caught in the quandary of definitions of terrorism, renowned media corporations like the BBC, CNN, and RFI skip the expressions "terrorists" or "freedom fighters" and employ the more neutral terms like "militants," "guerrillas," "assassins," "insurgents," "rebels," "paramilitary or militia." Thus, those labelled terrorists by governments or the media may be called freedom fighters, nationalists, liberators or revolutionaries later by the same governments and media. Having established the relationship between freedom fighters and terrorists above, it is necessary to define state/ political terrorism.

State terrorism is conducted by governmental agents or forces against its own people (Sultana, n.d.). The concept of "state terrorism" is as controversial as terrorism itself. Some schools of thought argue that political violence by the state should not be considered "terrorism." Corroborated by scholars like (Laqueur, 2003) and Hoffman (1998), who argue that the very existence of a state is based on its monopoly of power. For Cherry (2017), state or politically sanctioned violence aims to maintain general order. Described as a legitimate force, the state uses resources such as the military to perform acts of terrorism directly. Blakeley (2009) takes an opposite stance with the premise that state monopoly of violence is no justification for excluding it from studies on terrorism.

The police and military are state enforcers of the law. If they target civilians when the state should instead protect and thereby invoke terror in the broader audience, whether in armed conflict or peacetime, they commit acts of state terrorism. They violate principles enshrined in the international bodies protecting human rights: International Humanitarian Law (IHL) and International Human Rights Law (IHRL). Targeting armed enemy combatants is legitimate in warfare, but certain acts like killing prisoners of war and torturing or degrading treatment of prisoners of war are prohibited. Where the prohibited acts are violated, the state is guilty of state terror (Blakeley, 2009).

The deliberate use of violence and intimidation, especially against civilians by the state, is common in postcolonial African states like Nigeria, where dictatorships terrorise their citizens. In *Oil on Water*, the military orchestrate deadly force and intimidation tactics with impunity, their prime targets being ethnic minorities and indigenous people (Cherry, 2017). *Oil on Water* samples and examines state violence under the dictatorial regime of General Sani Abacha in Nigeria from 1993-1998. The military regime of Abacha was considered "The worst years of military dictatorship in Nigerian political arena" (Habila, 2010). Abacha exercised absolute control through his reign of terror that banned political activities and controlled the press. Zaq, a pro-democracy activist journalist working for the Star paper in Port Harcourt, reveals that it was during Abacha's reign that pressure on journalists and pro-democracy activists was at its most fervent pitch (Habila, 2010, p. 236). Most journalists, himself included, maintained two or three addresses to stay ahead of the military goons. He wrote fiery and fearless anti-military pieces that even "Our editor was hesitant to publish" (Habila, 2010, p. 122). He finally escaped to Burkina Faso to lie low and await Abacha's inevitable downfall. Abacha's reign was also characterised by human rights abuses, especially after the hanging of Ken Saro-Wiwa, an environmental activist who opposed the exploitation of Nigerian resources by a multinational petroleum company (Cedric, 2018). The regime provoked and heightened terrorism in Nigeria, such as torture, military brutality, capital punishment, and extrajudicial killings. Sergeant and the Major in the text are two military officers, symbols of fear, torture and repression. The root cause analytical framework will be implored below to examine the causal factors of terrorism and militancy in Irikefe Island.

Oil and Water Sourcing Conflict in Irikefe Island

Armed conflicts persist in post-independent African politics, and *Oil on Water* portrays how oil and water resources create a complex armed conflict in Irikefe Island as seen by Zaq and Rufus, two reporters, who embark on the kidnap trail of Isabel Floode, wife of a British petroleum engineer, kidnapped by militants (Habila, 2010, p. 31). They navigate the polluted water of Irikefe, observing and recording truths about the origin of the conflict between the oil companies and the Delta people, whose lands are exploited and ruined. They also have to contend with both the brutality of government soldiers who patrol the region and the militants who disrupt oil exploration to protect their environment. The root cause analytical (RCA) framework provides an in-depth understanding of the causes of conflict on the island. This concept identifies and addresses the root causes of problems to proffer plausible solutions to counteracting terrorism and militancy. It explores factors that cause individuals to join a terrorist group, for example, and thereby cuts down terrorist acts. Along with RCA, ecocriticism will be applied to the relationship between literature and the physical environment (Gloffelty,1996). The application of ecology and ecological concepts to the study of literature is entailed in ecocriticism (Rueckert, 1978). In this respect, it is posited that environmental degradation and pollution from petroleum exploration, with devastating effects on biotic and non-biotic elements in the Niger Delta Region of Nigeria, provided Habila with the subject matter in *Oil on Water*. The creative literary piece thus raises awareness of environmental issues in Nigerian communities.

A petroleum-rich local community, Irikefe Island allegorically represents the Niger Delta Region in Southern Nigeria. This region is economically significant as Nigeria depends on up to 90 percent of its foreign exchange from oil gotten from the area (Oluwadare, 2019), making oil from the region the lifeblood of the Nigerian economy (Ugwuanyi et al., 2014). Habila juxtaposes Irikefe oil wealth with its beautiful scenery, "Irikefe Island, also known as Half Moon Island, because of its distinct crescent-shaped coastline (Habila, 2010, p. 5). "It was a small village close to Yellow Island" (Habila, 2010, p. 42). "Yellow" is a symbol of glory conferred on inhabitants of the region by nature. Vivid imageries bolster this conferment of "crescent-shaped coastline creeks," "rivers," and "forest," indicative of fertility and diversity. Mangroves provide a carbon sequestration capacity to support various plant and animal life, making it ideal for agriculture and fishing for livelihood. The abundance accounts for the host communities' happiness, as Chief Ibiram declared, "They lacked for nothing, fishing and hunting and farming and watching their children growing up before them, happy" (Habila, 2010, p. 42). The people's attachment to the environment is captured in paradisiacal imagery "Once upon a time they lived in paradise… (Habila, 2010, p. 45) and were happy until when oil was discovered (Habila, 2010, p. 152). Contentment with what nature offers colours the people's ideology with paradisiacal ease "though they may not be rich," "the land had been good to them, they never lacked for anything" (Habila, 2010, p. 43).

An important cultural asset, land in Africa is cherished and preserved at all cost, wiring it with spiritual and economic significance. The people living in these communities are farmers, hunters, and fishermen, and their livelihood depends on the land (Lortyer, 2020). Any attempt to grab or invade it is met with resistance. The invasive implantation of an oil company on the island adversely affects the people's traditional mode of livelihood - fishing, besides degrading the land and forest, which in turn would affect their farming and hunting. Air, land and water pollution ensue. On this prism, Chief Malabo, custodian of tradition in a community meeting, warns his people about the environmental, cultural and economic consequences of selling their land to the oil companies. He reasons that it is their ancestral land and wonders, "What kind of custodians of the land would they be if they sold it off" (Habila, 2010, p. 44). For refusing to sell his land to the oil company, Chief Malabo is arrested and murdered by the military (Habila, 2010, p. 44). The forceful acquisition of the people's land and the assassination of their chief affects their identity and serves as a major cause of conflict in the region. The rich and beautiful Delta now becomes something only in the imagination of its people, who look back in anger and recount stories about their beautiful and collective past, "Once upon a time, they lived in paradise" (Habila, 2010, p. 42). This evokes the devastation of the polluted wetland by the greed for oil and money while the environment is being fragilised by oilfields and pipelines that meander snakelike across the Delta waters. The text applies narrative techniques like storytelling that englobe relevant historical information, upholding aspects of culture, and justifying conflict between the indigenes, the oil companies and the government, "So your question, are we happy here? I say how can we be happy when we are mere wanderers without a home" (Habila, 2010, p. 45). Irikefe being an island of river systems, swamps, rain forest and farmland, the insinuation of instability draws attention to itself.

The role and influence of culture on terrorism in general and terrorist ideology, in particular, have been neglected in terrorism studies, a rather regrettable neglect. Borum (2004) observes that one's social environment shapes one's worldview in various ways. For the most part, cultures have a formidable influence on personalities and development. Ignoring this means inviting trouble.

The setup is part of the world view of a people that should be considered. This explains why expropriating or damaging their land means rocking the boat. The oil companies not only acquire land but damage crops. In addition, they provide little compensation; the military kills those who protest this. The oil companies leave rusting pipelines, contaminated air and water, damage crops, and embitter the population despite the huge oil profits.

Besides the neglect, the implantation of the oil company devastates and renders the landscape barren (Habila, 2010, p. 39), adding to the absence of infrastructure, social services, non-oil industries and even petroleum products that typify the fishing, hunting, agrarian society. No developmental projects are introduced to boost the region's economy to replace their traditional occupations. Instead, the oil company's presence is signalled by pipelines that cover the entire village, like in a sci-fi movie "the meagre landscape was covered in pipelines flying in all directions, sprouting from the evil-smelling, oil-fecund earth. The pipes crisscrossed and interconnected endlessly all over the eerie field" (Habila, 2010, p. 38). The comparison of the village setting to science fiction (Sci-fi) typifies environmental changes that have taken place in the region, "We saw our village change, right before our eyes" (Habila, 2010, p. 45). The narrator wonders if this really is a village. The environmental ravages the oil industry brings are elaborated and hyped upon. Thus, oil is said to often spill from pipelines compounded by gas flares, devastate vegetation and animal life and cause an ecological disequilibrium (Babatunde, 2020). As detailed, "The land grew only gas flares and pipelines" (Habila, 2010, p. 43), rivers polluted and "useless for fishing" (Habila, 2010, p. 43). Crabs and bats, which the people caught and sold to fund their children's education, are no more. In a conversation with the narrator, Gloria worthlessly turns and points at the sky towards the oil fields, remarking, "Gas flares. They kill them. Not only the bats, other flying creatures as well" (Habila, 2010, p. 127).

Oil and water assume symbolic relevance in the text, water being a limpid liquid and oil, an unctuous mineral is not water-soluble. So, oil spills and gas flares affect marine life and the water resources on which the islanders depend for a living. The insolubility of oil in water becomes an agent of poverty and conflict. Poverty is manifested in a lack of education and resources for sustainable livelihood. Collaterally, hunger, malnutrition, social discrimination, and non-participation in decision-making ensue. Cédric (2018) notes that it is a paradox for a country, extremely oil-rich, to be incapable of making its population fully benefit from the wealth. Dr Dagogo-Mark is confronted by a village elder who looks at him in the face and tells that he is sick, the sickness being poverty, "Can you give me medicine for that?" (Habila, 2010, p. 152). Tamuno, the fisherman, and his son, Michael, who serve as guides to Zaq and Rufus in the kidnap trail, reflect this poverty too. Michael is stunted because of poor diet; his hair is reddish and spare, his arms bony like his father's, and they are both dressed in the same shapeless, faded, homespun shirt and trousers, their hands rough and callused from seawater; they smell of fish and look as elemental as seaweed (Habila, 2010, p. 7). The words "stunted," "poor diet," "reddish hair," "bony hand, rough and callused hands" are carefully employed to spell misery.

Springing from poverty are instability, insecurity, conflicts, violence, crime, and social tensions accompanying protest and restiveness in the region. Watching TV News at James Floode's residence, Rufus notes the picketing of youths holding placards in front of an oil-company building in Port Harcourt to protest poverty. Poverty pushes some youths to join militant groups. So Tamuno wants Zaq and Rufus to take his son, Michael, to Port Harcourt, for him to have a better future by learning a trade, driving, or schooling, "He no get good future for here I fear say soon him go join the militants, and I no wan that." (Habila, 2010, p. 41).

Unemployment also engenders terrorism in Irifeke Island. Though a university graduate, Salomon, James Floode's cook, "Like a lot of young men in the Delta, had been forced to take a job below his qualification while he waited for that elusive office job with an oil company" (Habila, 2010, p. 201). John and other unemployed youths hang out in backstreet barrooms to play cards and drink all day, always complaining about the government, "He had been full of anger before he left, the kind of anger that often pushed one to blaspheme or to rob a bank, or to join the militants" (Habila, 2010, p. 96). Rufus attests that he had seen that kind of anger in many of his friends with whom he went to school. Some of them are in the forests with the fighters, have made millions from ransom money, but many have died.

Illegal siphoning from petroleum infrastructures (Oluwadare, 2019) is a lucrative business that sustains the people. It is fuelled by poverty, lack of employment, neglect of the region, and greed. Since parents have lost their traditional fishing, farming and trading occupations, their children, who drop out of school, engage in illegalities like bunkering and oil theft, irrespective of the risk associated therein (Simon et al., 2014). Children steal fuel from vandalised pipelines to earn a living. Rufus's father and his friends buy stolen fuel from little children, as he tells his son, "This is the only business booming in this town. I buy from little children" (Habila, 2010, p. 64) a way of making money in a bastardised economy.

Floode complains, "Our pipelines are vandalised daily, losing us millions…

The people don't understand what they do to themselves" (Habila, 2010, p. 103). Floode's narrative voice demonstrates that capitalism is the dominant mode of production in Nigeria and for European bourgeoisie interest. Europeans and the West continue to control the political, economic and social life of Nigerians, thanks to the new leaders who readily step into the oppressive position of the departed colonisers.

Siding with the masses, the narrator blames the oil companies and the government for not responding to the people's plight, "I don't blame them for wanting to get some benefit out of the pipelines that had brought nothing but suffering to their lives, leaking into the rivers and wells, killing the fish and poisoning the farmlands...These people endure the worst conditions of any oil-producing community on earth ...They are just hungry and tired" (Habila, 2010, pp. 103-104). There is a vast chasm between Nigeria's multi-billion-dollar oil revenue and the standard of living for most Nigerians, the majority of whom are poor (Evaristo, 2010), which is why the class struggle between the exploiter and the exploited is endemic. Multinational oil companies, conniving with the ruling class, use government apparatus to exploit oil resources from the Island without ploughing a sustainable part of the revenue to develop the people and the island. No wonder militia groups crop up to prosecute the war against the state to secure their own share of the national booty for those who can brave the odds (Oluwadare, 2019).

Oil spills in Irikefe negatively impacted human health and livestock, raising the water's toxicity level. Dr Dagogo-Mark watches in dismay at how a whole village disappears, sharing the same story and diseases, "A man suddenly comes down with a mild headache, becomes feverish, then develops rashes, and suddenly a vital organ shuts down" (Habila, 2010, p. 156). To him, the services of graver diggers are needed more in the region than doctors. Because of the intoxication of the environment by gas flares and oil spills, he qualifies the islands as "A place of dying" (Habila, 2010, p. 151), symbolically represented by Zaq's death. Onunkwo, Nwogwu, & Ojiakor (2017) observe that air and water are polluted with oil fumes, exposing them to disease and death. Zaq's exposure to the unfortunate weather condition on the journey, he contracts the disease, which weakens and eventually kills him. Dr Dagogo-Mark wonders what he is doing in a region that is a death trap; there is nothing he can do to salvage the situation. The environmental devastation associated with the industry and the lack of distribution of oil wealth has been the source and a critical aggravating factor of numerous environmental movements and armed conflicts on the Island.

The novel reveals how postcolonial African leaders have failed in their responsibility to protect their citizens from imperialists who continue to exploit the people's wealth through their political leaders. It exposes the exploitative impact of neo-colonialism on indigenes for whom industrialisation fails to bring accompanying economic growth or provide jobs to ethnic groups who feel exploited. The benefits of the vast wealth created by petroleum extraction are not felt by the population who abandon their traditional agricultural practices because of environmental pollution. The majority of the people at Irikefe still live in abject poverty.

Therefore, leadership is seen as the major problem in Irikefe and Africa. As Achebe (1983) postulates, Nigerians are what they are because their leaders are not what they should be. Corruption, prebendalism, dictatorship, bad governance, bad economic policies, poverty, press censorship and violence all being societal ills that plague postcolonial African society in the 21st century giving rise to violence and terrorism in many parts of Africa.

This historical background informs some of the novel's thematic concerns, including neo-colonisation, oil exploration, environmental degradation, pollution, unemployment, poverty, rebellion, and terrorism. As history and context-bound, Helon Habila's *Oil on Water* is thus informed by socio-historical, political, and environmental concerns. The historical realities light up why the language of the text is harsh and the situation ominous. For bad leadership is what causes terrorism in the Niger Delta Region. Nigeria is supposed to be the wealthiest country in Africa because of its oil revenue. However, these profits are siphoned through corruption and collusion between the petroleum industries and the Nigerian government. Only a few have access to this wealth, as James Floode corroborates, Nigeria would "Become the Japan of Africa, the USA of Africa, but the corruption is incredible …The country was so corrupt only a few had access to that wealth… Corruption in Nigeria is incredible and sustaining the poverty" (Habila, 2010, pp. 102-103).

Although Irikefe is rich in oil and other natural resources, its people do not benefit from the riches. The underdevelopment results from poor leadership, corruption, armed conflicts and prebendalism. Political leaders in the region sacrifice the basic development needs of the masses on the altar of personal greed and aggrandisement. Leadership fails to control the oil companies regarding environmental pollution, and instead of engaging with the local communities on ways to improve their plight, it militarised the island. The government thus escalates violence between ethnic militia groups, the oil companies and the Nigerian military.

State Violence as Terrorism

Violence perpetrated by the state against its own citizens is a psychological and psycho-political strategy to disenfranchise citizens from pushing forth their political demands (Horgan, 2019). Modern states, especially dictatorships, expropriate the means of political organisations and domination, not excluding violence to establish the legitimacy of their rule. Torture, military brutality, extrajudicial killings and violence perpetrated by the state against its own people need examination. The Sergeant and Major in *Oil on Water* are military sadists, symbols of fear, intimidation, torture, and repression. Oil management in Irikefe is associated with high-level corruption and politically-sponsored violence to disenfranchise citizens from resisting their exploitation. This government terrorism does not necessarily oblige its citizens to engage in dialogue or submission. Instead, it illustrates a poor and distant relationship between the people and their leader.

Chief Malabo is accused of treason because he discourages his subjects from selling their land to oil companies. He is arrested, charged with supporting the militants, plotting against the federal government and threatening to kidnap foreign oil workers (Habila, 2010, p. 44). With his hands tied to his back as if he were a petty criminal, Chief Malabo is later killed; his body is wrapped with a white cloth in a raffia mat and handed to his people. This torture and extrajudicial killing expose the brutality and inhumanity of the system. Before Chief Malabo's burial, the oil company moves in with an army, "waving guns and looking like they mean business" (Habila, 2010, p. 44). Meanwhile, the government argues that "The pipelines are there for their own good, that they hold great potentials for their country and their future" (Habila, 2010, p. 103); that is, people who "Endure the worst conditions of oil-producing community on earth" (Habila, 2010, pp.103-104), a people whose natural environment has been damaged, exposing them to poverty. The state fails to show its citizens the benefits of oil exploration. Instead, it resorts to forcing them into acquiescence by its politically-sponsored violence as its only and dictatorial method of communication.

The assassination of Chief Malabo, expropriation of land, and gun-waving are acts of violence on the inhabitants of Irikefe, who identify with the victim. Brakeley (2009) opines that the deliberate use of violence and intimidation against individuals the state must protect are acts of state terrorism.

Like Chief Malabo, Karibi, another influential man in the village, is falsely accused and arrested by the military for fraternising with the militants. Over ten soldiers surround the smithy, silent but defiant man. His arrest is characterised by gunshots, non-verbal commands, and excessive force on a man who does not resist arrest or say a word, "A sergeant, stepped into the shed and pointed his rifle at Karibi who didn't struggle or say a word... They pinned his hands behind him and dragged him away through the village street" (Habila, 2010, p. 14). You would expect the military to start with verbal commands before using physical force against the suspect. Choosing to be physically violent on an unarmed civilian, being brutal or using excessive force is deliberate terrorism.

The presence of the military in the village, wielding whips, guns, and firing into the air, is intended to intimidate and cause civilian fear, as seen in the chaos it creates, "There was loud noise, dust rose and covered the tight passages, stalls and sheds; people rushed down the passages, knocking down tables and sheds as they went" (Habila, 2010, p. 13). A man running out of a hut, hands raised high in surrender, comes face-to-face with a soldier who reverses his rifle and swings the butt at the man's head. A terrified market woman, with her considerable mass, pins the narrator, who is lying flat on his back, to the dusty ground. Terrorism is caught in images: "wielding of whips and guns," "firing into the air," and "swinging the butt of his rifle at the man's head" "make everyone froze" (Habila, 2010, p. 13).

The military, which should enforce order and instil confidence in its citizens through collaboration and not violence, turns to terrorist tactics and attack on civilians. Contemporary Nigerian society is under surveillance by the military, which has become a panoptic machine to ensure the smooth functioning of power, instilling constant fear. The fear makes them refuse to give vital information on the missing woman and where the journalists could meet or contact the militants. Fear makes them indifferent to the happenings around them. They fear the fate of Karibi befalling them, the fate of informers. Thus, the community bears "The brunt of the oil wars, caught between the militants and the military. The only way they could avoid being crushed out of existence was to pretend to be deaf and dumb and blind" (Habila, 2010, p. 37). The Sergeant and the Major represent the panoptic machinery of people's lives subjected to constant and covert military surveillance.

Torture inflicts physical and psychological pains on civilians to punish, take revenge, or force information out of them. Zaq, Refus, Tamuno, the fisherman and his son, Michael, are caught by soldiers as suspected terrorists. Guns are raised at them, hands are bound, and they are led to a military camp on the island. There, the Major threatens to shoot Zaq and Rufus if they fail to prove that they are journalists, "I can shoot you right now and throw in the swamp and that's it" (Habila, 2010, p. 64). Rufus tries in vain to convince the Major to liberate Tamuno and his son, Michael, who has been working for them in the kidnap trail, "The old man and the boy... We've been together this past week, believe me, they are not rebels" (Habila, 2010, p. 155). The Major dismisses Rufus' request claiming to know them better, "I know these people. They understand only one language, force, that is all" (Habila, 2010, p. 157). When he pushes further to find out if these "prisoners" will be tried, the Major replies, "You journalists, with your fancy ideas about human rights and justice... all nonsense. There are no human rights for people like them...The best thing is to line them up and shoot them" (Habila, 2010, p. 157). The Major champions the abuse of human rights as proof of state terrorism. Seven suspects accused of being militants, including Tamuno and his son, Michael, are incarcerated, tortured every morning and being douched in petrol by Major. On their knees, the Major pours petrol on them, making sure the petrol finds every exposed surface on their faces, "You call yourselves freedom fighters? To me you are just crooks and I will keep hunting you down and shooting you like mad dogs" (Habila, 2010, p. 59). He mocks, "You can't stand the smell of oil? Isn't it what you fight for, kill for? Go on, enjoy. By the time I am through with you, you won't take money that comes from oil, you won't get in a car because it runs on petrol. You'll hate the name petrol" (Habila, 2010, p. 61). This violent strategy is to force suspects to change their behaviour, intimidate, create fear and defeat or deter opposition. Brakeley (2009) considers this as state terrorism. Rufus' stay in military custody allows him, as a journalist, to witness the brutality of the military in Irikefe Island. The reporter is enraged by the inhumane treatment of Tamuno, his son, and other prisoners in military custody. He promises to write about every detail, petrol trickle, and howl of pain inflicted on these suspects to expose military brutality. The Major is a sadist who derives pleasure from the torture.

The analysis above characterises the Abacha regime as a military dictatorship that employed political violence to quell every opposition from the people of Irikefe over environmental abuse. Nigeria is a signatory to international conventions that prohibit torture, and human rights abuse of prisoners in armed conflict is ignored in these perpetrations of human rights abuse by the military during the Abacha reign. The military incarnates repression and brutality rather than a defence force showing how postcolonial governance in Nigeria practices torture and violates the rights of supposed armed prisoners.

State monopoly or its legitimisation of physical force is often challenged by non-state actors by political insurgences or terrorist groups in self-defence. Like the government, freedom fighters or militants also use violence to achieve political goals. Believing that the political system in place will never respond to their peaceful demands, they resort to violent resistance. Thus, military brutality escalates violence and leads to militancy in Irikefe Island.

Militancy as Resistance Strategy Against Environmental Abuse

Irikefe, the hub of oil and gas production in Nigeria, carries the burden of development in other parts of Nigeria whilst their own human and material development needs are not being addressed (Ugwuanyi et al., 2014). Militancy is a form of resistance and war to protect their environment (Abianji-Menang, 2021). The military's assassination of Chief Malabo, a prominent figure of peaceful resistance, the militarization of the island, and the use of excessive force by the military show the political system in postcolonial Nigeria during Abacha's reign as irresponsive to the people's demands through peaceful protests and activism. This military brutality is challenged by militant groups who wield violence in self-defence to achieve a political goal. To attract and maintain publicity and to cause social change, they resort to kidnapping oil workers and expatriates for ransom, launching attacks on oil facilities, vandalising pipelines and using the media for propaganda.

The social responsibility media theory is employed here to show how in the era of global terrorism, militant groups exploit media/social networks for maximum publicity to amplify and be a force multiplier to influence the target audience (Bockstette, 2008; Okolie-Osemene & Okoh, 2015). This theory elaborates on the role of the media in investigative and objective reporting on facts during crises while enabling conflicting parties to express their grievances. It is a framework for examining the relationship between journalism and society in a given socio-political environment.

Habila's style in *Oil on Water* takes the form of investigative/journalistic writing done by Rufus and Zaq, who take pictures, record events and carry out in-depth interviews with traditional and militant leaders, oil company executives and military officers, kidnappers and the English woman, farmers and fishermen, women, medical practitioners, and religious leaders in order to present facts and uncover "the truth" about the causes of conflict in Irikefe Island. Rufus tells Zaq, "Our job is to find out the truth, even if it is buried deep in the earth" (Habila, 2010, p. 144). "What we really seek is not the kidnapped woman, Isabelle Floode and her kidnappers, but a greater meaning of the story which only a lucky few ever discovers that" (Habila, 2010, pp. 5-6). The forward and backward movement of the story reflects the reporters' meandering voyage through the vast Irikefe Island for factual reporting on "The abandoned villages, the hopeless landscape, the gas flares that always burned in the distance, and the brutal taking of Karibi" (Habila, 2010, p. 26), with the most powerful and important character in the story being the fetid, viscous and menacing landscape (Evaristo, 2010). Through vivid description, suspense, characters, and imagery, Habila weaves a beautiful, non-chronological story with Rufus' eyewitness account of environmental abuse and events that happen on Irikefe Island, which affects the lives of the inhabitants on the island:

> I looked outside of the forest and the abandoned boats on the water, the few thatched huts...the oil polluted water. The forsaken villages, the gas flares, the stumps of pipes from the exhausted wells with their heads capped and left jutting out of the oil-scorched earth, and the ever present pipelines crisscrossing the landscape, sometimes like tree roots surfacing far away from the parent tree, sometimes like diseased veins on the back of an old shivering hand, and sometimes in squiggles like ominous writing on the wall...the carcasses of the fish and crabs and waterbirds that floated on the desert of these tiny towns and villages and islands every morning (Habila, 2010, pp. 192-193).

The description of Irikefe qualifies it as a wasteland - barren and desolate because of oil pollution. It is a dystopian society of mass poverty, lack of trust, injustice, squalor, suffering and unimaginable violence (Onunkwo et al., 2017). From this prism, Dr Dagogo-Mark refers to the island as a dead place for dying (Habila, 2010, p. 151). The dystopian society of *Oil on Water* is an example where terrorism is justified as the narrator witnesses oil exploration's damage to the environment. Habila's engaging style draws the attention of the government and the multinational oil companies to the problems and conditions of the public that must be addressed. Environmental abuse is the prism through which events unfold in the novel.

Henshaw, whom Rufus and Zaq meet at the military camp under custody, and Ani Wilson, whose gang name is "Professor" (Habila, 2010, p. 157), are militant leaders and environmentalists. They are disgruntled with the environmental abuse and became militants to fight for change, "We are the people, we are the Delta, we represent the very earth on which we stand" (Habila, 2010, p. 163). The Major explains that Professor, a militant kingpin, "Used to work for an oil company and one day he grew disgusted with the environmental abuse and became a militant to fight for change" (Habila, 2010, p. 156). This declaration by a government agent testifies to the genuineness of Professor's environmentalist fight. It resonates with Chief Ibiram's view that oil production and state-sponsored violence led to militancy in the region. Their ideological argument makes them eco-terrorists, theirs being the people's fight and qualifying them as freedom fighters.

Ideology is key in militant targets in *Oil on Water*, justifying their violence.

They displace the responsibility on either their victims or those they hold responsible for the state of affairs, which they claim led them to adopt violence (Drake, 1998). Their violence involves kidnapping, vandalising pipelines and attacking the military base.

The kidnapping of oil workers and expatriates for ransom is part of the militants' strategy to communicate and influence their target audience - the oil company and the government. Isabel Floode is the wife of a British petroleum oil company engineer in Port Harcourt, James Floode. A man and his wife, a foreign family whose names are not mentioned, were kidnapped, a Filipino contractor and an Italian worker, respectively (Habila, 2010, p. 223; p. 54; p. 200). The targeted victims of terrorist attacks are carefully selected for their shock value and impact. Sandler (2014) opines that kidnapping for ransom is a criminal act of extortion when the kidnappers are not pursuing or financing a political agenda. However, it is a terrorist strategy utilised by militant groups to raise funds to secure their operations and pursue their political aims.

Kidnapping is also a significant source of financing and livelihood to militants and the Irikefe inhabitants. Joseph, a militant, reveals that Professor sent Monday and other gang members with guns to Port Harcourt to kidnap a foreign oil worker and bring him to ask for ransom. (Habila, 2010, p. 213). The money would pay for a consignment of guns he was expecting from overseas. Ransom money is often paid by the oil company or its country of origin, not individuals. From this premise, Jambo, a police officer, sees the kidnapping of oil company workers and expatriates as "Plucking money off a money tree" (Habila, 2010, p. 220). Depicting oil companies as money tree justifies kidnapping as a source of livelihood, an appropriate analogy considering that the money comes from their oil, "So we would be getting back what was ours in the first place" (Habila, 2010, p. 221). Before they were released, their company paid three million ransom cash for the foreign family kidnapped (Habila, 2010, p. 223). However, Professor arrests and kills Salomon, Jambo and Bassey as criminal elements who loot and kill under the guise of freedom fighters, considering them enemies (Habila, 2010, p. 232) who destroy the image of the struggle.

Ideologically inspired, the locations of militant attacks are also carefully selected to produce the desired effects on the government and the oil companies. Terrorist ideology creates a class of legitimate targets, deemed as enemies, thereby placing blame on the victim, who is viewed as responsible for the violence in the first place (Drake, 1998; Hoffmann, 1998). Since their grievances are against the oil companies and the government, they target pipelines and bomb oil companies in Port Harcourt, overrun police stations, and syphon oil. These acts are amplifiers to convey a broader message and influence a wider audience (Schmid, 2006). "Victims of terrorist attacks are therefore considered targets to put pressure on the government and oil companies to change. Militants never strayed too far from the pipelines and oil rigs and refineries, which they constantly threaten to blow up" (Habila, 2010, p. 7). James Floode moans, "Our pipelines are vandalised daily, losing us millions…" (Habila, 2010, p. 103). This is evinced by the abandoned oil-drilling paraphernalia strewn around the platform, "Some appeared to be sprouting out of widening cracks in the concrete, alongside thick chumps of grass. A weather-beaten signboard near the platform said, "Oil well. No. 2. 1999. 15000 meters" (Habila, 2010, pp. 8-9). Eco-terrorism or militancy is thus a variant of terrorism specific to Nigeria.

The psychological warfare technique of propaganda is used by freedom fighters/militants who employ modern media to reach mass audiences and to coerce the government and oil companies. Okolie-Osemene & Okoh (2015) opine that the advent of new digital media and ICT gadgets in the age of terrorism not only enhances the nefarious activities of militant groups but also uses them to amass and disseminate information while promoting militant activities. The manipulation and exploitation of the media by terrorist groups play a crucial role in their propaganda (Wilkinson, 1997). Eager for publicity, kidnappers in *Oil on Water* would invite a selected team of reporters to their hideout to confirm that the hostages are alive and unharmed. Afterwards, they would make long speeches about their environment and reasons for taking up arms against the oil companies and the government. Finally, they would send a ransom demand through one of the reporters. After a week or so, depending on how quickly negotiations go, the oil company would pay up, and the hostages would be set free, unharmed (Habila, 2010, p. 54). This is how James Floode receives over a dozen ransom demands from different Irikefe groups. For example, they request five million dollars and ask him to send "Five reporters to confirm that his wife, Isabel, is alive and well" (Habila, 2010, p. 35). In an unaddressed letter to him, there is some of her hair to confirm that she is the one, alive and unharmed. Floode is willing to negotiate with the kidnappers. That is how Zaq and Rufus, two journalists, are contacted to engage in a kidnap trail in search of Isabel Floode.

When Rufus finally meets Professor, he is given an opportunity for an interview with the English woman and her driver, Salomon. He gets first-hand information on the abductors, the quasi-kidnappers of Isabel (Salomon, her driver, in complicity with his friends Bassey and Jambo, a police officer), and later the militants, the real kidnapper. Salomon is disgruntled with Mr Floode for impregnating his girlfriend, Koko, and with the oil companies for not employing graduates like him. While it is true that some youths join the militants because of the lack of employment, many, like Salomon, Bassy and Jamabo, exploit the situation for financial gain without minding the cost (Onunkwo et al., 2017). Professor hands an envelope to Rufus to take to Isabel's husband with a five-million-dollar demand for ransom, "It contains more of her hair. Tell him his wife is safe, but after two days, if we don't hear from him, we can't guarantee her safety anymore. We are getting impatient. Two days, final" (Habila, 2010, p. 231). Armed groups exploit the media in the era of global terrorism to attain their target audience and achieve a political agenda. Although considered manipulative and exploitation, the media are an expedient technique utilised by armed groups to reach mass audiences and coerce the government and oil companies. Bockstette (2008) points out that in the 1990s, militant groups communicated with their audience(s) by traditional means such as journalistic interviews, face-to-face interviews, fax, propaganda and even press conferences. With technological advancement and the rise of Al-Jazeera at the end of the 90s, a shift in the primary strategy emerged. The Al-Jazeera television network became a channel known for broadcasting terrorists' messages. Al-Jazeera would provide tapes to CNN and other international news corporations. This depicts the extent to which the media mutates from its role in critical reporting to play a more active role as a conflict participant.

Professor reveals who he is to the narrator and their reasons for engaging in terrorism. He asks Rufus to write only the truth, "Tell them about the flares you see at night and the oil on the water, and the soldiers forcing us to escalate the violence every day. Tell them how we are hounded daily in our own land. Where do they want us to go, tell me, tell me, where? Tell them we are going nowhere. This land belongs to us. That is the truth, remember that. You can go" (Habila, 2010, p. 232). Professor's discourse realistically exposes the causes of terrorism in Irikefe Island. He emphasises the fact that they are not terrorists, "We are not the barbarians the government propagandists say we are. We are for the people. Everything we do is for the people. What will we gain if we terrorise them? (Habila, 2010, p. 232). Professor's declarations corroborate Henshaw's view that they are not terrorists but freedom fighters. Their being labelled as "rebels," "terrorists," "kidnappers" (Habila, 2010, p. 156) is pejorative government propaganda to discredit them. His rhetorical questions are intended to appeal to the journalist's conscience for him to be objective in his reporting by presenting only the truth of what he has witnessed and observed. It is also intended for him to make a valid judgement on whose side to believe - government propagandists who call them terrorists or justify their role as freedom fighters in the ongoing war against environmental degradation.

Though Rufus leaves Irikefe Island without Isabel Floode, he feels fulfilled that he has evidence of her being alive and enough scoop to write the meaning of the story (the abduction of the English woman, the factors that give rise to militancy and youth restiveness in Irikefe Island) which only a lucky few ever discovers (Habila, 2010, p. 5).

The death of Zaq, Rufus' mentor, reveals that environmental pollution from oil exploration at Irikefe Island does not only affect the terrestrial, aquatic and arboreal habitat but human denizens as well. Rufus returns to Port Harcourt as a hero who does not only contend with the brutality of the military and the militants but the deadly environment caused by oil pollution that has rendered Irikefe a wasteland and dystopian society:

> The village looked as if a deadly epidemic had swept through it. A square concrete platform dominated the village like some sacrificial altar…the next village was almost a replica of the last: the same empty squat dwellings, the same ripe and flagrant stench, the barrenness, the oil slick and the same indefinable sadness in the air, as if a community of ghosts were suspended above the punctured zinc roofs, unwilling to depart, yet powerless to return. Eager for a drink, I bent under the wet, mossy pivotal beam and peered into the well's blackness, but a rank smell wafted from its hot depths and slapped my face (Habila, 2010, p. 8).

Terrorism is a charged term; the violence and ferociousness associated with it giving off a negative connotation, morally wrong whether utilised by government forces or non-state armed groups for whatever political goals. From the investigations, records of events, and in-depth interviews with traditional and militant leaders, oil company executives, and military officers, kidnappers, farmers and fishermen, women, medical practitioners, and religious leaders, Rufus uncovers the truth and presents an objective report of the causes of conflict in Irikefe Island, of Professor, who is a symbol of militant resistance in Irikefe Island. Rufus says, "Professor is not a madman who shot people for fun. He is a man with an agenda, and he would treat anything that could help him in that pursuit with respect. I am that thing, and the more firmly I believe that and act accordingly, the safer I would be" (Habila, 2010, p. 229). He justifies Professor's militancy in Irikefe Island as resistance to an ecological problem that erupts in the Niger Delta region of Nigeria against the state, petroleum industries, and the host communities due to environmental pollution. It views militant terrorism in Irikefe Island as a necessary retaliation against environmental degradation under the repressive military regime of General Sani Abacha, a regime with no freedom of expression.

Their actions are justified on ideological and political bases, qualifying them as freedom fighters. "Terrorism," like beauty, thus rests in the eye of the beholder. So that one man's terrorist is another man's freedom fighter. In brief, the armed conflict in Irikefe would have been resolved through a peaceful dialogue were the Nigerian government sensitive to the people's plight by providing basic developmental needs. Instead, the regime of General Sani Abacha impressed on inhabitants of this island that the political system in place would never respond to their demands through peaceful protest or activism but through the barrel of the gun. Military repression is thus no solution to political issues. It only escalates violence and insurgency. Any government facing violent acts from a resistant movement usually condemns such acts as terrorism, even when such attacks target only military, security forces, or objects of their demand.

Abstract

Though freedom fighting is associated with terrorism, rebellion and insurgence, the "freedom fighter" and "terrorist" are different things to different people and countries with militant groups. The politics of a given setup may make the terms interchangeable labels for groups of people fighting for their rights or the liberation of their people by an armed struggle. Scholarly debates are split over the categorisation of freedom fighters versus terrorists. In Helon Habila's *Oil on Water*, terrorists are locked in an ecological war in Irikefe Island against the state, petroleum industries, and the host communities. The insurgence in Irikefe seeks to guard the rights of a people against the government's insensitivity. They are terrorists, as viewed by the Nigerian government for daring to protest against environmental degradation. Their struggle's ideological and political bases justify their actions as freedom fighters. Labelling them as terrorists estranges them from being reached out for by the Nigerian government. If the Nigerian Government had responded to the people's plight and provided basic developmental needs, the armed conflict at Irikefe would have been resolved through peaceful dialogue. Instead, the regime of General Sani Abacha forced Irikefe inhabitants to believe that his regime will never respond to their demands even when expressed by peaceful protests. The indigenes, therefore, resort to the barrel of the gun to force the government to respond to their predicament. Against this narrative, the root cause analytical framework is employed to highlight the causal factors of terrorism and militancy in the world of the novel, while the effects of gas flares and oil spillage on the environment in literary discourse are examined by ecocriticism. Since the media are vital in understanding these concepts, social responsibility media theory highlights the media's role during armed conflicts to relay information and opinions to the public in a professional manner that does not instil fear or socially harmful emotions.

Keywords: Terrorism, Freedom fighter, Propaganda, Militancy, Asymmetric warfare

References

Abianji-Menang, O. A. (2021). War for the Environment in Helon Habila's *Oil on Water. Epitome: International journal of multidisciplinary research,* 7(21), 1-15.

Achebe, C. (1983). *The Trouble with Nigeria.* Enugu: Fourth Dimension Publishing.

Babatunde, A. O. (2020). How oil and water create a complex conflict in the Niger Delta. *The Conversation.*

Blakeley, R. (2009). State terrorism in the social sciences: Theories, methods and concepts. In R. Jackson, E. Murphy, & P. Scott (Eds). *Contemporary state terrorism: Theory and practice. Critical Terrorism Studies* (12-27). Routledge: Abingdon.

Bockstette, C. (2008). Jihadist terrorist use of strategic communication management techniques. *George C. Marshall European center for security studies.* Paper series (20), Retrieved from http:www.marshallcenter.org.

Borum, R. (2004). *Psychology of terrorism.* Tampa: Florida.

Cherry M. (2017). State racism, state violence, and vulnerable solidarity. In N. Zack (Ed.). *The Oxford Handbook of Philosophy and Race.* Retrieved from https://www.myishacherry.org. DOI10109/oxfordhb/9780190236953.013.3

Cédric C. (2018). In this country, the very air we breathe is politics: Helon Habila and the flowing together of politics and poetics. *Commonwealth Essays and Studies* [online]. Retrieved from http://journals.openedition.org/ces/289. DOI/https://doi.org/10.4000/ces.289.

Drake, C.J.M. (1998). The role of ideology in terrorists' target selection. *Terrorism and Political Violence,* 10(2), 53-85.

Evaristo, B. (2010). Topical and urgent tale of environmental and rights Abuse in the Niger Delta on *Oil on Water* by Helon Habila. Retrieved from http:/www.theguardian.com.

Ganor, B. (2002). Defining terrorism: Is one's man's terrorist another man's freedom fighter? *Police Practice and Research: An International Journal,* 3(4), 287-304.

Glotfelty, C. (1996). Introduction: Literary studies in an age of environmental crisis. In C. Glotfelty, & H. Fromm, (Eds), *The Ecocriticism Reader: Landmarks in Literary Ecology.* Athens, Georgia. The University of Georgia Press.

Habila, H. (2010). *Oil on Water.* New York: Norton.

Hoffman, B. (1989). The contrasting ethical foundations of terrorism in the 1980s.

Terrorism and Political Violence,1(3), 361-377.

Hoffman, B. (1998). *Inside Terrorism*, New York: Columbia University Press.

Horgan, J. (2019). Psychological warfare. *The psychology of terrorism*. (2nd Ed). London: Routledge.

International Humanitarian Law and International Human Rights Law: Similarities and differences. (2003). Retrieved from www.icrc.org/Web/Eng/siteeng0.nsf/htmlall/57JR8L/$FILE/IHL_and IHRL.pdf?OpenElement

Laqueur, W. (2003). *No End to War: Terrorism in the twenty-first century*. New York: Continuum.

Lortyer, M. T. & Agabi J. N. (2020). Environmental degradation, corruption and militancy in Helon Habila's *Oil on Water*. *Greener Journal of Language and Literature Research*, 6(1), 19-24.

Oluwadare, A. (2019). "Militancy and criminality in the Niger Delta Region of Nigeria." *Crime and law and society in Nigeria: Essays in Honour of Stephen Ellis*. 37. In R. Akinyele, & T. Dietz. (Eds.). Brill, Leiden; Boston. 158-174.

Okolie-Osemene, J. & Okoh, R. I. (2015). The nature of terrorism reports on social networks. *Glocalism Journal of culture, policies and innovation*. (n.p.). 1-18.

Onunkwo, C., Nwogwu E. U., & Ojiakor, T. (2017). Quest for recognition and freedom: An Archetypal study of Helon Habila's *Oil on Water*. LWATI: *A Journal of Contemporary Research, 14*(2), 44-72.

Rueckert, W. (1978). Literature and Ecology: An experiment on ecocriticism. *Iowa Review, 9*(1). 71-86.

Sandler, T. (2014). The analytical study of terrorism: Taking stock. *Journal of Peace Research, 51*(2), 257-271.

Sandler, T. (2015). Terrorism and counterterrorism: An overview. *Oxford Economic Papers*, 67(1).1-20. Retrieved from https://doi.org/10.1093/oep/gpu039.

Schmid, A. (2006). Magnitudes and focus of terrorist victimization. In U. Ewald, & K. Turkic. (Eds.). *Large-scale Victimisation as a Potential Source of Terrorist Activities: Importance of Regaining Security in Post-conflict societies*. 13. 3-19. Amsterdam, IOS press.

Simon, E. D., Akung J. E., & B. U. Bassey, B U. (2014). Environmental degradation, Militancy/kidnapping and oil theft in Helon Habila's *Oil on Water*. *Mediterranean journal of social sciences, 5*(2), 383-388.

Sultana, A. M. (n.d.). Indian foreign policies and the contemporary world. Dept. of political science, CPBU. Course 204.

Ugwuanyi B. I., Obaje I, Ohaeri C. S, Ugwu C. E & Ohagwu C. A. (2014). Militancy in the Niger Delta Region of Nigeria: A reflective discourse on the causes, amnesty and imperatives. *Review of Public Administration and Management. 3*(6). 76-86.

Wikan, V.S. (2018). Is one man's terrorist another man's freedom fighter?

E-international Relations. Retrieved from https://www.e-ir.info/2018/11/29/is-one-mans-terrorist-another-mans-freedom-fighter/

Wilkinson. P. (1997). The Media and terrorism: A reassessment. *Terrorism and Political Violence*. London, Frank Cass, *9*(2), 51-64.

Wilson, T. (2022). Perspectives on the application of terrorism as a useful term: Through the lens of the West and its self-appointed 'terrorists.' *Political Reflection Magazine*. Retrieved from politicalreflectionmagazine.com.

United Nations Office on Drugs and Crime (UNODC). (2018). *Education for Justice. University Module Series: Counter-Terrorism*. Vienna.

TEN

Post-Apartheid Multiracial Democracy and 'New' Patterns of Social Inequality in Nadine Gordimer's *The House Gun* and Nicholas Mhlongo's *Dog Eat Dog* and *After Tears*

ETIENNE LANGMIA FORTI

The question of inequality in South Africa is as old as the country's history, for it originates from the very concept of apartheid, which promoted inequality. Before 1994, the country was built on the governance philosophy of apartheid upheld by the Afrikaners. This minority group ruled South Africa for close to four decades, and, according to Christopher O'Reilly (2001), the policy adopted by this racist oligarchy was informed by the socioeconomic advantages they benefitted from as a numerical minority. The spirit of such a weird policy set the pace for the degree of inequality that Black South Africans would experience throughout the reign of the Afrikaner Nationalist Party. The ensuing devastating degree of inequality and its long-lasting ramifications on the country becomes much clearer when one adds to O'Reilly's view, that of Desmond Tutu (2000, p. 99), who states that successive apartheid regimes "demolished many black townships and uprooted many settled communities and dumped God's children in poverty-stricken Bantustan homeland resettlement camps, what really came to be no better than dumping grounds. [...] Three and a half million people were forcibly removed in an attempt to unscramble the racial omelette that was South Africa." The outstanding degree of inequality instituted and perpetuated by the racist regime(s) is most glaring in Tutu's description of the fate of settled communities dismantled by this invader-settler Afrikaner community. Thus, by dislocating and relocating whole black communities, the apartheid regime(s) destroyed the livelihood of these communities it wanted to exploit. Actually, an understanding of the far-reaching consequences of their respective racially motivated acts becomes frightfully evident when, like Tutu says above, three and half million people were severed entirely from their different sources of existence.

With these wicked actions, it becomes clear that the socioeconomic chasm observed in the country - between those who once enjoyed absolute power and their victims - will remain widespread for generations in post-apartheid South Africa. Consequentially, the frightful levels of fragmentation which apartheid engendered in South Africa's socioeconomic spheres are very perceptible in the fictional works of Gordimer and Mhlongo and constitute the thrust of this chapter which looks at the problem from the perspective of what it terms 'new' patterns of social inequality. It is termed 'new' patterns of social inequality, for it is an attempt to contextualise the issue within the overall new political and social dispensation. This attempt, according to the paper, derives from the conclusions of some socio-political analysts who hold that unlike in the early 1920s to the later part of the 1980s when racism was the basis of the broad issue of inequality and particularly social inequality, in the South Africa of the early 1990s to the present, the question is not determined by an official policy but rather accentuated by the legacy of apartheid which continues to thwart the country's attempt to reinvent itself.

'New' Patterns of Social Inequality in Nadine Gordimer's *The House Gun* and Nicholas Mhlongo's *Dog Eat Dog* and *After Tears*

The observation that the issue of the 'new dimensions' to the old question of inequality in post-apartheid South Africa's socioeconomic landscape is still very much conditioned by its past derives from Gordimer's and Mhlongo's fictionalised portrayal of the numerous problems the 'new' nation faces. Some aspects of these social challenges facing the new South Africa described by the two authors are homelessness, poor living conditions in state prisons, extreme unemployment rate, the prevalence of poverty and the upsurge of class distinction amongst blacks. The preponderant attention these authors give to the problems mentioned above indeed derives from their negative impacts on the quest for nationhood, as seen in South Africans' opinions on national priorities discussed by Rule and Langa (2010), who indicate that South Africans strongly think that the most important challenges facing their nation today are unemployment, poverty, crime and HIV/AIDS. In addition to these, Rule and Langa hold that after ten years of the advent of multiracial democracy in the country, the disparity in wealth distribution as well as the high level of poverty among South Africans, greatly influences the outlook of her citizens as to the areas that need the government's urgent attention. The critics believe that poverty alleviation and efficient service delivery are some of the delicate issues the government needs to redress in the prelude to its nation-building aspirations (Rule & Langa, 2010, pp. 20-29). The crucial observation made by Rule and Langa seems to explain Gordimer's and Mhlongo's focus on unemployment as one of the major problems confronting contemporary South Africa.

Rule and Langa's (2010) observation on the problem of unemployment, which occupies a central stage in the priority areas that need quick and concrete solutions from the post-apartheid leadership, dovetail with Mhlongo's stance as portrayed in the number of appalling examples the author raises in his novels. Talking about such examples that abound in the author's novels, the first which vividly stands out is the plight of one of Njomane's friends and classmates, Thek, whose brothers are all unemployed. Njomane reveals that Thek is the fifth child in a family of eight, who, like most of her brothers and sisters, depends solely on their mother for survival, "Her two brothers were both unemployed. The eldest brother lived with his 'vat en sit' lover and two children in one of their back rooms. He made a living by mowing other people's lawns for cash. Her other brother, Neo, was along our street […] I had helped him to scrawl several advertisements on old pieces of cardboard that we nailed on telephone and electricity poles to attract potential customers" (Mhlongo, 2004, p. 65). This glaring picture of misery depicted through the said family could be considered the consequence of unemployment, probably caused by the country's apartheid past, which did not allow blacks to have a decent education or open up businesses. Due to this, most blacks are forced to find refuge in their menial jobs to earn a living since their parents' meagre salaries cannot satisfactorily sustain their large families. The plight of Thek's family, as described by the narrator, paints a vivid picture of the high rate of unemployment that has ploughed blacks such as Thek's brothers into abject misery.

In addition to the plight of this family is that of the miserable homeless white man whom Mhlongo (2004) describes. His fate illustrates the view, as stated by Rule and Langa (2010) as well as Petersson (1998), that the prevalence of unemployment in the country is one of the worst crises facing her socio-political growth. In effect, the white man who now frequents the streets of Johannesburg is actually a victim of the prevailing high rate of unemployment which has hit the country, as evidenced by the message inscribed on the cardboard he carries, which reads "Unemployed. Five dependants, Two Epileptic, One Asthmatic. Wife has Cancer. House Repossessed. No Food. No Shelter. Please Help. God Bless You" (Mhlongo, 2004, p. 67). From the message inscribed on the cardboard, it is quite glaring that the character is a victim of unemployment and the country's current high cost of living, and since his means cannot match the latter, he is thus forced to beg in the streets. This white character, from a global standpoint, can be viewed as being symbolic of the masses living in the new South Africa who cannot meet up with the exigencies imposed on them and the nation by the spirit of consumerism. Consequently, he, like others, is forced into the streets as a beggar in order to provide for his apparent large dependent family, who are not only financially impaired but also physically due to their respective precarious health conditions. This is the most pathetic part of the dilemma of the poor South Africans, illustrated by the image of desperation embedded in the message on the cardboard as it announces his helplessness due to his inability to have a job that can permit him to cater for his dependents. This image is important because it presents a very acute picture of the sad reality and challenges confronting the country and its citizens.

The plight of the white South African is not a peculiar case since unemployment has become a common phenomenon in the country by virtue of its centrality to the major thematic preoccupations of Mhlongo's novels. Njomane exposes this national concern when he recounts a scene that he and his friends witness while drinking in a bar. According to Njomane, a beggar nicknamed Stomach Ache begs from the group and, most importantly, from Thek, with whom the former is quite familiar. During the exchange between the beggar and Thek, her friends realise that the beggar sounds very educated, and they are perplexed because they cannot comprehend how such an educated man could end up as a beggar on the streets. It is against this atmosphere of disbelief that the global nature of the issue of unemployment becomes vivid, given that Thek, who knows the beggar tells her friends that her sister, who was the beggar's classmate at the university, had told her that he was excluded from the institution because he could not afford the fee set down by the university. The beggar's predicament evidently exposes the pertinent nature of unemployment confronting not just the nation's citizens but also its nation-building process if one were to look at Thek's admonition directed to her friends who at one point consider Stomach Ache to be lazy: "You think it's easy out there in the real world, don't you? But that's because we are protected by these varsity walls. Once we are let loose in the real world you'll realise that life is a matter of dog eat dog" (Mhlongo, 2004, pp. 217-218). According to Thek, post-apartheid South Africa has become, figuratively speaking, a cannibalistic society where only those who are capable to survive enjoy the proceeds of multiracial democracy while the majority who are financially impaired, such as Stomach Ache live in abject poverty and misery. Symbolically, the beggar's story brings to the limelight the immense difficulties confronting South Africans such as the beggar who cannot live up to the new standards brought about by multiracial democracy. Concretely, what Thek means is that instead of a democratic South Africa being a society where everyone has the minimum means of survival, it has become a hostile environment mostly to the poor, who are metaphorically devoured by the democracy they all fought for.

Thus the image of post-apartheid South Africa, according to Mhlongo (2004), is that of a Darwinian primal environment where the strong eat up the weak, better still, where the strong class can survive due to their financial power while the weaker class, such as the beggar and all poor South Africans lead a life of abject poverty and misery. At this stage in the discussion on the difficulties facing the new nation, it is worth noting that this is the most central image in Mhlongo's *Dog Eat Dog* since it is contiguous to how the author handles the same issue in *After Tears* (Mhlongo, 2007). This central image which constitutes the title of the novel, *Dog Eat Dog*, is employed by the author in his bid to portray post-apartheid South Africa as a new nation where the rising cost of living and its consequences, one of which is the frustration born of the inabilities of South Africans to rise above the poverty level, have rendered life synonymous to that experienced in a primal jungle where metaphorically speaking, only the strong (rich) can survive while the financially impaired (weak) such as Stomach Ache continue to sink into the abyss of misery.

Stomach Ache's story equally highlights the theme of the deferred dream as the emergence of multiracial democracy, which many believed would bring about a remarkable improvement in the lives of all South Africans, has, ironically, brought about misery to the majority of this population who have historically lived below the poverty line. The element of the dream deferred is reinforced by Thek's continuous analysis of the difficulties facing South Africans as seen when she tells her friends, "you know the expectations our families have when we are still studying. Our unemployed siblings and retrenched parents expect us to graduate and make big changes to our appalling family conditions. And if we fail to fulfil those expectations, the frustration will pile up in our hearts and the weaker of us will become drunkards or even resort to crime" (Mhlongo, 2004, p. 218). From Thek's observation, it is clear that Stomach Ache's story occupies a symbolic universal dimension within the context of the numerous problems facing post-apartheid South Africa. He is central to the theme of dream deferred as illustrated by Thek's lesson to her friends wherein she uses him as an example to demonstrate the physical and psychological consequences of the prevailing unemployment-engendered hardship on the country's populace. Thek's opinion above, therefore, becomes a lucid picture of both the physical and, most significantly, psychological consequences of the high unemployment rate on young South Africans, who often turn to alcoholism or crime as a means of drowning their frustration. In fact, the character's observation paints a bleak picture of life in post-apartheid South Africa, where hopelessness has become an integral part of its multiracial democracy. Thus, the new leadership has to look for quick and concrete solutions to the problem if it must create a sense of belonging to a socially and politically united entity in all South Africans.

From a postcolonial perspective, the country and its nation-building process seem to be witnessing an entrenchment of a new, subtle and more dangerous form of the Centre /Margin binarism caused by the high rate of unemployment. This observation, informed by the examples from Mhlongo (2004), seems to confirm Petersson's (1998) view on the key areas that need the government's action. Petersson (1998), like Mhlongo (2004, p. 4), thinks that "Critical for South Africa's future is its ability to enter a new phase of growth, to tackle the problems of unemployment and inequality and to give all South Africans the opportunity to improve themselves and their living standards. This will require more public expenditure favouring the African majority in areas such as education and human resource training, health, water, energy and housing facilities." In Peterson's view, like Mhlongo's (2004) description of the alarming state of unemployment-engendered inequality in the country, the future of South Africa and its democracy largely depends on the present leadership's abilities to salvage the problems of unemployment and inequality. This can be achieved if the government redirects its public spending on priority areas, which are the provision of quality education and human resource training, health, water, energy and housing facilities to the black majority in dire need. The similarity between Petersson's opinion and Mhlongo's stance emanates from the importance the latter attributes to these problems. In this wise, the poor housing conditions in the country, the deplorable situation of Thek's family, and that of the street beggar with five dependents can be viewed as the priorities that need the government's urgent action. One can therefore claim that the disturbing image of the country as painted by Mhlongo (2004) is the author's deliberate efforts at suggesting to the new leadership what they need to do in order to forge a spirit of nationhood in all South Africans. This is because the author's delineation of these problems sharply reflects the view of a political analyst such as Waldmeir (2006, p. 281), who thinks "Black South Africans are not demanding revolutionary change; opinion polls consistently reveal relatively moderate expectations. My private, unscientific inquiries always yield the same response - overwhelmingly, black South Africans want jobs, not handouts. Their reasonable expectations of what government can achieve are pitifully limited. They have so little that any improvement [...] makes a huge difference. Patience is not unlimited; but it is considerable." The most significant part of the analyst's, like Peterson's (1998) view is her caution to the new leadership, which has to solve the basic problems of blacks and, by extension, all South Africans such as those described by Mhlongo (2004) if it has to achieve the desired goal of a united South Africa where all its citizens would see themselves as belonging to one indivisible political entity. From the examples above, it is evident that unemployment and poverty go hand in glove, as the absence of jobs creates an imbalance in wealth between the country's former broad racial groups. The black population is a victim of this prevailing state of affairs, for a majority of them live far below the poverty line, while the general white population seems not to be concerned, as demonstrated by Mhlongo.

Gordimer (1999, p. 14) vividly describes the pervasive poverty which plagues the new leadership's initiatives in its bid to establish a united and egalitarian society. This problem is lucidly exposed in the image the narrator paints of Claudia's poverty-stricken black patients. According to the narrator, these black patients who turn up for consultation and treatment "every week have eyes narrowed by the gross fatty tissue of their faces and others continue to present the skin infections characteristic of malnutrition." The appalling picture which emerges from the narrator's description of Claudia's malnourished patients reveals one of the most disquieting difficulties which the new leadership has to redress if it wants to convince everyone, especially the majority of black South Africans who fall in this category, to get involved in the nation-building endeavours. Most of these patients cannot procure the most basic foodstuff necessary to maintain a healthy body. Their precarious fate becomes very vivid when the narrator says, "They eat too much or they have too little to eat. It's comparatively easy to prescribe for the first because they have the remedy in themselves. For the second, what is prescribed is denied them by circumstances outside their control. Green vegetables and fresh fruits - they are too poor for the luxury of these remedies, what they have come to the clinic for is a bottle of medicine" (Gordimer, 1999, p. 14). The implication of the narrator's claim is well understood when one analyses the subtle allusion to the legacy of the apartheid era on the present inherent in the reference to circumstances beyond the control of these patients. This is to say that the sort of poverty and misery which these patients typify can be explained by the consequences of the continued impact of the socioeconomic and political restrictions that apartheid had imposed on them in the past.

A similar example to that of the poor black patients is that of the haggard-looking black youth who helps the Lindgards to find a parking space in the streets of Johannesburg. The global nature of poverty plaguing post-apartheid

South Africa is further illustrated in the image of this street boy who comes too close to the window of Harald's car for some compensation after helping them. The picture of the boy, which emerges from the narrator's description portrays the despicable fate of a pauper who spends his entire days in the city's streets begging for money. The boy, at this point, assumes a symbolic dimension within the broader historical context of contemporary South Africa when the narrator describes him as "the familiar face, the city's face of a street boy" (Gordimer, 1999, p. 180). The universality of his fate explicitly expresses the broader symbolism of this example as a black who has to turn to the streets as a beggar where the only source of livelihood is the benevolence of the rich such as the Lindgard family (symbolically a white family) but which ironically is far from providing him with the desired comfort. It therefore becomes disquieting that the street boy's efforts to seek help from the street all end in futility, and his only source of momentary escape from the overbearing hardship is found in drugs. Drug addiction thus becomes a momentary escape when the boy realises the enormity of his predicament, as noticed when the narrator observes that "The boy has his glue-sniffer's plastic bottle half-stuffed under the neck of the garment he's wearing, his black skin is yellow, like a sick plant. What's left of his intelligence darts quickly at the coin, his survival is to see at a glance if it is enough" (Gordimer, 1999, p. 180). Actually, the narrator's description of the piteous fates of such street children accentuates the pathetic picture of a black South African living in abject poverty and misery who, ironically, seeks solace in drugs as a way of making up for the sort of comfort that wealth would have provided to him. This pathetic aspect of the boy's fate is most acute in the image the narrator creates of a human being on the brink of physical and psychological self-destruction, as seen in the analogy between the boy's drug-destroyed health and a plant that has begun to wither. In effect, the boy is described as looking wasted, not just as a result of poverty and the consequent long hours in the scorching sun of the city streets but also - most poignantly - as a result of the glue he sniffs for some sort of momentary comfort and escape from his state of being. Ironically, the glue he sniffs for comfort and company is instead destroying him because it seems to have imprisoned him in its vicious cycle of self-destruction. The boy's predicament, like those of Claudia's black patients (Gordimer, 1999, p. 14), exposes the degree of inequality in post-apartheid South Africa.

The image of poverty Gordimer (1999) portrays is very similar to Mhlongo's (2004), except that poverty is central in the thematic preoccupations of the latter's novels more than in the former's. This difference might be explained by Mhlongo's (2004) strong affinity for life in the township(s) by virtue of his racial background, which must have given him a first-hand experience of the suffering of this group of South Africans. Hence, the shocking image of misery characteristic of South Africans who live in the townships such as Soweto is preponderant in Mhlongo's novels. This historic township and the misery that characterises it becomes a broader symbol of the lives of black South Africans, whose lamentable well-being is vividly exposed by the main protagonist and narrator, Njomane (Mhlongo, 2004). The character brings out this problem when his request for a bursary from the University of the Witwatersrand is turned down repeatedly by the said institution because the personal information the character provides does not qualify him for a bursary. This premise is a symbolic mirror that the author uses to expose the poverty and misery in the black community. Through Njomane, the despair of a people comes to light, especially when he wonders if the university bursary committee had bothered to read his bursary application given that "I thought I had supplied everything that the Bursary Committee needed: copies of my father's death certificate and my mother's pension slip, an affidavit sworn at our local police station giving the names and ages of the nine other family members who depended on my mother's pension, as well as three other affidavit confirming all movable and immovable property that we owned. Although unfortunately, my family did not own any immovable property as the house in Soweto that we had been living in since 1963 was leased to us by the apartheid government for 99 years. What more information do these people want about the poverty that my family is living in" (Mhlongo, 2004, p. 8). Njomane's desperation symbolically becomes a cogent expression of the misery that exists in the black townships in a country that is emerging from the socioeconomic and political constraints of the past imposed on them by an amoral government whose beliefs in the superiority of the white race influenced them to deprive the supposedly inferior black race of any source of livelihood. This allusion to apartheid's legacy is present in the character's subtle reference to the creation of the township of Soweto by the apartheid state in 1963 with its attendant ramifications, which seem to have spilt over into the post-apartheid era. Therefore, the author's argument, as seen in the fate of Njomane lies in the view that the sort of poverty the narrator and his family are victims of is an acute depiction of the excruciating degree of misery and hopelessness prevailing in the country. And from which it is pretty difficult for black youths such as Njomane to distance themselves since he is unable to have the necessary bursary which would enable him to study conveniently at the university, which in turn would give him the possibility to obtain a decent job that could guarantee him and his family a life of comfort. Thus, university studies and qualification constitute a symbolic escape channel which any youth such as Njomane is bound to take if they must shun the life of poverty that staying in the townships would signify. Unfortunately, the past continues to be a stumbling block to such escape because poverty that was bestowed on blacks by apartheid gave them practically no possibility to meet the challenges of a free post-apartheid South Africa.

It is due to this glaring inability of black youths such as Njomane to rise above the morass of poverty epitomised by his township that makes him lament, "Did this mean I would be forced to hook up again with those hopeless drunken friends of mine? Was I going back to that life of wolf-whistling the ladies who passed by in the street, calling them izifebe (prostitutes) if they did not respond the way we liked? I felt like I was being pushed back into a gorge filled with hungry crocodiles" (Mhlongo, 2004, pp. 8-9). The desperation of black youths such as Njomane is glaringly evident when one analyses the symbolic implication of the number of rhetorical questions the character poses, coupled with the recurring cannibalistic image of post-apartheid South Africa, which life in its townships such as Soweto symbolises. Against this background, one seems to understand the characters and, by extension, the black youths' predicaments, most of whom live in the townships. The extent of this poverty-driven inequality is inherent in the bigger image of life of any black aspiring youth such as Njomane who remains in the townships like Soweto. The protagonist thinks living in Soweto is synonymous with sinking into a metaphoric abyss filled with crocodiles ready to devour him, especially if he cannot obtain a bursary from the university. Therefore, this metaphoric image of the township explains the character's desperate wish to go away from the former and from the hopelessness that has become part and parcel of this historic location.

This image of doom which is part and parcel of life in the townships is further accentuated when Njomane declares that his admission to the university marked the beginning of a life of hope, which is absent in Soweto and other townships where despair is the daily companion of its inhabitants. Thus, the only means for him, as for other youths, to shun this endemic misery characteristic of the townships is to have an admission to a university and the necessary bursary that would enable him to study conveniently as it is the only outlet to a better future for any youth in the new South Africa. This element of hope inherent in a black youth obtaining a university qualification is illustrated by the contrastive comparison that Njomane makes between life in the townships and that in the university hostel. Njomane narrates, "That month that I had been allowed to stay at the [university hostel] I had tasted the cheese life. I had my own room, and although I was sharing it with my newly acquired friend Dworkin at least I enjoyed some privacy unlike at home in our four-roomed Soweto house. At home I still slept in the dining-sitting room although I was twenty years old [...] at home I was woken up at four o'clock in the morning by the footsteps of my two brothers on their way to the kitchen to boil water before they went to work" (Mhlongo, 2004, p. 9). The contrast between life in Soweto and that of the university hostel justifies his outcry when he is faced with the prospect of returning to the township due to his inability to obtain a bursary. In other words, Njomane's contrastive description of life in both environments indicates the low prospect for a black youth succeeding in the townships where the living conditions, symbolised by the character's household, do not create the atmosphere necessary for success in the lives of their inhabitants.

The image of abject poverty and hopelessness Mhlongo describes seems to corroborate the view of Kayode Soyinka (2004, p. 9), who attests that during his visit to South Africa after its first multiracial elections of 1994, he "saw a country where the two extremes of the world met. There was third world poverty on a large scale especially among the blacks and an amazing first world wealth among the whites. I visited villages where most blacks live. I was invited into the boardrooms of some of the biggest companies in the country." Underneath Soyinka's observation, one can get the undertone of blame pointing toward apartheid's legacy of imposed inequality within the black community. This claim is given credence by his comparison of the lives of blacks and whites in their respective worlds created by the former apartheid regimes. And this is illustrated in Mhlongo's novel through the apparent subtle comparison of life in the black community represented by Soweto and that in a former white-dominated community here represented by the university that the protagonist wishes to integrate. The fact is that Soyinka, like Mhlongo, considers the poverty that controls the lives of blacks as one of the consequences of apartheid's imposed socioeconomic disparity.

Poverty so far has been discussed from an individual dimension, such as the personal experiences of the various characters, but any such analysis of the issue would be incomplete without a global view of this problem. Hence an exhaustive discussion on this challenge to nationhood necessitates a bird's eye view analysis of the collective experience of the black populace. This holistic picture of poverty in the country is portrayed through the symbolism of the historic township of Soweto described in the works of Mhlongo, especially in *Dog Eat Dog*. In this regard, the appalling picture of the narrator's life in the township is accentuated by the more general image, which reinforces the story of the other poverty-stricken blacks. This general image of the townships is brought to the limelight when Njomane journeys through Soweto in a train which takes him closer to the sad reality of life in the said township. Njomane declares that as he travels by train through his township, what strikes him at first sight, are the appalling living conditions of its inhabitants, "As the train pulled out of the New Canada Station, I managed to peer through the window at the horizon, hoping for a whiff of fresh winter air. But all I could see was the murky sky of Soweto, God's worst ghetto, obscured by a layer of smoke from the Welcome Dover coal stove used by the residents to cook and warm their houses. The smoke from the Welcome Dover coal stoves was complemented by that made by the homemade mbawula coal stoves in the tin shacks squashed into the yards of each and every block of Soweto houses" (Mhlongo, 2004, p. 179). The above description of Soweto paints a picture of squalor, where survival is a matter of sheer luck and God's mercy. This disgusting image of Soweto heralding its inhabitants' experience achieves a symbolic dimension within the scope of the general plight of black South Africans living in the impoverished sections of the nation's periphery (margin), better known as townships. In effect, this symbolic view of life in the country through Soweto is influenced by the historical significance of the latter in the collective endeavour of all South Africans and, most significantly, blacks against apartheid. From this premise, it is evident that the emergence of multiracial democracy has not changed much in the lives of the country's populace, who continue to live side-by-side with abject misery, and death as their daily companion even though the agent of the latter has at least changed from having a human face, symbolised by the once apartheid state, to a more challenging and invisible adversary which is poverty. Such a seemingly metaphoric view of death becomes clearer when one analyses the fate of the narrator's classmate and family. One notices this through the narrator's reminiscence when he says that the appalling picture of Soweto always reminds him of his classmate "who had passed away the previous weekend. He and six members of his family were killed in their sleep by the inhalation of coal smoke from their mbawula stove in their Orange Farm Shack [...] living in constant contact with danger has become normal for the five million people who live in God's worst ghetto" (Mhlongo, 2004, p. 179). The story of Njomane's classmate and family is a frightening image of the fate of most South Africans - predominantly blacks - who still occupy the periphery (margin) characterised by excruciating poverty at the dawn of their country's multiracial democracy. At this juncture, one could say that Mhlongo, through Njomane's insightful portrait of the lives of blacks, seems to expose the irony that characterises South Africa's ambition to attain nationhood.

The ironic picture of the country becomes most apparent when Njomane reveals that in such slums as Soweto, it is not uncommon to see signs of a certain economic prosperity existing in the country which is yet to spill over to the poorer section of its population. This irony is visible on the billboard which carries the advertisement "PEPSI WELCOMES YOU TO ORLANDO EAST" (Mhlongo, 2004, p. 183), and it is acute when one juxtaposes the announcement of economic prosperity with the conspicuous signs of wreckage and abandonment characteristic of the lives of Sowetans and blacks in general. And this may confirm the view held by Greg Barrow (1994, p. 14) when he observes that "to visit rural communities is to be forcefully reminded that South Africa remains a deeply divided country. The division may no longer be between black and white. But the division between rich and poor [which] is growing alarmingly wider." The analyst's view is equally enhanced by Patti Waldmeir (2006, p. 283), who states, "When South Africans- stepped through the looking glass, it did not emerge in Wonderland. It emerged in the real world, where poverty is the biggest challenge to all democratic governments, and where there are tougher problems to solve than apartheid." Both analysts agree that poverty is one of the biggest challenges to the unity of the new South Africa, and in this regard, one would think that Mhlongo, like Barrow (1994) and Waldmeir (2006), seeks to expose the herculean task and responsibility that confront the new leadership in its endeavour to reconstruct social justice in South Africa.

The same global image of social inequality is also raised in Mhlongo (2007) set three years after the country's accession to multiracial democracy. In other words, three years after the formal implantation of multiracial democracy, the country, particularly the black community, continues to be plagued by an apparently insurmountable degree of poverty. Unfortunately, this bleak picture of contemporary South Africa is brought out through the novel's main protagonists, the narrator and relatives - Bafana, Dilika, Zero and Uncle Nyawana. Actually, the said challenge is announced in the novel when the disillusioned Dilika tells his group of friends that "the cost of living has seriously become higher after these tears of apartheid. We teachers are still paid peanuts by our own black ANC government. That's why I can't even afford proper shoes" (Mhlongo, 2007, p. 15). According to Dilika, the new South Africa, which they all thought would bring about remarkable changes in their lives, has not done so but has ironically replaced the hopelessness of the past with an equally remarkable disillusionment since they now suffer under a multiracial leadership. This new sort of suffering which may not be seemingly different from that imposed by apartheid, except that they now suffer under a free environment, is caused by the high cost of living, which does not match the financial means of ordinary South Africans. Dilika's fate symbolically – because it is worth mentioning that the novel's title derives from his observation of the current state of affairs in the country as described above - is an overt illustration of the overwhelming degree of poverty and misery which now beset the common South African. In fact, working-class South Africans such as Dilika cannot meet the ever-rising cost of living that multiracial democracy seems to have brought about. Worst of all, he, with other blacks, cannot live comfortably because the salary the new leadership pays its civil servants is not commensurate with the cost of living, which keeps rising at a geometric proportion.

This disparity between the poor and rich in the country is quite alarming if one were to corroborate Dilika's observation with Zero's when he tells Bafana, Uncle Nyawana and Dilika that there is no need for common black South Africans such as them to aspire for a change in their way of life because "If you're black and you failed to get rich in the first year of our democracy, when Tata Mandela came to power, you must forget it ... the gravy train has already passed you by and, like me, you'll live in poverty until your beard turns grey. The bridge between the stinking rich and the poor has been demolished. That is the harsh reality of our democracy" (Mhlongo, 2007, pp. 14-15). Zero's humorous description of the dilemma of blacks is a depiction of one of the saddest realities of the 'rainbow nation' where the advent of multiracial democracy under the tutelage of a black majority leadership, instead of bridging the gap between the very poor populace and the very rich, has rather ironically widened it to the point that the poor are getting much poorer while a rich few are getting richer. Even though it might appear ironic for Zero to think blacks could improve their living standards and conditions during Nelson Mandela's presidency rather than under Thabo Mbeki's, the view expresses a basic fact about post-apartheid South Africa. Zero seems to be saying that the new South Africa, during its first four years of existence, was a little better than the present, where the situation has ironically grown worse even though she has entered her second phase of maturity with the second democratic leadership under the tutelage of Thabo Mbeki. It is worth noting that the subtle allusion to the latter can be traced to the novel's setting, which was published during his tenure. It is equally important to note that the element of disillusionment with the post-apartheid situation is not only inherent in Zero's disgust with the economic chasm between the poor and the rich but also in the metaphor of the gravy train which he employs to distinguish between Mandela's reign and Mbeki's.

In Mhlongo (2007, p. 164), Zero can be considered the populace's mouthpiece by virtue of his profession as a taxi driver, which enables him to come in constant contact with the preoccupations of all South Africans. As such, the country's deplorable economic situation he describes to Bafana contains first-hand information from the vantage point of a citizen who is in constant touch with the realities of the country as seen when while driving through Soweto, he points out to Bafana "a heap of waste at the side of the road that separated Eldorado Park from Pimville [who notices] ... two green-and-white pikit-up trucks dumping waste while people stood by and watched." In this case, Zero draws Bafana's attention to another aspect of the sad reality of life in post-apartheid South Africa, which is further reinforced when he tells Bafana, "Every day, I used to compete with about a thousand other people scavenging for paper and plastic ... just like those people you can see over there. I worked at Goudkoppies seven days a week for almost eight years, but I only ever made about R100 or R200 a week. I used to have sugar water and bread every day ... I think I know what poverty is ... I used to dodge medical waste - used syringes, drips, bloody sheets and bandages - at the dump. I used to inhale toxic fumes from the degrading chemicals. We competed with well-fed scavenging rats" (Mhlongo, 2007, pp. 164-65). In this instance, Zero's allusion to the past can be viewed as a subtle comparison of life under apartheid and that under the present political order with the intention to expose the poverty-engendered misery that has become endemic in the black townships after the advent of multiracial democracy. Evidently, Zero's allusion to his life under apartheid – symbolic of most blacks' – is an attempt to point out that multiracial democracy is finally a South African reality with its attendant benefits, which unfortunately have not reached the masses. Hence the image of the democratic South Africa which emerges from Zero's description and comparison, as in the case of the examples from Mhlongo (2004), is one where very little has changed even though the country has witnessed a positive political drift from the apartheid past. This considerable bearing of the country's past on the present is noticeable in subtle references to apartheid's legacy, which still forces blacks to forage on rubbish heaps, hoping to find a source of sustenance amidst battles with scavengers and existing health dangers from hospital waste. Consequently, the image of the historic township of Soweto in Mhlongo's novels symbolically portrays a South Africa dominated by poverty and misery.

This depiction of despicable poverty in the author's novels corroborates Waldmeir's and Shaun Irlam's assessments of the levels of transformation South Africa's multiracial democracy has created in the country. According to Waldmeir

(1997, p. 280), "even if both racial and political reconciliation can be achieved, a huge task of economic reconciliation will remain. Unless the haves and have-nots can be reconciled, nothing else will matter. For South Africa finds itself in the middle of a revolution, not at the end of one. The inauguration of Nelson Mandela brought about political liberation. But in the economic sphere, it was largely a revolution without change. That cannot remain true if the ANC is to retain its popularity – and if racial reconciliation is to endure." Waldmeir's observation is quite relevant within the scope of the issue of inequality as raised by Mhlongo and Gordimer, especially when one considers the political analyst's opinion on the level of the country's political and economic transformation. She holds that even though racial and political reconciliation can be achieved, the economic disparity between the rich and poor has not yet been resolved despite its significance in the whole history of the struggle against apartheid. The most important part of her observation is when she states that South Africa, after 1994, finds itself in the middle of a revolution and not at the end of it. She seems to be saying that the end of apartheid and the emergence of multiracial democracy, which came with the election of Nelson Mandela, brought about a political liberation which is just part of the nation's journey to total freedom and equality since the other parts of that journey, which find expression in the social and economic spheres, are still far from being complete. Like Waldmeir (1997), Irlam (2004, p. 697) holds that "Whatever transformations have taken place at the level of political institutions and national iconography, the inescapable fact is that little has changed in the material conditions defining South African Society since the end of apartheid." Irlam's view seems to reflect Zero's portrait of the townships and the unchanged nature of the lives of those who live in these forsaken parts of the country, constituting one of the consequences of apartheid's legacy. As such, the country's transformation, particularly in the lives of its population, has not really taken place, and if the country hopes to remain a united multiracial nation, this socioeconomic disparity must be resolved. This is because a new and dangerous pattern of Centre /Margin binarism created by poverty is actually implanting itself in the country's social sphere.

Another aspect of social inequality that could impede the country's nation-building initiative, as portrayed in Mhlongo (2004, pp. 81-82), is the conspicuously poor housing conditions for poorer sections of the country's populace - predominantly blacks. The extent of the problem is vividly illustrated when Njomane says that "people use the names of famous political leaders to attract the government's attention to the urgent need for housing." The reaction of the homeless is a symbolic reminder being issued to those in power to know that the freedom they fought for so relentlessly is still far from being complete, as the masses for whom these liberators fought for still live in sub-human habitations. Through the act of naming some of the new up shoots of shanty towns after famous figures of the historic struggle - Sisuluville, Sobukwetown, Mandela Views - the black masses seem to be reminding the new leadership that one of the important essences of the struggle for multiracial democracy is still very much a part of the new nation since shanty towns are still part of the black experience. This is observed when Njomane remarks that in his Soweto Township: "Next to the main road I saw children playing hide and seek. They ran into the dumpsite between the shacks. One child wearing a tattered blue T-shirt hid behind a tin shack with No 3814 painted on the outside" (Mhlongo, 2004, p. 82). What emanates from the image of the deplorable living conditions of blacks in the townships around the country is the fact that the black population still lives in shacks like in the days of apartheid, even though the difference between the periods lies in the voluntary nature of such up shoots of shanty towns which now predominate the suburbs of Johannesburg.

Like in *Dog eat Dog*, Mhlongo (2007, p. 52) also raises the same problem when Bafana describes the dispute between his family and Mr Sekoto over the ownership of the former's supposed family house. The conflict which ensues from the dispute symbolically brings to the limelight the enormity of the housing problem confronting the new nation. This symbolic aspect of the conflict stands out when Bafana goes to the Housing Department to inquire about the rightful owner of the disputed house. Once there, he realises that many black South Africans are homeless. The narrator's realisation seems so disquieting when he declares that "By half past nine I was at the housing department's offices in Newgate Centre. As I entered, I saw the corridor was already full of people. The majority had come to register for the low cost RDP houses that the government was building." The multitude of homeless black South Africans describes the major challenge facing the new leadership and its nation-building aspiration, which can only become a reality if such a multitude is made to feel as part of the new South Africa. And this is only possible if the government provides them with decent homes as it occupies a central stage in the country's political life considering her apartheid history characterised by the massive uprooting and displacement of the racially 'inferior' groups from their aboriginal homes.

The degree of social inequality in post-apartheid South Africa, as exposed by Gordimer and Mhlongo, is further compounded by the upsurge of class distinction within the black community. The entrenchment of this phenomenon in the country's socio-political and economic landscape is reflected in Hein

Marais' assessment of the state of South Africa's transition to democracy when he opines that "the ANC government's economic policy had acquired an overt class character and was unabashedly geared to service the respective prerogatives of national and international capital and the aspiration of the emerging black bourgeoisies, perhaps above all - at the expense of the impoverished majority's hopes for a less iniquitous social and economic order" (quoted in Lazarus, 2004, p. 616). Concretely, Marais' description corroborates the picture of the country portrayed by Mhlongo (2007), where the upsurge of the spirit of consumerism has brought about class distinction and its attendant consequence of disillusionment characteristic of those who occupy the lower strata. This new phenomenon is depicted by Zero and the narrator, who, while driving through the city of Johannesburg in the former's old taxi, sees a young girl in a luxury Silver Audi A3 in a lane next to theirs. According to Bafana, this daunting discovery of the existence of a class of a rich minority amidst a poor majority such as Bafana and Zero, drives the latter very angry as observed when he tells the former, "That's what I have a problem with, Advo [...] you see what Tata Mandela and President Mbeki have done to us black men? This crazy system of theirs means the young black women drive expensive cars while we black men still belong to the working class" Mhlongo (2007, p. 126). From a symbolic standpoint, Zero's observation seems to suggest that the advent of multiracial democracy has created a class of rich minority who now form a new sort of majority ruling class who are enjoying the spoils of multiracial democracy at the new 'centre' while the majority are languishing in poverty and misery at the 'margin.' Consequently, post-apartheid South Africa has brought about an elitist class made up of a minority at the 'centre' of economic growth among a majority of the once dispossessed who are still living below the poverty line. In Zero's view, such a marked disparity among black South Africans in a young democracy as theirs is the ironical and paradoxical reality of the much sought-after multiracial democracy which Nelson Mandela and others fought for tirelessly for decades.

According to Mhlongo (2007), this phenomenon of consumerism, though a marker of prosperity, has become a force that seems to lure almost all poverty-stricken black South Africans living in the country's townships who wish they could join the new class of wealthy South Africans. Like Zero, Uncle Nyawana is a symbol of such poor South Africans, evidenced by his desperate craving to join this new rich class of South Africans, observable when he tells Bafana that the latter's graduation from university with a bachelor's degree in law is a stepping-stone for them to join the class of the rich. This, according to him, would mark a break-away from the poverty imposed by illiteracy which is predominant in the townships. "Our days as part of the poor working class of Mzansi will soon be over. We're about to join the driving class, with stomachs made large by the Black Economic Empowerment. Yeah, we'll be fucking rich. Stinking rich [...]" (Mhlongo, 2007, p. 14). Though humorous, Uncle Nyawana's aspiration, which is a cogent wish to join the class of rich black South Africans at the 'centre' of economic growth, is a satirical depiction of the country's nation-building process. Ironically the birth of the country's multiracial democracy has instead favoured the growth of class distinction, which seems to have and is entrenching the Centre/Margin and Self/Other binarisms among ordinary South Africans who feel left out by the new leadership. This can be appreciated through the character's humorous description of this new class of rich black South Africans as men with large stomachs resulting from what he calls "Black Economic Empowerment." In fact, multiracial democracy has ironically created an elitist class of a minority who are excessively rich while the majority is abysmally poor. Hence Uncle Nyawana's desperate craving is a deliberate attempt by Mhlongo to expose the incongruity that epitomises their new democracy and its attempt at fostering nationhood when those who should work selflessly toward its achievement have instead grown fat while the populace they are supposed to serve has grown thinner.

Like Mhlongo (2007), Gordimer (1999) equally exposes a similar situation while describing such class stratification characteristic of post-apartheid South Africa. This new class of rich blacks is symbolised by Motsamai, who now lives in one of the residential areas hitherto reserved for the successful white upper class. What is ironic about Motsamai's fortune is not so much the fact that the narrator indicates that it is difficult to say if Motsamai admires the architectural beauty of the house or not but rather that "it provided a comfortable space for a successful man and his family and was now supplied with current standard equipment, electrically-controlled gates for their security against those who remained in the township yards and city squatter camps" (Gordimer, 1999, p.167). The narrator, in this case, seems to point to the existence of class distinction which now characterises the country where a few blacks, such as Motsamai, who form an elitist class, have barricaded themselves behind security fences at the 'centre' while calling on the majority at the 'margin' who are poor to contribute, better still believe in the country's nation-building process. This ironic twist stands out when the narrator subtly intimates that these elitist South Africans have tended to adopt the ways of their former masters. They now barricade themselves in maximum security villas for fear of reprisal from those post-apartheid has not changed their poor status quo. Consequently, Mhlongo and Gordimer, in these examples from their respective novels, show that an ironic new form of Centre /Margin binarism now exists in post-apartheid South Africa. The bottom line is that these examples from the authors' works confirm Chijioke Uwah's view on the irony surrounding the new South Africa's multiracial democracy and nation-building process seen when the critic holds that "the benefits of independence have been hijacked by the new black elite who assumed power from the colonial masters, while the majority of people continue to wallow in abject poverty, homelessness and unemployment" (quoted in Andrew Foley, 2007, p. 130).

Consequently, the pervasive outgrowth of disillusionment that has set in among blacks barely a few years after the inception of multiracial democracy, which promised a remarkable improvement in their lives, is equally demonstrative of the critical socioeconomic and political challenge threatening South Africa's nation-building process. In Gordimer (1999), this state of affairs emerges during the buffet organised by Motsamai in his house when one of his brothers disapproves of the new trend of affairs in the country. The element of disillusionment stands out when Motsamai's brother is told that Harald is a representative of banks that issue loans to blacks to build houses and other developmental projects but based on very stringent conditions. Motsamai's brother considers these conditions for loans as being very prohibitively stringent to blacks who are practically unable to provide the necessary collateral security these banks demand. According to this character, the black populace is caught up in a dilemma since they "don't have capital. What is this 'collateral' but capital? For generations we've never had a chance to create capital, tonight's Friday, every Friday people have had their pay packet and that's what they ate until the next pay day. Finish. No bucks. Collateral is poverty, a good position, not just a job. We couldn't have it - not our grandfathers, not our fathers, and now we're supposed to have this collateral after two years of our government" (Gordimer, 1999, p. 171). Motsamai's brother's desperate outcry highlights the plight and predicament of black South Africans who have never been given a chance to own capital that could have permitted them to benefit from the opportunities offered by the advent of multiracial democracy. This is to say that the bleak fate of blacks living in the present democratic South Africa, according to the character, was sanctioned by the vile system of apartheid, which provided blacks - most of whom were labourers - with only the barest minimum that was meant to keep them healthy enough to work for their white masters. The despondency which this has created is noticed in the black community's inability to change their miserable status quo, although the political scene has witnessed a change of policy which seems to be in their favour. It is therefore, through this historical allusion to the apartheid past and its legacy in the contemporary democratic environment that one gets to comprehend the paradoxical nature of post-apartheid multiracial democracy and its nation-building process. The new conditions imposed on banks meant to ensure a certain degree of accountability are ironically prohibitive to those – blacks – whose miserable conditions the government, via the banks, seeks to redress.

From a postcolonial dimension, the blacks symbolised by the character in question see themselves as still occupying the 'margin' that was imposed on them by apartheid and which post-apartheid has not abrogated completely but instead continue to render them, subalterns, even when they are supposed to have been freed from such binaries with the advent of multiracial democracy. This apparent historical link between the authors' depiction of their country's state of affairs is based on the similarity that exists between their preoccupations raised in the discussions above and the blame which Durrheim (2010) attributes to the ramifications of the country's past on the present when the critic states "Apartheid policies in South Africa put a system of race-based exploitation and marginalisation into operation, according to which people were provided with segregated, inferior and inadequate education and health, and barred from certain categories of employment, as well as from accessing recourse such as land, housing and finance. In other words, the policies of apartheid and colonialism before them laid the framework for an extensive system of affirmative actions for whites, which left in its wake widespread race-based poverty, exclusion and inequality" (Durrheim, 2010, p. 31). In Durrheim's view, apartheid's policies and the legacies thereof are responsible for the different socioeconomic inequality in South Africa where the black population is the most hit by these apartheid-created problems.

Conclusion

At the close of the discussions on the new patterns of social inequality in post-apartheid South Africa, one notices a continuous impact of apartheid's legacy in the lives of the country's black population, who were the main victims of the racial policy upheld by the Afrikaner National Party throughout its close to four decades of reign. In this regard, the question of social inequality in the present democratic dispensation is very much linked to the initial objectives of the Boers, which were informed by the desire to fully exploit the rich natural resources of Africa. Thus, the advent of a multiracial democracy has not eradicated the legacy of the economic goals that instituted socioeconomic and political inequality.

Abstract

This essay focuses on the new patterns of social inequality prevalent in post-apartheid South Africa and draws its inspiration from the novels of Nadine Gordimer and Nicholas Mhlongo. Its discussion of the deplorable socioeconomic state of affairs in contemporary South Africa and possible ramifications on the country's reconciliation and reconstruction processes is based on the fictionalised examples evident in *The House Gun*, *Get a life*, *Dog eat Dog* and *After tears* by Gordimer and Mhlongo respectively. These novels portray 'new' dimensions to the age-old question of inequality in South Africa, which seems to have 'accompanied' the country into its new political era. It is worth noting that though the country after 1994 emerged as a united political entity, socially and economically, South Africa is still a divided nation due to the continued appalling socioeconomic situations of a cross-section of its population. Against this backdrop, Nicholas Mhlongo and Nadine Gordimer think that such multidimensional challenges could have devastating consequences on the political endeavour to construct a multiracial democracy. Though the clarity of the issues discussed in this paper is informed by new historicists and postcolonial theoretical considerations, it is equally worthy to indicate that the authors' fictional representations of contemporary South Africa are not in total conformity with the actual socioeconomic reality and its impact on the reconciliation and reconstruction process in the country in question.

Keywords: Inequality, Post-apartheid, Multiracial Democracy, Nationhood and Nation-building, Centre/Margin

References

Barrow, G. (1999). BBC Focus on Africa magazine. In T. Porteous, G. Jammy, J. Phillips, L. Bellers, R. White, & K. McCririck (Eds.), *Beyond the Rainbow* (pp. 11-16). Kent: BBC World Service.

Durrheim, K. (2010). South Africans' social attitudes, 2nd report: Reflections on the age of Hope. In R. Benjamin, M. Wa Kivilu, & D.Y. Derek (Eds.), *Attitudes towards racial redress in South Africa* (pp. 31-42). Cape Town: HSRC Press.

Foley, A. (2007). "Truth and/reconciliation: South African English literature after apartheid." *Conference Paper University of Western Australia*, pp. 124-144.

Gordimer, N. (1999). *The house gun*. New York: Penguin.

Irlam, S. (2004). Unravelling the Rainbow: The remission of nation in post-Apartheid literature. *The South Atlantic Quarterly, 103(4)*, 695-718.

Lazarus, N. (2004). The South African ideology: The myth of exceptionalism, the idea of Renaissance." *The South Atlantic Quarterly, 103(4),* 607-628.

Mhlongo, N. (2004). *Dog eat dog.* Cape Town: Kwela Books.

Mhlongo, N.(2007). *After tears.* Cape Town: Kwela Books.

O'Reilly, C. (2001). *Post-colonial literature.* Cambridge: Cambridge UP.

Petersson, L. (1998). Post-Apartheid South Africa: Economic Challenges and Policies for the Future. In L. Petersson (Ed.), *Introduction* (pp. 1-18). London: Routledge.

Rule, S. & Zakes, L. (2010). South Africans' social attitudes, 2nd report: Reflections on the age of hope. In R. Benjamin, M. Wa Kivilu, & D.Y. Derek (Eds.), *South Africans' views about national priorities and the trustworthiness of institutions* (pp.19-30). Cape Town: HSRC Press.

Soyinka, K. (2004). Africa today: Voice of the continent. In K. Soyinka, W. Adebayo, M. Akintunde, J. Mukela, J. Mwalulu, G. Nkrumah, M. L. King & O. Oredein (Eds.), *South Africa's success story* (p.9). Lagos: Afro Media (UK) Ltd.

Tutu, D. (2000). *No future without forgiveness.* New York: Doubleday.

Waldmeir, P. (1997). *Anatomy of a miracle: The end of apartheid and the Birth of the new South Africa.* London: Norton and Company.

ELEVEN

Politics of Gender in African and African American Dramaturgy
A Study of Selected Plays by Athol Fugard and August Wilson

NGONG JOSEPH SAM

This chapter examines the politics of gender exclusion in the selected plays of Fugard and Wilson. The issue at stake is that men and women in Africa and America are not given equal status in the domain of political, social, economic and cultural life. The chapter is based on the premise that Fugard and Wilson skilfully and subtly fashion strong female characters who attempt to bridge the gap in gender inequality. In addition, most black women in their plays function mainly in secondary roles and in reaction to men. It is realised that public discourse about crisis among African American men and women is unabated and that the situation of Black women in African American communities has worsened. For instance, Cole and Sheftal (2003, pp. 71-73) posit that most Black women live in single-parenthood, largely female-headed households, compared with one in four American children in the general population. Also, sixty-eight percent of African American children are born to unmarried mothers. Furthermore, the decline in Black marriages, the increase in women raising children alone and higher divorce rates can be explained to some extent by an increase in Black male joblessness and other economic factors such as low wages, violent crime, homicide, drugs and incarceration. Moreover, Duffin (2021) contends that a higher percentage of Black children in the United States live with single mothers. Against this backdrop, the activities carried out by women when the men are away from their homes are examined in this chapter. Thus, it is evident that the Black woman in America is confronted with both a woman's question and the race problem. The chapter is structured into two parts: the first section handles gender exclusion in the selected plays of Athol Fugard's apartheid and post-apartheid plays, while the second part dwells on the selected plays of August Wilson.

Gender Exclusion in the Selected Plays of Athol Fugard

South Africa, like most African countries, is characterised by gender inequality. The men in South African drama are highly patriarchal and are at the forefront of activities in Fugard's Apartheid plays. Fugard's *Sizwe Bansi is Dead* (1986, p. 44) portrays the South African woman as a housewife:

> Man: So Nowetu, for the time being my troubles are over. Christmas I come. In the meantime Buntu is working a plan to get a Lodger's Permit. If I get it, you and the children can come here and spend some days with me in Port Elizabeth. Spend the money I am sending you carefully. If all goes well I will send some more each week. I do not forget you, my dear wife.
> Yours loving Husband
> Sizwe Bansi.

From the above quotation, the woman has been excluded by the man and society because Nowetu can only see her husband during Christmas. A woman who sees her husband yearly is restless. She is always disturbed because she cannot handle the children alone. She needs love and her husband's attention, but none are within her reach. Consequently, she is excluded from jollification, which makes her suffer from schizophrenia. In addition, she cannot get a Lodger's Permit because only men can obtain it. Here, the woman is excluded from town life. Life in the village is also good, but the woman does not intend to remain with the children in the village without hospitals, good living conditions and other social amenities such as water, schools and electricity. Moreover, the woman's position in the play is that of a caretaker because she is not allowed to work in the mines but can work as a cleaner or cook. As a result, she remains traumatised in her home with the children. Thus, she undergoes repression, suppression and depression. According to Freud (1920), the mechanics of repression acts to direct instinctual desires and impulses towards pleasurable instincts by excluding the desire from one's consciousness and holding or subduing it in the unconscious. The woman in the said play yearns to join her husband in the city, but her dreams are disenchanted due to unfulfilled desires.

In the play mentioned above, it is noticeable that men play a dominant role in South African society. They take up active political roles while the women remain at home and think about their men. Kolawole (1997, p. 29) points out that one of the obnoxious apartheid laws which have shaped women to be what they are is the destructive migrant law. This law has undermined the family structure so that women suffer from the politicians and men. A critical reading of *Sizwe Bansi is Dead* reveals that all activities from the beginning to the end are centred on the men, not the women. The woman is mentioned at the end of the play in Sizwe Bansi's letter. Collins (2000) contends that her position is that of a "Mammy." Fugard does not bother about how Black women care for their children in the absence of men. It can be insinuated here that there is gender exclusion in the play. But a critical examination of the situation reveals that the predicament of the Black South African woman is the struggle for sustainability in the absence of the man. The household is usually governed by women who are regarded as single mothers.

South Africa is governed by patriarchy, a system that has existed for thousands of years (Muthien, 2012). In the Introduction to *Sizwe Bansi is Dead*, Fugard presents the *Coat*, based on an actual incident where the man leads in the political, economic and social spheres. The man in the *Coat* represents many who had been found guilty of a banned political party and sentenced to five years imprisonment (Fugard, 1986, p. vii). Although the man has abandoned his wife for five years, the woman cannot forget him. The man's coat now serves as a mental picture that will enable her to remind and console herself that she has a husband. The coat in this context symbolises patriarchal domination. Therefore, it is remarked that men play a dominant role in South African society.

In addition to the problem that most women manage their families without the support of men, Fugard's *The Island* (1986, pp. 70-71) presents the woman as an object of sexual gratification. John remembers when they were picked up and when they were released from prison. Winston reminds John that whatsoever a man is, he cannot do without a woman. John usually slips through the backdoor and makes his way to Sky Place at 10 pm because of women. That is where he used to have fun with them.

The above view bears witness to the issue that the Black South African woman's image, like many women in the world is that of sadomasochism. Winston tells John that his people will welcome him with a woman when he is released from prison. The language seems obscene, but it depicts a situation where one finds a released prisoner having a "wild fuck" with a woman. Winston is governed by the libido in Freud's psychoanalysis which states that behind every human action, there is a sexual motive. Since Zachariah possesses a high sexual drive, he cannot regulate it. Consequently, the woman has been reduced to a mere object that can be used for sexual pleasure. Fugard uses pornographic scenes to objectify the woman's status in *The Island*.

Besides, Fugard's *Bloodknot* (1974) presents Zachariah and Morris, who centre their discussion on economic empowerment but think that a woman can only be used as an object of sexual satisfaction. For instance, the men think that when they receive their salary, they will go out and look for a woman. Zachariah is psychologically worried about the absence of a woman in his life. He forgets about the sum of money they are counting and thinks about having fun with a woman. This expresses his libidinal tendencies. "Zachariah: You are not going to make me forget. I won't. I'm not just going to. We had woman. I tell you. Woman. Woman! Woman!" (Fugard, 1974, p. 11). The libido is used in psychoanalytic theory to describe the energy created by sexual instincts. According to Sigmund Freud, the libido is part of the id and is the driving force of all human behaviour. While the term libido has taken an overt meaning in the play and the world today, to Freud, it represented all psychic energy, not sexual energy. Zachariah is controlled by the libido. He does not want to listen to Morris but keeps shouting a woman's name.

It is realised that Zachariah has spent a whole year without a woman because he considers her as an object of sexual satisfaction as he compares human love relationship to donkeys. Sexual objectification is treating a person as an instrument of sexual pleasure. It also means treating a person as a commodity or an object without regard to their personality or dignity. Objectification is most commonly examined at the level of society but can also refer to the behaviour of individuals. Szymanski (2011) contends that sexual objectification, particularly the objectification of women, is an important idea in psychoanalysis derived from feminism. Hence, many feminists regard sexual objectification as deplorable and as playing an important role in gender exclusion.

Similarly, Zachariah recalls the flashback of his affair with Connie in the bushes and thinks talking about a woman can help relieve him of his sexual desires (16). It is ridiculous that the mere act of Zachariah's sexual drive is aroused because he sees donkeys mating. Zachariah has gone out with uncountable women and derives pleasure from going out with new women. The women vicariously mentioned by Zachariah, in most odious terms, are not given their rights as women. Thus, they are denied any choice of empowerment in their narrated situations. Undermining women's status in absentia can be considered a deliberate act of exclusion. It is remarked that most of the plays written by Fugard before the end of apartheid relegate women to the periphery of society while the men are at the centre.

Fugard's *Master Harold...and the Boys* (1984, pp. 2-3) unravels a negative attitude toward women. This is portrayed in the play by Willie and his girlfriend. A woman is presented as a deceiver who extorts money from men as Willie reveals in his song at the beginning of the play. Sam thinks that a woman's role is to make a man happy, that is, for self-gratification. He visualises a handsome man with a woman in his arms smiling at him and a beautiful lady in an evening dress. A woman's role such as Hilda in the play, is to entertain the men. According to Willie, women are like shoes that men have to wear. Now that Hilda is likened to size twenty-six. He has to look for a different size. At this juncture, it is observed that the women in *Master Harold ... the Boys* play secondary roles. Hally's mother is to accompany his father to the hospital. Women have not been given important roles compared to men. Their role is to gratify men. Fugard excludes women in the casting. The three main characters on stage are Hally, Sam and Wille. Hilda and Hally's mother are mentioned in the background. The audience only hears about them, but they do not see them physically in the play. This method of casting is referred to as the politics of gender exclusion.

Besides, Fugard's *Hello and Goodbye* (1974, p. 108) presents a woman who has been excluded from the home. Johnnie is Hester Smit's brother, but he owns the home alone. Hester has left home to the street, but when she returns to the family, she is regarded as an outcast, while Jonnnie is the caretaker. It is noticed that Johnnie does not want Hester's presence at home. He ignores the sister's arrival because he thinks she does not have a role in the family's affairs. He is like Walter Lee in Lorraine Hansbury's *A Raisin in the Sun* (1994), who contemptuously advises Beanetha to marry instead of dreaming of becoming a medical doctor. Hester has been away for many years because she is disgruntled with how the father and son handled the family. Johnnie is so concerned with the family wealth to the extent that he does not bother about the arrival of his sister, but Hester reminds him that by birthright, she has to own a share in the inheritance. Hester believes that half of the house belongs to her mother. She finds their parent's Marriage Certificate, remembers her departed mother in a flashback, and declares that her mother's mistake was getting married to their father. This implies that the father did not give the mother fair treatment, leading to her death. Hester informs Johnnie that she saw the look in their mother, who fell in her grave, looking tired and frightened. This exhaustive look results from the psychological trauma she encountered in her matrimonial home. The home here symbolises the socioeconomic, cultural and political realities in South Africa that have excluded women. Hester's mother would have taken what she wanted and kicked the father out of the house. As a result, Hester is suffering because their mother was not greedy. She thinks that their mother was stupid.

Freud believes that human behaviour is caused by hidden and unconscious motives (Eagleton, 1996).

Furthermore, Hester thinks that the men in their family have unfairly treated the women. It is in this connection that she declares: "... And I am his daughter and you're his son and I'm your sister. Where's our mother? Well, I'm also ME. Hester... something is going to be mine. Just mine...no sharing with brothers or fathers" (Fugard, 1974, p. 123). Johnnie replies that Hester has been talking about gender relations for twenty years. In Freud's Electra complex, the girl child is often attracted to the father while in Oedipus complex, the boy child is attracted to the mother. Here, it is the reverse because of the patriarchal norms. The girl child is instead interested in the mother. Consequently, she is excluded from the family because of the mistreatment given to the mother by the father. So, Hester ruminates that if she is not careful, what happened to the mother may befall her because their father does not bother about her as she yearns for a sense of belonging. All she needs from her father is her inheritance. Women do not have the right to property in *Hello and Goodbye*. The female child has just called home to greet and go away because the father and the brother have excluded her.

It is critically observed that there is gender equality in Fugard's post-apartheid plays such as *Sorrows and Rejoicings* (2002), *Coming Home* (2010) *and Valley Song* (1986). In *Sorrows and Rejoicings*, the audience faces the lives of two South African women and inheritance. Dawid Olivier has returned home to die, so one witnesses what happens after his death in a flashback. Allison wants to obtain her husband's poems so that she can publish them, but Marta and her daughter have burned the poems. It is realised that the women in *Sorrows and Rejoicings* have been living in distress after the death of Dawid.

South African society is characterised by the cultural expectations of the widow. Most women become widows at an early age. The consequences are that these widows are often infected by HIV and AIDS. Sometimes these widows undergo cleansing after the death of their husbands. Also, the South African widow, like any African widow, has financial problems. For instance, a widow cannot even be sure she would be allowed to keep the money and property she worked for and earned when her husband was alive. If inheritance is available, such as houses, cars, cattle or money, the widow's family often claims it. In Fugard's *Sorrows and Rejoicings*, Marta is excluded from inheriting the property of someone she had a child with.

Another problem in the play is the plight of illegitimate children. Rebecca has been taught never to mention the word father, daddy or pa to protect the father from imprisonment. The girl child is not allowed to mention her father's name because the men do not treat women fairly. Besides, illegitimate children should not mention their fathers' names because society forbids any relationship between blacks and whites. Rebecca symbolises children who have not enjoyed fatherly love because they have been taught by their mothers to hate men. Her mother thinks Rebecca should not think about her father because men are "useless things." Rebecca's mother is, in turn, protecting herself, her daughter and Dawid. However, Rebecca believes that some women who think like her mother are selfish because they do not mind about fatherly love or fatherly bond as Sigmund Freud's psychosexual development will always hunt the girl child in the tenet of Electra Complex. That is the natural tendency of the girl child to be interested in her father. This is the kind of trauma which Rebecca goes through. Although her mother has cautioned her to remain silent about her father, she cannot suppress her parental relationship. Consequently, she becomes neurotic to the extent that she cannot control her emotions. So, she burns what her father has reserved for her. As if it is not enough, she angrily tells her mother to abandon the house.

The society in Fugard's *Coming Home* is that of single motherhood. Men have become irresponsible and wretched. Veronica is left alone to look after Mannetjie. The men seem to lack a sense of direction (Fugard, 2010, pp. 16-17). The man in the play is very pessimistic and irresponsible. Alfred lives a second-hand life in that he is a celebrated bachelor. What he does is think about getting an old bicycle in post-apartheid South Africa. Here it is noticed that the woman has the upper hand over the man. One also realises that single parents head the majority of post-apartheid families. Women raising children alone may have little or no time to be highly involved in politics. This is another kind of exclusion because they are reduced to caretakers. In this vein, Collins (2000, p. 160) points out that Black women alone want loving relationships with Black men but instead end up alone. Therefore, they are blamed for how Black women are rejected and excluded.

Fugard's *Valley Song* takes place in 1996, just after the demise of apartheid. Yong Veronica Jonkers has dreams of singing in Johannesburg because she wants to become famous like the women she watches on television through the window of one of her neighbours. There are two main physical characters in this post-apartheid play: Abraam Jonkers and his granddaughter, Veronica Jonkers. This is the first time that Fugard becomes gender sensitive in his play. Here, he juxtaposes the male and female characters.

During the post-apartheid period, women do not need passes to go to cities in search of greener pastures. Unlike the period before apartheid, the laws did not give passbooks to women. Veronica's mother contracts AIDS in the city because she does not have the skills that will permit her to get a job. Veronica's father symbolises irresponsible South African men who have excluded women from having a better lifestyle. It can be argued that there is gender sensitivity and equality between men and women in Fugard's New South Africa.

From the above analysis, it is perceived that Fugard excludes female characters in apartheid plays such as *Sizwe Bansi is Dead*, *The Island*, *The Bloodknot*, *Master Harold...and the Boys*, *Statements after an Arrest under the Immorality Act*, *Hello and Goodbye*, and include them in post-apartheid plays, notably, *Sorrows and Rejoicings*, *Valley Song* and *Coming Home*.

Gender Exclusion in August Wilson's Selected Plays

In some of his plays, August Wilson juxtaposes men and women on a scale balance. He contends that men and women play complementary roles, as highlighted in the following quotes: "A woman is everything a man needs. To a smart man he is water and berries" (Wilson, 1984, p. 46). "A man that believe in himself still need a woman that believe in him. You can't make life happen without a woman" (Wilson, 1986, p. 28). From these quotations, it is evident that women play fundamental roles in Wilson's plays. We shall look at each selected play in turn.

Fences (1994) is a play about an African American family. One learns about Troy's dreams and aspirations, but little or nothing is known about his wife's dreams. He is loved and admired by Bono, his dear friend and Rose, his wife. Wilson portrays the man's achievements in the African American community, but nothing is mentioned about the woman's achievements. The most influential women in the play are Troy's wives. When Troy reaches the North of America, he meets his first wife and fathers a son, Lyons. While stealing to feed his family, he commits murder and is sentenced to fifteen years in the state penitentiary. During his incarceration, his first wife continues to struggle without him. Here, Wilson focuses his attention on the man and excludes the hero's first wife from the rest of the plot. However, the luck of Troy improves when he meets the woman who will later become his second wife. Nothing is mentioned about how the first wife survives in the absence of Troy. As Wakefield (2003, pp. 42-43) points out that "powerful economic fences are constructed which separate the family members from one another." Thus, the fence in the play symbolises the division between white men and white women and black men and women. Troy is physically and psychologically excluded from mainstream American life, but he builds fences to exclude himself from his family. He is fenced off from his wife and children because he sees them as subordinates.

Notwithstanding, Rose represents the traditional African American woman. She lives a satisfactory life with Troy until her status in the family is abused: she is conformed to traditional gender roles. In her wrath, she explains to Troy that she has been patient as a wife for eighteen years:

> Rose: I've been standing with you! I been right here with you Troy. I got a life too. I gave eighteen years of my life to stand in the same spot with you. Don't you think I ever wanted other things? ...I took all my feelings, my wants, and needs, my dreams... and buried them inside you. I planted a seed and watched and prayed over it. I planted myself inside you and I waited to bloom (Wilson, 1994, p. 2279).

From the above quotation, it is remarked that Rose's effort to make a good and prosperous home and to keep a good husband has ended in futility. On a sad note, she reminds her husband that women also have wants because she is excluded from matrimonial issues such as decision-making. This statement is made in reaction to Troy's behaviour. He is self-centred; he thinks only about himself and does not care about others. In other words, he is an irresponsible husband.

What baffles one in *Fences* is how Rose heads her family after the death of Troy. Although Troy dies at the end of the play, there is every indication that Rose, like any African American woman, will head the family, for it is noticeable that 54% of single women head African American households (Baribun, 2002, p. 16). Wilson does not forecast the life of the woman after the demise of the man. This implies that the playwright has also destroyed the woman. Her existence in the text is thanks to the man. Thus, when the man dies a physical death, the woman also dies a psychological death in the author's mind. This act is considered the politics of gender exclusion.

The Piano Lesson (1990, p. 52) elucidates how Wilson involves perspectives of gender stereotypes. Berniece enters the play with an eleven-year-old daughter, Maretha. She reminds her brother that he always talks about his father but nothing about his mother. She forgets that her father had excluded her from the management of the home, as observed in the expression, "...you always talking about your daddy but ain't stopped to look at what his foolishness cost your mama." Berniece has become the custodian of the family's culture. Her brothers are money-minded and do not bother about their cultural artefacts. Hence, Wilson illustrates that the culture of African Americans can be better preserved through African American women. However, Boy Willie addresses Berniece as a 'woman' to remind her that she plays a secondary role in decision-making.

In a similar dialogue between Berniece and Avery, Berniece debunks the view that a woman cannot be something without a man. Everybody is worried to know how she takes care of herself and her child without the assistance of a man:

> Berniece: You trying to tell me a woman can't be nothing without a man. But you alright, huh? You can just walk out here without me - without a woman and still be a man... "How Berniece gonna take care of herself? How she gonna raise that child without a man? Wonder what she do with herself. How she gonna live like that? ...Everybody telling me I can't be a woman without a man. Well, you tell me, Avery you know how much woman am I? (Wilson, 1990, p. 67).

From the above quotation, the female character demonstrates that a woman can live successfully without a man. Berniece proves that some women are stronger than some men. She is proud of being a single mother and stands up for her rights. She incarnates maternal positioning, and she is an empowered female figure. In brief, she fights against the exclusion of women in socio-cultural issues. Thus, it is noted that the image of the Mammy and the subservient Black woman has been transformed by making maternity a source of power to reckon with.

The women in Wilson's *Joe Turner's Come and Gone* (1984, pp. 65-66) play secondary roles compared to the men. Selig looks at women as horses that men can ride and abandon. He thinks that all a man needs is a good life, and when a man tells a horse to get up or stop, it does so. Also, he thinks that when a man is with a woman, he should grow bigger every day. However, he once abandoned his wife because he observed that he was decreasing in shape. Later, in a flashback, he recalls an incident in his marital life in Kentucky. His wife was so disgruntled that he went out and looked for a prostitute. The horse in the play is a metaphor for sex workers. Thus, it is evident that Selig uses women for sexual gratification. Washington (1987, p. 74) asserts that the most common attack on the image of Black women is to portray them as immoral women who are licentious and oversexed. The forgone symbol is reminiscent of what happens in the said play.

In another tête-à-tête between Jeremy and Bynum, Bynum reminds Jeremy that a woman has a strategic role to play in a man's life. One of the issues that excluded women from men in the nineteenth century was slavery. The slave master in *Joe Turner's Come and Gone* took away the men and abandoned the women with their children. Sometimes the slave masters had to make Black women pregnant. As a result, the men worked in the fields for many years without seeing their wives. This hurt the characters in the plays. Selig testifies that they have been bringing people together. So, the effect of slavery and its aftermath is still felt. As represented by Selig, Wilson portrays the negative effects of slavery in that it caused the separation of families. When it was abolished, blacks could not meet their loved ones. In the play, Selig seeks missing ribs and brings them together. Nonetheless, when the men meet the women, they exclude them from important job opportunities.

When a woman is ignored, it implies that she is not considered in decision-making, and everything she does passes away like the wind. According to Bynum, the woman is a metaphor for the whole world with everything, and he opines that a woman is everything a man needs. After Bynum's advice, Jeremy changes his mind about women. He now acknowledges the importance of women as he courts Molly:

> Jeremy: ...with a woman like you a man can make it nice in the world.
> Molly: Moll can make it nice by herself too. Molly don't need nobody leave her in the cold in hand. The world rough and enough as it is.
> Jeremy: ... A woman like you can make it anywhere she go. But you can make it better if you got a man to protect you... With a woman like you it's like having water and berries. A man got everything he need (Wilson, 1984, pp. 65-66).

From the above dialogue, Jeremy, formerly controlled by the id, gains consciousness and, like any other African American man, is sensitised on the virtues of womanhood and manhood. After excluding the importance of the woman in the world, he now includes her, as he claims repetitively, "with a woman... it like having water and berries" (p. 66). Exclusion, in this vein, is rejecting the virtues of a woman and accepting them. It does not mean that a woman is a necessary evil but an important force to reckon with because no man can succeed without a lady of substance behind him.

Gender in Wilson's *Gem of the Ocean* (2003) can be examined in the character of Aunt Ester. There are seven characters in the play, but there are only two women: Aunt Ester and Black Mary. One may think that the women have been crushed numerically, but when one reads closely, one realises they play predominant roles because they possess strong matriarchal powers. In a flashback, Aunt Ester informs Black Mary that she was empowered by Miss Tyler, who lived with her for many years before she died. Before dying, she had initiated Aunt Ester into the sacred world (Wilson, 2003, p. 6). This view has to do with the initiation of African American womanhood. Although the playwright has used only two female characters against five male characters, the female characters do not play secondary roles like in other plays. So, we can say that Wilson has unconsciously excluded some women from the casting because there is no gender equity.

With regards to Wilson's *Ma Rainey's Black Bottom*, Ma Rainey is an active working-class woman who does not depend on her husband for sustenance. The image painted in the play is that of a successful African American woman who is not easily suppressed and excluded from white society by white men or black men because she is a woman of substance. Before the nineteenth century, African American women and even white women had no say in public matters. So, Ma Rainey represents the rise of women in political, social and economic issues. In a related way, Butake (1989) presents Mboysi, who is looked upon with disdain by the police officer simply because she is a woman. However, she fights back as Ma Rainey does. The white producer in the play wants to exclude and deprive Ma of her songs, but Ma fights back. She is already aware of how white producers exploit black women (Wilson, 2000, p. 593).

From Ma Rainey's perception, White producers and Black men exploit Black female musicians. This goes in line with the issue of triple colonisation. The Black woman is marginalised by white men, white women and black men. As seen in the above excerpt, Ma Rainey fights against any exclusion. Wilson's observation on how Black women are treated by black men and white men respectively is also one of the concerns of Shange (2010). In her play, she describes in detail the victimisation of black women by black men and comments on the violence perpetrated by black people against other blacks in the frustration of being excluded from white society.

However, Wilson presents Floyd and Red Cartar in the *Seven Guitars* (1986) as unfaithful African American men who consider African American females second-class citizens (Wilson, 1986, pp. 102-103). Vera explains how a woman feels when a man abandons her. She thinks the man has never stopped asking himself how a woman feels because every night, the man abandons her in a room on an empty bed. She does not understand how a man should abandon her for a long time and think of coming back. Hence, it is evident that any man who abandons a faithful wife must regret it. The woman does not understand why someone can abandon her and return later.

On the other hand, the place of motherhood is very instrumental in the lives of African American men, as demonstrated in the quest for the mother by men. In addition, African American women, like their men, suffered from abject poverty. Floyd's mother experienced poverty throughout her life. "My

Mama lived and died she ain't had nothing...My Mama ain't had two dimes to rub together. And ain't had but one stick. She got to do without the fire. Some kind of warmth in her life" (Wilson, 1986, p. 97). African American women in the 1940s were poor because they were excluded by white men and white women. Black men relegate black women to subordinate positions in the family. Hence, from the period of slavery up to the twentieth century, African American women like Floyd's mother in *The Seven Guitars* were poor. The situation is different today because African American women have been empowered. Many powerful African American women are in mainstream American socio-economic, cultural and political spheres of life. Some of these women include Oprah Winfrey, Condoleezza Rice, Kamala Harris, Ketanji Brown Jackson and African American female authors.

The woman in Wilson's selected plays possesses a maternal position. The woman's place is a sanctuary for men and children, and above all, African American men can only gain hope through women. In Wilson's plays, the place of the African American woman has been reconstructed and restored. Porter (2001, pp.56-62) asserts that the African American woman has been crucified. She is assailed on the one hand by white patriarchy and, on the other hand, by the sexiest black men and racist white women. He adds that the African American mother was repeatedly bought, sold and raped, and she scrubbed floors in the houses of white men. Besides, Porter notes that in America's past, as it is in the present, the reality of African American women is a reality of oppression because the woman has suffered from psychological mutilation, the violence of rape and forced breeding; she reared the oppressor's children and performed menial and degrading jobs. So, this was the foundation for the African American woman.

The portrait of the African American woman has been restored in Wilson's plays. The face of the black woman, and grandmothers that had been relegated to nursing homes, where she exists in loneliness as she awaits death, is ignored by the white power structure and has been given a positive image. Nowadays, several black playwrights have written about the predicaments of black women. It should be noted that very few of these writers have portrayed women sensitively and realistically. It is evident that black women's accomplishments were not recognised in the struggle against apartheid but were underlooked in the colonial and patriarchal society of South Africa (Grabowski, 2013, p. 3).

From the above discussion, it is realised that gender inequality exists not only in some countries but in most countries. Collins wonders why African American women and their ideas are unknown and not believed in. She argues that the knowledge produced by black women has been suppressed, which makes men rule women. In addition, she states that the invisibility of black women and their ideas occurs not only in the United States of America but in Africa, the Caribbean, Europe and other places where black women live. Hence, there is a very minimal amount of literature written by Black women. Despite suppressing black women's knowledge, U.S. Black women have managed to write intellectual works and have their ideas matter. Some women, notably Sojourner Truth, Anna Julia Cooper, Ida Wells Barnet, Mary McLeod Bethune, Toni Morrison, Barbara Smith, and others, have continuously struggled to make themselves heard. African women writers such as Ama Ata Aidoo, Buchi Emecheta and Ellen Kuzwayo have used their voices to raise important issues that affect Black African women (Collins, 2000, p. 3). Ngozi Adichie has projected the African female voice on gender issues from 2003-2023.

Conclusion

This chapter examined the misrepresentation of women in the selected plays of Fugard and Wilson. From the foregone analyses, it is noticed that the representation of women in Fugard and Wilson's plays is not given equal weight as compared to men. So, there is bound to be gender inequality because the role of the men in their plays surpasses that of the women. Slavery has also contributed to separating African American men from their women. Even though slavery was abolished, the negative impact on the African American family is still felt today. The plays inform readers and the audience that men and women have complementary roles. However, some African American men still believe women can be used as a horse. The characters in the plays educate each other on the virtues of womanhood. Thus, it is noted here that no man succeeds without a woman behind him. Many women succeed in raising children alone without the support of men. In other words, about seventy percent of African and African American women take care of their families singlehandedly. Thus, when women raise children alone, they have little or no time to be highly involved in political matters.

Gender becomes a political issue in that women's position in society is decided by men and women in various ways. So, each society has its manner of handling women fairly or unfairly. Therefore, gender equality depends on the society of the writer. In most societies in the world, women are excluded from mainstream issues. Women struggle for their rights by empowering and liberating themselves as time passes.

It is also realised that love relationships between African American men and their women are often unreciprocated because most men end up in prison.

Consequently, men and women become unfaithful to each other. Wilson counters traditional beliefs and stereotypes about black women at this juncture. White writers presented them as immoral and oversexed. So, Wilson maintains that women were also separated from men by white society. Thus, the negative image of the black woman has been restored in Wilson's *The Piano Lesson, Gem of the Ocean, Joe Turner's Come and Gone, Ma Rainey's Black Bottom* and *The Seven Guitars*. Wilson has used juxtaposition, flashback and irony to give the African American woman the place she deserves in her community. Therefore, Wilson and Fugard have contributed immensely to feminist political discourse in that gender remains a global challenge.

Abstract

Most women in Africa and America have been psychologically and physically mutilated in the socioeconomic, political and cultural spheres. Thus, this essay discusses the exclusion of women in the selected plays of Athol Fugard and August Wilson. Using the psychoanalytical and feminist theories, the paper argues that the misrepresentation of women is not given equal weight in the plays of both authors. The playwrights skilfully fashion female characters who play secondary roles. However, the same dramatists reclassify women to hold strategic positions in their plays as time is no longer on their side. Fugard has been writing for over fifty years, and his position towards women has changed drastically when comparing his apartheid and post-apartheid plays. Wilson, on his part, handles women with mixed feelings. Thus, it is observed that the conspiracy to annihilate women in male fiction functions unabated. Therefore, Wilson and Fugard have contributed immensely to feminist political discourse because gender remains a global challenge.

Keywords: gender, psychoanalysis, politics, objectification, misrepresentation

References

Barbarin, O. (2002). African American males in kindergarten. In J.U. Gordon (Ed.), *The African American male in American life and thought*. New York: Nova Science.

Butake, B. (1989). *The survivors*. Yaounde: SOPECAM.

Cole, J., & Beverly, S. (2003). *Gender talk: The struggle for women's equality in African American Communities*. New York: Random House Publishing Group.

Collins, P. (2000a). *Mammies, matriarchs, and other controlling images in black feminist thought: Knowledge, consciousness and the politics of empowerment*. New York: Routledge.

Collins, P. (2000b). *Black feminist thought: Knowledge, consciousness and the politics of empowerment*. New York: Routledge.

Duffin, E. (2021). Number of Black families with a single mother in the United States from 1900 to 2020. New York: Statista research department.
Eagleton, T. (1996). Ed. *Literary theory: An introduction*. Oxford: Blackwell Publishers Ltd.
Freud S. (1920). *A general introduction to psychoanalysis*. New York: Horace Liveright
Fugard, A. (1974). *Three Port Elizabeth plays. The blood knot, Hello and Goodbye, Boesman and Lena*. Oxford: Oxford University Press.
Fugard, A. (1984). *Master Harold…and the boys*. New York: Penguin.
Fugard, A. (1986). Statements: *Sizwe Bansi is Dead, The Island, Statement after an arrest under the Immorality Act*. New York: Theatre Communication Group.
Fugard, A. (1996). *Valley song*. New York: Theatre Communication Group.
Fugard, A. (2002). *Sorrows and rejoicings*. New York: Theatre Communication Group.
Fugard, A. (2010). *Coming home*. Theatre New York: Dramatists Play INC.
Grabowski, A. (2013). She's a brick house: August Wilson and the stereotypes of black womanhood. Retrieved from https://cupola.gettyburg.edu/student/99
Hansberry, L. (1994). *A raisin in the sun*. New York: Vintage Books.
Kolawole, M. (1997). *Womanism and African consciousness*. Asmara: Africa World Press. Inc.
Muthien, B. & Annika, S. (2012). *Gender-based violence in South Africa: Interview with Bernadette Muthien*. Fair Observer Make Sense of the World.
Porter, M. (2001). *The Conspiracy to destroy black women*. Chicago: AAI.
Shange, N. (2010). *For colored girls who have considered suicide/when the rainbow is enuf/a*. New York: Scribner.
Szymanski, D. M, Moffilt, L. B & Carr E. R. (2012). *Sexual objectification of women: Advances to theory and research*. Knoxville: Sage.
Wakefield, T. (2003). The family in twentieth-century African American drama. New York: Peter Lang Inc.
Washington, M. (1987). *Invented lives: Narratives of black women 1860-1960*. New York: An Anchor Press Book.
Wilson, A. (1984). *Joe Turner's come and gone*. New York: Theatre Communications.
Wilson, A. (2000). *Ma Rainey's Black Bottom*. In G. Plimpton (Ed.) *Playwrights at work: The Paris Review* (346-368). New York: Morden Library.
Wilson, A. (1994). Fences. In N. Baym, R. Gottesman & L. Holland (Eds.) *the Norton anthology of American literature 4th* ed. Vol. 2. (pp. 2246-2292). New York: Norton Company.
Wilson, A. (1986). *The Seven Guitars*. New York: Theatre Communications Group.
Wilson, A. (1990). *The Piano Lesson*. New York: Plume.
Wilson, A. (2003). *Gem of the Ocean*. New York: Theatre Communications Group.

TWELVE

The Intricacies of Racial Stigma
A Self Reconstruction of the Sublime in Maya Angelou's I Know Why the Caged Bird Sings

NYE GRACE NFORMI

Maya Angelou chronicles her life experiences and struggles in *I Know why the Caged Bird Sings*, which gives an insight into Maya's life as a young African American girl who grows up in a society where discrimination is rife. The novel discusses various forms of oppression that she faces. Gross (2014) claims that Angelou's book is an interesting story of her own experiences and a portrayal of a modern Black community in the 1930s of the American South. Megna (1998) backs up Gross' claim in her critique of the importance of the novel as a historical book and also discusses how Angelou intended the autobiography to target the historical circumstances of the time. However, these two analyses portray the novel in two completely different ways. Gross (2014) describes it as a well-written story that was carefully thought out, and racism has a visible impact on the main character's life. He regards the autobiography as a beautiful story that depicts the warmth and understanding within the Black community, whereas Wallace contends that Angelou's autobiography is a means of exposing the horrific racism that pervaded her childhood. She focuses on Maya Angelou's struggle and the tragic events that made her the woman she is, irrespective of the antithetical angles from which both critics review Angelou's work. However, both reveal the paradox existing between fiction and reality. The cruel horrors of racial stigma and priceless beauty in the inestimable worth of the African American identity and the inability of these extremes to be dichotomised rather than harmonised in a single continuum are the primary cause of the irreconcilable gaps that exist between the cruel reality of institutionalised systems and the idealism of African American identity.

In order to effectively appraise Maya Angelou's novel, we will screen out two critical tools as assessment labels. These include African American criticism and feminism. At the upstream, African American criticism delves into the African American experience handling issues such as the question of freedom from the warping forces of oppression, the surviving spirit of sustenance in the cruel south under segregation, the bending hardship of economic survival, and the sacred importance of the family and the community as a necessary force for social cohesion. The goal here is to reconstruct the misinterpretation preconceived by the African American experience from the corrosive stigma of racism. To achieve this, it is imperative to penetrate and overlap the psychology of subjugation, defiance, and resistance. Reginald (2016, p. 727) reckons that:

> several historically and pedagogically important events happened to literature written by Blacks and the black authored criticism of that literature of the 60s, black writers writing for a black readership...Many black professors labored during the 40s, 50s and early 60s to show how similar Gwendolyn Brooks' Annie (1949), was like T.S Elliot's *The Wasteland* (1922)...or labored to show how similar in content, structure, style, theme and intent Ralph Ellison's *Invisible Man* (1952) was to James Joyce's *Portrait of the Artist* (1916) as a way of proving Ellison's literary worth.

This excerpt shows how African American writers of the 40s, 50s, and 60s worked hard to copy white writers in order to be recognised as good writers. Here, Martin argues that there had to be something unique about African Americans in their way of judging and seeing literature. Following the same traces, methods, themes and intent as white writers who do not have the same background experiences as African Americans kills realism. Also, Yogita (1999, p. 1) holds that:

> African American literature begins with a meditation on the meaning of slavery and freedom... The reconstruction era prompts the literature of racial uplift... During the Harlem Renaissance and Black Art era, writers turned to realist protest fiction that combats continuing segregation and Jim Crow disenfranchisement.

This presents the evolution of African American critical theory. In the beginning, African American writers focused on slavery and freedom and over time, it moved to the search for identity, recognition and African American dignity. Similarly, Griffin (2004, p. 2) upholds that:

> The past 30 years have witnessed an explosion of literary production by people of African descent. Black writers have been publishing their works for centuries, this has been an era of institutionalizing and diversifying literature, identifying and creating a market for it and formalizing its study.

According to this article, there have been great improvements and achievements in African American literary studies. There was a time when African American writers wrote only for freedom, but today, there's great diversity. African Americans do not only write to be recognised but to identify and create works that they commercialise.

Turning to feminism, the dilemma of the African American woman is also a fertile ground for black feminists to err and expose the grievances of the female folk. Also, it becomes a yardstick for black feminists to troubleshoot a glorious hope, vision, and future for the upcoming generation. Guerin (1992) does not share an optimistic view of African American women's falsehood, believing that there is no glorious hope for African American women in their observation that black women are thus in a double bind. They do not expect gender solidarity from White women or radical solidarity from African American men, two group recognition and African American dignity, on which they should have been able to rely for assistance.

Despite the cruel truth that alienates African American women in a state of helplessness and hopelessness, whether from White women's or African American women's solidarity, it is implied that the solution to the problem of African American women is beyond race and gender. If these two indicators are quantitative criteria that condition externalities, they do not determine an individual's happiness when internalised as qualitative criteria. If two wrongs do not make a right, then every shortcoming must indeed allow for adjustment as long as life provides the opportunity. Collins (1990, p. 22) believes that: as long as Black women's subordination within intersecting oppressions of race, class, gender, sexuality and nation persists, Black feminism as an activist response to that oppression will remain needed. If African American women are continuously relegated to the background, it is of essence that they will always protest for social changes. True happiness is first, an individual matter before it extends collectively. True happiness is rendered and complete when those around contribute to it. This is what makes it worth cherishing.

Gender Inequality and Feminist Assertion

Due to American society's patriarchal organisation, women's place and role in society have always been controversial. However, following the feminist movements, women have been able to turn their silence into speech as a way of carving their own identity. The African American woman's plight is different as she lives in a society wherein she is doubly marginalised: marginalised because of the colour of her skin and because she is a woman. Hurston (1937, p. 14) writes, "De nigger woman is the mule uh de world. The white man throws his bag at the black man, and the black man leaves it for the woman to carry."

Many female authors are now bringing issues concerning female experience into the limelight, thereby breaking the long silence. Maya Angelou portrays strong-willed female characters like Annie Henderson, Vivian Baxter, and herself. The African American woman is seen as the cornerstone of her society. Most often, these women are deserted by the men who, more often than not, are swept away by the complexities surrounding them. Single-handedly, these women brave the storm, raise their children, and walk relentlessly for the betterment of their communities.

Annie Henderson is the only person (a woman) to own a store in Little Rock, Arkansas. "My grandmother had owned the only Negro general merchandise store since the turn of the century" (Angelou, p. 104). This is thanks to her years of hard labour. She takes her destiny into her own hands after three unsuccessful marriages. She is married first to Mr. Johnson, who leaves her with two sons to raise, then to Mr. Henderson, and then to Mr. Murphy, who turns out to be reckless and hopeless. When Mr. Murphy goes to the stamp shop, Uncle Willie and Bailey would stay at home and keep an eye on him for fear that he may steal everything in the store.

This series of abandonments only increase Momma Johnson's desire to make it in life. Angelou (1969, p. 122) confesses, "I saw only her power and strength." This power and strength are not directed for her own sake but for the betterment of the Negro race. Maya asserts that "Momma Johnson intended to teach Bailey and I to use the paths of life that she and her generation and all the Negros gone before had found and found to be safe ones." Thus, Annie Henderson single-handedly grooms her children and her grandchildren. Bernstein (1996, p. 18) reiterates this aspect, "we are our mothers' daughters, our mothers' sons, and our mothers live inside of us as we go beyond and extend the meaning of their lives." This helps the next generation to recognise their identity, oneness and to pass this strength to other generations. The chain must continue so that their children shovel and not be wayward.

Her determination to have her granddaughter treated by the dentist presents her as a woman capable of braving all hurdles in life: "Since there was no Negro dentist in Stamps, the nearest Negro dentist was in Texarkana, twenty-five miles away. Annie Henderson takes her granddaughter to the dentist, Lincoln (a white). A man she has been lending money to" (Angelou, 1969, p. 188). Mrs. Henderson believes that because she has been rendering services to dentist Lincoln, she will not have to go too far to plug Maya's tooth. Dentist Lincoln refuses to treat Maya. "Annie, my policy is that I'd rather stick my hand in the mouth of a dog than a Nigger's" (Angelou, 1969, p. 189). After using these words, he goes back to his office. Annie Henderson follows him, catches him by the collar of his white jacket, and says, "Stand up when you see a lady, you contemptuous scoundrel. Do you think you acted like a gentleman by speaking to me like that in front of my granddaughter?" (Angelou, 1969, p. 190). The dentist has no choice but to stand. She shakes and pushes him back into his dentist's chair. He trembles terribly. Mrs. Henderson deals with him accordingly. She teaches him to respect her first because she is a woman.

In the same light, Vivian Baxter's will and determination portray her as a woman determined to shape her own destiny in life. In the face of adversity and separated from her husband, she takes up odd jobs and earns a living for herself. Angelou says this of her: "Life is going to give just what you put into it. Put your whole heart into everything you do and pray, then wait" (Angelou, 1969, p. 269).

Thus, these women serve as role models for Maya. They are Maya's folk heroines. Maya's mother, Dane Weston, affirms that "for Maya, the greatest heroines are the women in her family" (Angelou, 1969, p. 220). This is because these women can transcend patriarchy and forge ahead while simultaneously reconciling their individual wills to the collective wills of their people, who are confronted by racial discrimination and social injustice. Maya thus grows up with a philosophy of hard work and determination inculcated in her by these two women. She works hard enough, graduates at the top of her class, and celebrates her victory. "My work alone had awarded me a top place and I was going to be one of the first called in the graduating ceremonies... No absence, no tardiness, and my academic work was among the best in the year" (Angelou, 1969, p. 172). Here, Maya seems to suggest that independent of race and gender, hard work and determination are keys to success for any woman. Though the road may be difficult, a woman can shape her destiny by pushing past taboos and working hard. Such is the message passed across by Morrison and Hurston in their works, *Beloved* and *Their Eyes Were Watching God,* respectively. According to them, a woman's destiny lies in her hands. It suffices for her to seize every opportunity and break through the octopus grip of patriarchy and racism. This is what Sethe does in *Beloved*, and Janie does the same in *Their Eyes were Watching God*.

Maya's journey from childhood to maturity reveals the stages undergone by the African American woman in a racist society. Female vulnerability to external forces is evident, and for her, the woman can define her identity in relation to her own individual will first, then to the will of the community. All through the novel, female characters show mastery of their environment and emerge victorious at the end. In an article, Hallway (2014, p. 4) adds,

> One adult who had a very positive impact on the author was Mrs. Flowers, a neighbour. She was better off economically than other blacks; she was refined, pleasant to everyone and was noted for her kindness. The role she played in Maya's identity is enormous. Mrs. Flowers made Maya proud to be a black woman simply by being herself. She became committed to helping the psychologically troubled Maya overcome her inability to speak by teaching her to read aloud from books.

This is to emphasise the role Mrs. Flowers plays in Maya's life. She is not out to appreciate and encourage Maya but goes beyond by giving her books to read and spend time listening to her read aloud. This constant practice helps Maya regain her voice (identity). This is re-emphasised when Maya says: "I was liked, and what a difference it made. I was respected not as Mrs. Henderson's granddaughter or Bailey's sister, but for just being Marguerite Johnson" (Angelou, 1969, p. 100). This shows the powerful impact that reading has on the individual. This makes her discover many things. Mrs. Flowers does it with much love, something Maya has hardly experienced from people around. Maya is always referred to as ugly. The love Mrs. Flowers shows her contributes to uplifting her identity and helps her believe in herself.

Bloom (1998, p. 2) notes a similar view: "Angelou tells us that she read widely as a child, saving her young and loyal passion for the African American poets Paul Laurence Dunbar, Langston Hughes, and James Weldon Johnson." All of whose voices can still be heard in her own poetry. She cites Dunbar, whom she cites first, as providing her with her most famous title. Reading extensively made Maya learn more about others, prompting her to come up with the title of this book, taken from Paul Laurence Dunbar's poem, "Sympathy."

Reconstruction of the African American Identity

This section identifies the ways and measures through which African Americans seek to reconstruct their self-identity. Bulkin (2016, p. 3) writes:

> Confronting the giants that obstruct our path is the most challenging nightmare we can experience on our journey towards glory, caught between the rocks and without facing them, nor can one prolong our confrontation with them. If we don't want them to get the better of us at the verge of our glory.

This reflects the fate that befalls African Americans who are striving to overcome the wall of stigma built by racism. The greatest challenge for African Americans is to reach a point of self-awareness where the full knowledge of our identity has experienced the sublime (the ideal). The sublime becomes the key that unlocks the door of social injustice to a dimension of accomplishment where self-esteem and identity reconstruction are perfected. Knowledge of this enables one to perceive the sense of salient concepts that constitute it.

First and foremost, one of the criteria through which African Americans strive to reconstruct their identity and experience the sublime is through religion. Religion becomes an instrument that creates a balance between society, morality (ethics), and spirituality. Through religion, Angelou questions the actions of Whites towards Blacks as condoning, inappropriate, and unfair. Fulfilling the role of a spiritual medium, the voice of moral conscience transmits values of belief and virtues that conform to godliness and righteousness. Angelou exploits it as one of the sensitive thematic concerns of her novel, and it remains a critical weapon she uses to expose the missing puzzle that fits in as the solution to the problems brought about by race and identity.

Despite the emotional turmoil and imbalance, Marguerite and her brother suffer from their parents' separation; the upbringing Momma Johnson (Angelou's grandmother) gives them at Stamps and Arkansas helps them to be morally upright. In the absence of their parents, as a code of moral values, religion becomes the spear that sharpens an ideal character of virtue, that is, a long-lasting legacy, and also approving in the sight of God and man. Momma Johnson does not hide her intentions, so she encourages them to go to church. She advises them to "go to church. You've got to feed the soul like you feed your body. I'm taking the children too. Raising a child in the way he should go, and he will not depart from it" (Angelou, 1969, p. 121).

From the above observation, it becomes evident that educating children in the fear of God becomes inevitable. It represents the voice of wisdom that defines the beauty of grey hair that accompanies old age. If the older generations, gifted with the wisdom of experience, do not adequately educate the younger generation, there will undoubtedly be no life-lasting legacy since the younger generation is a prototype of the future generation. It is proper and legitimate that the older generation should pass on to the younger generation a life-lasting legacy of wisdom. This is an urgent call to both generations. They have to sit up and assume their respective roles towards each other. To the old, she urges them to educate the young since they hold the keys to wisdom and success needed by the younger generation to make history. She is compelling the young to develop the listening ear of humility and learn tirelessly from the old.

Even though parents dominate their children in life experiences, they should not take this advantage as pride to oppress and discourage them. As a result, while children owe them respect, parents should treat them with love in a godly manner. Momma Johnson believes that encouraging children to attend church daily is the right thing to do. Her reason for bringing them to church is to develop and maintain a genuine relationship between them and their creator.

Also, she esteems that experiencing the joy of salvation will set them free from the chains of social injustice. Further, she reckons that children not only need physical food to make their bodies healthy, but they also need to be fed with spiritual food (the work of God) for their souls and spirits to experience the joy of salvation. As Christ himself said to Satan, man must not live by bread alone but by every word that comes from the mouth of God (Matt 4 verse 4). Momma Johnson, as an elderly woman, is aware of the fact that the physical challenges that children face are colossal and complex. They need the creator to lead them. She holds that, even as children have to be fed and satisfied, the food that satisfies their body will perish. She maintains that the spirit is fed with the word of God, and that is what will not perish.

Momma Johnson, through this, emulates the perfect incarnation of godly virtues transmitted from one generation to another. To her, it is her heritage that immortalises timelessness. Furthermore, Momma Johnson's encounter with the perverted White girls at the store is another form of education she passes on to Angelou while experiencing racism in Stamps, Arkansas. While performing her sales routine, Momma Johnson encounters a shock wave confrontation with a group of Whites who call Momma Johnson and Willie by their first names, infuriating Marguerite. The attitude of Momma Johnson in relation to this incident draws one's attention to the legacy of wisdom she wants to pass on to the younger generations.

In the first place, Momma Johnson sends Marguerite to the store to avoid a direct confrontation between Marguerite and the White girls. It is said that every parent knows the attitudes and behaviours of their children and how to deal with them. This is the case for Momma Johnson, who acts instinctively with the grace of wisdom to respond immediately by sending Marguerite inside the store. She knows Marguerite is still a young girl experiencing growth with a rash temper. She senses that allowing Angelou makes things worse. Seeing danger coming from a distance (the White girls), she anticipates the occurrence of a greater one than Angelou's rebellious reaction against the White girls. Momma Johnson's decision to send Angelou behind the store is not a sign of weakness but strength. Striving for peace at a priceless cost requires immeasurable sacrifice, even if it involves going and placing our integrity on the head. Are the White girls' attitudes toward Momma Johnson appropriate? Of course, it is not. Is Marguerite's reaction against the White girls towards Momma Johnson justified? Yes, they are. To Momma Johnson, the problem here is not the misbehaviour of the White girls. The real problem is Marguerite's reaction and the consequences in the long run. Momma Johnson does not only use wisdom to protect her granddaughter from the dangers of racism; she also passes such knowledge to Maya in order for her to learn the way she ought to deal with the fact that two wrongs do not make any right. She wants Angelou to learn that our response to a mistake can be an action with a reaction of anger. We do not measure the consequences of our actions. In the end, it becomes clear that anger ends up pushing the offended to a state of regret. Momma Johnson esteems that Angelou will understand the reason behind her actions when she grows older.

Again, Momma Johnson displays sound maturity against the girls' racist attack by not responding to violence with violence but with passivity. We do not expect children to show disrespect for the elderly simply because their race makes them superior. Having the white colour does not indicate by any means that one's soul is pure and void of sin.

If that is the case, the White girls would disrespect an aged woman. It may be easy to teach someone how to hate, but it is much more difficult to teach someone how to love. As an elderly person, natural logic gives her the right to rebuke them since their actions are wrong. When children are not corrected while young, it becomes difficult to correct them when they grow old. These girls have been taught to hate African Americans by their White parents, regardless of age and gender. Ironically, Momma Johnson does not confront them but distances herself from them to avoid doing the unthinkable. Knowing the consequences of a hasty reaction, she resorts to passivity and silence. Silence is perceived here as a powerful weapon of self-control. Silence also allows African Americans to experience an internal fulfilment of peace, serenity, and a sense of belonging.

Silence contains a certain degree of wisdom that quenches every storm and transforms them into stepping stones. Mary Louise Roth in *Morale Booster* comments on the importance of silence when she discloses that silence is to the spirit in the same way sleep is to the body. It is necessary that we regain our breath, name our forces, and select our thoughts. It permits one to be linked to their spirit and inspires us with ideas in our hearts where the voice can guide us. For a balanced and conscious life, it is primordial that we reserve ourselves for moments of silence. During such moments of deep intimacy with oneself, we perceive the essential. Silence enables us to be present in life (Angelou, 1969, p. 137).

For Momma Johnson, the White girls' behaviour signifies that first: they are still kids unaware of their actions, and the ignorance of youthfulness renders them blind to reality. Second, it shows that she has the power to maintain her self-esteem through the too-loud barking noise of racial stigma.

Besides, sending Marguerite to the store to avoid her from doing the unthinkable, Momma Johnson resorts to singing hymns. This may sound ridiculous at first sight that an attacked person resorts to singing instead of reacting. Is it not ironic? Given that an attack is considered a serious offence to one's self-esteem, one does not expect the victim to sit with their arms crossed.

Like many African Americans, Momma Johnson is confronted with the mountain of racial prejudice that dehumanises them and robs them of their identity. Due to this, they develop self-pity and low self-esteem. The result of these negative feelings is that they give more attention to the opposition than to God.

Momma Johnson, an ardent woman of the Christian faith, is aware that the White girls are the forces of opposition she needs to overcome. At this point, these girls do not just represent young White girls who are innocent; at a deeper level, they symbolise the forces of racial prejudice that stigmatise African Americans. Momma Johnson uses wisdom and faith to outshine their threatening presence by singing hymns to praise God. Her focus on God does not mean she does not face opposition or that the resistance is not great. It simply demonstrates that she relies more on God's supernatural force to overcome things than on human strength. This approach should be considered a pivotal force to reckon with by most African Americans. Most African Americans trapped in the deep sea of racism have sunk not because they are weak. It is because they have given racism an undesirable place in their lives to conquer their souls and spirits. According to African Americans, they have not given God the rightful place. We do not say that one should not fight for their rights, for that is legitimate, but that our reliability, ability and dependency on God should be utmost. Until African Americans learn to disregard their understanding and step down with their inferiority, the superiority of God's wisdom will not step in to defend their course.

In addition, Momma Johnson's singing praises to God rather than allowing the White girls' threats to overshadow her belief affirms that praise makes the enemy to flee. Who is the enemy? This enemy, who is certainly not a friend to one's progress or well-being, can lead to one's stigmatisation, if care is not taken. In the case of Momma Johnson, the White girls' racist provocation, their obscene provocation is an external force of racism that threatens the self-esteem of African Americans so as to give them reason(s) to belittle them more. One of the weapons or tricks of the enemy is to arouse doubt, uncertainty, and fear.

Sometimes, one allows the opposition to triumph, not because they are infallible and cannot be overcome, but because one gives them the power to override one. When Momma Johnson starts praising God, the segregated wall of racial stigma, the White girls, built into her complex, are recompleted and rendered abstract since the initial purpose of their provocation is to divert her attention from praising God. Her new approach and strategy create confusion. Her response to them (with a system of faith and love) is the perfect weapon that causes the White girls to flee.

The girls flee because Momma Johnson's faith in God outweighs the number and purpose of their wicked schemes. This is undoubtedly what African Americans can do to overcome the wall of stigma built against them.

Conclusion

A keen look at Maya Angelou's *I Know Why the Caged Bird Sings* reveals her authorship as one of the most skilful female African American writers of her time. Like most of her contemporaries, Angelou has ingeniously documented the sad realities of the African American experience using *I Know Why the Caged Bird Sings* as a medium of language expression.

The work has established the complexities of racial stigmatisation that have strained human relationships. It is rightly said that the factor of race is a social indicator that favours the externalities of colour rather than the genuine inner worth of the individual. This is where the powerful hierarchical elements of racism come to the fore. This chapter has highlighted the stigma of being an African American in a racist society. Nature has made us equal. It is humankind that creates divisions in society for their benefit and stigmatisation. For that reason, it serves the purpose. But it also creates boundaries at the interpersonal, intergroup, and international levels that are often impossible to penetrate. Some commit crimes, and others only reap the consequences of being associated with the negative, whether in terms of their work, shared social identity, family, religion, or something as simple as being a scapegoat for the injustices that project their way into society.

What is important to learn from all these is that they reflect a sheer loss of human ability to distinguish between the good and the bad and the basic human essence of being kind and helpful toward others. And if this continues, it will serve no fruitful purpose in the long run, for we are all humans first, and the association we share with our family, religion, profession, socioeconomic status, and many more come later.

Since stigma remains a cancer to building healthy self-esteem, African Americans must learn to look beyond this misrepresentation. This power of transcendence gives humans the dominion to perceive identity reconstruction as a prime necessity for happiness. Given that the power of positive change lies in the hands of the beholder, African Americans have the power to project their identity to the forefront.

Abstract

Maya Angelou's *I Know Why the Caged Bird Sings* is a social weapon of self-awareness to voice the ills and grievances of such an institutionalised social system. The novel is a configuration of American society after the abolition of the slave trade, which paradoxically is still subject to racial discrimination and gender inequality. The African American woman has been marginalised as a passive victim of racial discrimination and gender inequality. Maya Angelou, who incidentally happens to be one of these women, reiterates this in her work. The absence of the duality of these two coexisting components has inevitably caused a significant disruption in American society's self-construction of the sublime. As a product of historical misconception, this constraint remains problematic and a stumbling block to social cohesion and integration. This chapter serves as a conduit for conscientising these individuals in order to re-ignite a never-die spirit of hope and belief in the American dream. In *I Know why the Caged Bird Sings*, she serves as the authorial voice of the female folk as a means to eradicate the warping forces of patriarchy. In this work, African American criticism and feminism are utilised as a screen to access the dimensions in which Angelou tailors to overcome patriarchy.

Keywords: racial stigma, gender, self-construction, sublime, African American criticism, feminism

References

Angelou, M. (1969). *I know why the caged bird sings*. New York: Random House.

Bernstein, J.B. (1996). *Karen Donnelly*. Westport, CT: Bergin Garvey.

Bloom, H. (1998). *Maya Angelou's why the caged bird sings*. Philadelphia: Chelsea House Producers.

Bulkin, N. (2016). I wish you were here. New York: Nightmare Magazine.

Collins, H. P. (1990). *Black feminist thought: Knowledge, consciousness and the Politics of Empowerment (2nd ed.)*. London & New York: Routledge.

Guerin. L. W. (1992). *A handbook of critical approaches to literature*. Oxford: Oxford University Press.

Griffin, F. J. (2004). Celebrating thirty years of black American literature and literary Studies: A review. *Journal of Black Studies, 35*(2), 165-175.

Hallwas, J. (2014). *Identity issues in I know why the caged bird sings*. US: The McDonough County Voice.

Hurston, Z. N. (1937). *Their eyes were watching God*. New York: Joshua Ballinger Lippincott

Lori, P. S. (2002). *Topdog/underdog*. New York: Theater Communications Group.

Morrison, T. (1987). *Beloved*. New York: Vintage International

Murphy, R. (1997). *The Bedford glossary of critical literary terms*. New York: Bedford Books.

Reginald, M. (2016). Past and current thoughts in African-American literary criticism. *International Journal of Education and Human Development, 2*(4), 34-37.

Gross, R. (2014). *Newsweek's original review of Maya Angelou's I know why the caged bird sings*. New York: Random House.

Yogita, G. (1999). African American literature, criticism and theory. In S. Ray, H. Schwarz, L. J. Villancanas, A. Moreiras, & A. Shemak (Eds.), *The Encyclopedia of Postcolonial Studies*. New Jersey: Blackwell.

THIRTEEN

On the Margins of National Heritage:
Colonising Conspiracy and Economic Misery in Helon Habila's Oil on Water

KOUBLI NOUANWA

The economy of a country, region or continent is the most vital and delicate sector where riches are crystallised and money concentrated. Great empires rest upon their economic prosperity to establish their hegemony and domination over the world. The success of Western empires, for example, hinges upon imperialism, which has been well blueprinted by colonial ideologists since the exploration period and the transatlantic slave trade. This is the case of the USA and many other Western empires that had colonies. Capitalist countries anchor their development on the economic exploitation of the underdeveloped countries or the colonised societies constituting the Third World. The so-called independent nations are deprived of their economic opportunities and plunged into economic malaise. This concept initially used to describe the USA's economic stagnation or recession of the 1970s is used in this study to paint the economic ordeal of the colonised peoples economically exploited by the capitalist powers. Rodney (1972) denounces colonialism as a harmful enterprise depriving the colonised societies of the benefit of their natural resources and labour: "African and Asian societies were developing independently until they were taken over directly or indirectly by the capitalist powers. When that happened, exploitation increased, and the export of surplus ensued, depriving the societies of the benefit of their natural resources and labour. That is an integral part of underdevelopment in the contemporary sense" (p. 16).

As stated earlier, the hegemonic position of the colonising empires is explained against the backdrop of the economic exploitation of poor nations. Memmi (1974) observes: "The deprivations of the colonized are [. . .] the direct result of the advantages secured to the colonizer" (p. 8). Because of these continued deprivations, imperialist exploitation of lands, fauna and flora and the economic dictatorship of the capitalist powers, most countries in Africa, Asia and Latin America are the worst economically backward of the globe. Placed into the exploitative hands of the capitalist world, the colonised nations are not given any chance to advance economically. According to Wa Thiong'o (1993, p. 68), neo-colonialism is materialised in "the dominance of the IMF and the World Bank in the determination of the economies and hence the politics and culture of the affected countries in Asia, Africa and Latin America" (p. 68). This is what economically maintains the colonised world in the lowest rung of development. Colonised societies are so politically and economically controlled and dominated that they cannot undertake their development freely and easily. Denouncing this harmful economic domination of the Western world in her seminal work, "Can the Subaltern Speak?" Spivak (2003) argues that: "The phased development of the subaltern is complicated by the imperialist project" (p. 25). This famous postcolonial scholar applies the term subaltern to the colonised to indicate how colonialism has subdued the colonised and left them powerless and voiceless, which impedes the development of their societies. Nowadays, this imperialist exploitation is unfortunately well maintained in the relations between the Western world and the Third World countries via neo-colonialism.

Neo-colonialism is the new form of economic, socio-political and cultural domination orchestrated against the so-called independent countries by their former colonial masters. Spivak (1985) refers to it as "the imperialist project, displaced and dispersed into more modern forms" (p. 243). This new facet of imperialism is often operated with the consent of the political leadership of the Third World. Analysing this, Ashcroft, Griffiths, and Tiffin (2002) argue that the twenty-first century is an economic, cultural and political legacy of Western imperialism (p. 216). In the twenty-first century (the neo-colonial era), the colonising empires connive with the puppet governments of the so-called independent countries to thieve away the economic wealth of the native populations. Habila's *Oil on Water* is written against the backdrop of the colonising agglomerate's continued economic exploitation of poor nations in connivance with the local government. With a postcolonial spirit, Habila in the text under consideration criticises the harmful diplomacy the Federal Nigerian Government entertains with the colonising capitalist world to pirate away the oil dividends of the Nigerian masses. When the latter insurrectionally react against the oppressing colonialist schemes, they are systematically eliminated. This is the cause of most political crimes, internal displacement and exiles observed in the seemingly decolonised world. Grossberg (1996) describes it as a "place subsumed within a history of movements and an experience of oppression" (p. 92). Due to this, the so-called decolonised Nigeria remains "an armed and commissioned camp to keep Negroes in slavery and kill the black rebel" (Du Bois 1935, p. 12).

Therefore, postcolonial literature of resistance and protest is committed to denouncing such tragedy perpetrated against the silenced masses. The likes of Habila are thus concerned with liberating the dominated "societies from economic injustice, social backwardness, and political reaction" (Ashcroft et al. 2002, p. 129). Given that what occurs to Nigeria occurs to many other colonised nations, this colonising conspiracy should be viewed as the major impediment to Nigeria's economic development and the general root cause of contemporary underdevelopment in the neo-colonised world.

Conspiring against the masses

As underlined earlier, this underdevelopment is today perpetrated against the neo-colonised societies by the metamorphosed form of colonialism called neo-colonialism. This new colonising ideology is the refined economic instrument of domination of the capitalist world over the poor nations. It keeps plundering the economy of poor countries since the formal end of colonisation. Since the 1960s, the so-called independent people's hopes to be free are proved illusory as they remain "The Wretched of the Earth." According to Wa Thiong'o (2009), the colonised remain "ensnared in neocolonialism, cold-war politics, and globalization" (p. 81). For the scholar, the two most visible facets of imperialism today are neocolonialism and the leadership of the USA. It should be recalled that the USA and the other colonial powers of Europe, which form the colonising world, connive criminally with the political leadership of the Third World, constituted of the economically poor and dependent countries. Owing to this conspiracy, the economic resources of the colonised subjects are monopolised by the colonising empires and their colonial agencies placed in the colonised areas. Informed by this, postcolonial writers like Habila are eager to speak for their voiceless subaltern fellows through postcolonial literature.

Oil on Water opens with the description of a fire accident which has claimed many Nigerian lives and left many physically handicapped and disfigured. This notorious event testifies to the continued criminal effects of colonial exploitation in Africa as the oil is exploited by the colonising multinational companies in total connivance with the Federal Nigerian government. This is materialised via the metropolitan agents such as James Floode, Black Suit, who criminally plot with the Nigerian State to cart away the oil riches and plunge the Nigerian people into immiseration. This colonising enterprise meets the postcolonial crusade launched by different groups of nationalist militants such as Black Belts of Justice, The Free Delta Army and the AK-47 Freedom Fighters (pp. 34-35).

In their well-tailored neo-colonial plan, the former colonial masters pass through the puppet government, which lubricates the way to the economic exploitation of the masses. Through *Oil on Water*, Habila exposes the selfish and subservient government which accepts and signs the exploitative economic partnership with European oil corporations to heist the natural riches, and the economic assets of the native population. Once the malicious imperial authorities are officially permitted to exploit the resources of the natives, forced and unholy pacts and negotiations with the local land custodians follow. Habila denounces this as he writes: "One day, early in the morning, Chief Malabo called the whole village to a meeting. Of course, he had heard the murmurs from the young people, and the suspicious whispers from the old people, all wondering what it was he has been discussing with the oilmen and politicians. Well, they had made an offer, they had offered to buy the whole village, and with the money—and yes, there was a lot of money, more money than any of them had ever imagined—and with the money, they could relocate elsewhere and live a rich life" (pp. 42-43). The postcolonial writer unmasks here a double-faceted colonising mechanism: the colonisers had first pauperised the colonised and then cynically appeared as a generous spirit to aid and assist economically the poor they had created. In addition to the mental, and cultural colonisation, they want to colonise the lands with all their amazing economic assets. And if the local authorities, the custodians of lands, oppose conspiring against their people, refuse to sell their land because it is where "they'd been born here, they'd grown up here, they were happy here, and though they may not be rich, the land had been good to them, they never lacked for anything," (p. 43) they are oppressed and suppressed. This is the case of Chief Malabo. As the latter refuses to sign the colonising agreement because it is "their ancestral land, this was where their fathers and their fathers' fathers were buried" (p. 43), the oil officialdom, in collaboration with the Nigerian bureaucracy, scheme anew hostilities and reprisals denounced as follows: "And already far off in the surrounding waters the oil company boats were patrolling, sometimes openly sending their men to the village to take samples of soil and water. The village decided to keep them away by sending out their own patrols over the surrounding river in canoes, all armed with bows and arrows and clubs and a few guns. But daily, Chief Malabo was feeling the pressure... One day the patrol came upon two oil workers piling soil samples into a speedboat. There was a brief skirmish, nothing too serious—one of the workers escaped with a swollen jaw, the other with a broken arm...but the next day the soldiers came" (pp. 43-44). As the land custodian has rejected the offer, and has opposed conspiring against his own people, the imperialists, aided by their political stooges, plot the intrusion into the natives' lands. To find a legal reason to oppress and suppress the natives and take their lands, the cunning colonialists use this seemingly mild violence by despicably exploiting the oil against the owner's consent. This aims at igniting the wrath and the violent reaction of the natives, which will be legally used against them.

Furthermore, the colonisers use false accusations and fake news to subdue the colonised. As a matter of fact, "the next day the soldiers came. Chief Malabo was arrested, his hand tied behind his back as if he were a petty criminal, on charges of supporting the militants and plotting against the federal government and threatening to kidnap oil workers. The list was long" (p. 44). Once the native occupants are dispossessed of their lands, rendered homeless and placeless, the colonisers can occupy the place and exploit the natural resources for pleasure and leisure. Unfortunately, the learned people amongst the natives, especially political intellectuals and lawyers, instead of succouring the powerless and defenceless natives, side selfishly and subserviently with the white invaders. While for instance, the Nigerian lawyer unpatriotically advises the natives to "consent to the oil company's demands, sell the land," (p. 44) the politician uses the blindfolding demagogy, assuring them trickily that: "their situation was receiving national attention, it was in the papers, and he was going to fight for them to see that their chief was returned safe and sound" (p. 44). It is worth underlining that this demagogue and traitor, who introduces himself as a senator, comes from Abuja, the political capital of Nigeria (p. 44). Such politicians, who are paradoxically the people's political representatives mainly living in cities, are disconnected from the local realities and the suffering conditions of colonised subjects. They just visit them for political harangues and manipulations. The said politician accompanies "two white men, oil executives" (p. 44) in order to hoodwink his colonised subjects into accepting the colonising pact of oil exploitation. Such colonial agents, in collaboration with the colonising force, re-tailor the colonising schemes whenever a postcolonial wall is erected against them. Fanon (1963) decries this stating: "Now, in the colonies, the economic conditions are conditions of a foreign bourgeoisie. Through its agents, it is the bourgeoisie of the mother country that we find present in the colonial towns" (p. 177). This bourgeoisie eliminates every postcolonial resistance.

Since Chief Malabo has become an impediment to economic exploitation, he is unjustly arrested, jailed and murdered in prison. It is narrated pertinently that "Chief Malabo, whenever they went to see him, told them not to give in, not to worry about him – but they could see how he was deteriorating every day. And then they went to see him one day and were told he was dead" (p. 44). This unfortunate situation occurs to Chief Malabo because within "the context of colonial production, the subaltern has no history and cannot speak" (Spivak 2003, p. 28). Chief Malabo is brutally murdered because he ventured to speak for his people, defending them against the invading forces of colonialism. It is worth stressing that within the framework of neo-colonialism, nationalists like Chief Malabo, who dare speak back to their colonial masters are pitilessly suppressed.

In addition to directly obstructing the economic opportunities of the Third World, the conspiracy between the colonised governments and the colonising empires blocks other health opportunities. When the medical investigations of medical experts are not given attention, when a whole population and the entire environment are ill because of oil toxins poorly managed by the powers that be, economic development is de facto nullified. Habila underlines this criminal act through the testimony of this medical doctor: "Well I did my duty as their doctor. I told them of the dangers that accompany that quenchless flare, but they wouldn't listen. And then a year later, when the livestock began to die and the plants began to wither on their stalks, I took samples of the drinking water and in my lab I measured the level of toxins in it: it was rising, steadily. In one year it had grown to almost twice the safe level. Of course, the people didn't listen, they were still in thrall to the orange glare. When I confronted the oil worker, they offered me money and a job. The manager, an Italian guy, wrote me a check and said I was now on their payroll" (p. 153). This medical doctor's testimony proves that the conspiracy against the masses is so intricate that the solution to the misery of the colonised is hard to be found. Despite the medical alert launched by the said doctor, the heartless colonisers, abetted by the sycophant local government, simply carry on with their criminal oil exploitation. When the local doctor takes the matter to the Nigerian government, they thank him and dump the results in some filing cabinet (p. 153). Even the international community, as well as the clergy, join in colonialist machinations by remaining silent. The doctor testifies thereof: "More people died and I sent my results to NGOs and international organizations, which published them in international journals and urged the government to do something about the flares, but nothing happened. The church also folded when Brother Jonah got a job as a clerk with the oil company. Almost overnight I watched the whole village disappear, just like that" (p. 153). This shows that the colonised Nigerian government, the colonising oil multinationals and Non-Governmental Organisations, as well as the church operate in tandem to economically oppress and suppress the colonised. Demagogically and hypocritically, they show their compassion for the colonised, but, in truth, it is humanitarian simulacrum.

The oppressing and suppressing violence of colonialism in exploiting the colonised is best understood against the backdrop of the colonial ideology, which conceives the non-Whites as their opposing human race to be dominated. Said (1979) writes in this regard: "There are Westerners, and there are Orientals. The former dominate; the latter must be dominated, which usually means having their land occupied, their internal affairs rigidly controlled, their blood and treasure put at the disposal of one or another Western power" (p. 36). From this desire to dominate the colonised, the colonialists developed the criminal desire to erase them through socio-political, cultural and economic oppression and suppression. According to Spivak (2003), the project of colonialism is "to constitute the colonial subject as Other. This project is also the asymmetrical obliteration of the trace of that Other in its precarious Subjectivity" (pp. 24-25). This elimination is much more effective in the economic domain, granted that without the economy, the existence of an individual or a society is reduced to nothing. Thus, colonialists work towards eliminating the colonised economically. This explains why their economy is under erasure (Spivak 2003, p. 24). All this aims at achieving their colonialist project of economic hegemony. Because of the erasing force of colonialism, the independence of the colonised is fruitless for them. Wa Thiong'o (1993) highlights the fruitlessness of independence entangled in the neo-colonial network when he states: "Independence which at the very least should have meant the liberation of a people's productive forces from foreign control was in most cases merely a change of form from colonial economic and political arrangement and practices to a more vicious neo-colonial arrangement" (p. 44). The productive forces of the colonised remain paralysed by the imperialist control of the colonising world. This is materialised through the conspiracy between the colonising powers and the subservient political leadership of the colonised world. According to Nkrumah (1963), colonialism "is creating client states, which it manipulates from the distance. It will distort and play upon, as it is already doing, the latent fears of burgeoning nationalism and independence" (p. xvi). Disenchanted and ensnared in neo-colonial schemes, the pauperised colonised populations are bound to resort to unorthodox and unethical ways and means to survive.

Plunging the Masses into Immiseration and Unethical Practices

The scientific oil process by the oil multinationals terribly endangers and damages the health of the surrounding humans, animals, plants and land fertility (because of the toxins, chemicals and fires emanating from the scientific oil process). This prompts economic crimes as it places the exploited subjects on the margins of their national riches and plunges them into abject poverty and wretchedness. The economically marginalised populations, being economically incapacitated, are exposed to instability, homelessness, placelessness, juvenile delinquency, and joblessness. They resort miserably to rural exodus, prostitution, unorthodox and illegal activities for survival.

As indicated above, oil pollutants and toxins jeopardise biodiversity. The negatively exploited environment is characterised by "the barrenness, the soil slick and the same indefinable sadness in the air as if a community of ghosts were suspended above the punctured zinc roof, unwilling to depart, yet powerless to return" (p. 10). It is worth underscoring that the barrenness of the soil, and the emptiness of the place are caused by the oil pollutants and toxins, the military violence used by the government soldiers and the postcolonial activists. Owing to this violence, there is economic malaise, as activities such as market and commerce are slowed down and stopped. This is illustrated by the case of a market woman who is on the run, having left all her goods behind to save her endangered life. The narrator discloses that: "For a moment, everyone froze. As I turned to ask the old man what was going on, a terrified market woman suddenly appeared in front of me, her eyes blinded by fear. The next minute, I was flat on my back and considerable mass was pinning me to the dusty ground, thus she was up on her feet and away, agile, almost airborne. Long afterward, I remembered her marketplace smell and her unseeing eyes above mine, and the moaning, terrified sound coming continuously from her mouth a sound she was unaware she was making" (p. 13). This is typical of terror-stricken places in neo-colonial regimes. In such a milieu, markets, the economic centres are reduced to ghost towns, shops and goods are dismantled and burned, which escalates into a severe economic crisis. Because of this economic malaise, the populations are relegated to abject poverty, even the richest, like kings and queens, businessmen and entrepreneurs, are exposed to economic downfall and wretchedness. Such is the example of Chief Ibiram whose house is as poor as his subjects'. His homestead is described as a dwelling with no "furniture and one large open window. The floor was covered with old straw mats on which we sank as if they were cushions of the softest down. The big man sat in the only chair in the room" (p. 17). Due to oil exploitation, a whole family with all properties may be found "all dead and decomposing" (p. 9). This is vividly narrated as follows: "Behind one of the houses we found a chicken pen with about ten chickens inside all dead and decomposing, the maggots trafficking beneath the feathers. We covered our noses and moved on to the next compound, but it wasn't much different: cooking pots stood open and empty on cold hearths, next to them stood water pots filled with water on whose surface mosquito larvae thickly flourished. It took less than an hour to traverse the little village, going from one deserted household to the next, taking pictures, hoping to meet perhaps one accidental straggler, one survivor to interview" (p. 9).

This ecological disaster provoked by the colonial exploitation of the oil not only damages people and their living conditions but also wildlife. The illustration is the case of the water environment, where lies the natives' natural wealth. Habila describes it as "expressionless water there were no birds or fish or other water creatures—we were alone" (p. 11). It is worth indicating that, because of the oil pressure, water, the most vital liquid has lost its naturalness. It is described as "snake, twisting and fast and slippery, poisonous. [...] old jute rope, frayed and breaking into jagged, feathery end ends, the fresh water abruptly replaced by a thick marshy tract of mangroves standing over still" (p. 37). Water, which in due course harbours an immense wealth of the population has become a disgusting place where the fishy smell is replaced by "the foul smell of the swamps," (p. 37) where are seen oddities such as "a piece of cloth, a rolling log, a dead fowl, a bloated dog belly-up with black birds perching on it, their expressionless eyes blinking rapidly, their sharp beaks savagely cutting into the soft decaying flesh [...], a human arm severed at the elbow" (pp. 37-38). It is worth recalling that the toxins and pollutants emanating from the oil production are not the only threats jeopardising the health of the colonised; they are dangerously entangled with the government soldiers on the one hand and the militants on the other hand. Owing to this, the masses are bound to live below the poverty line, unstable and despaired as they cannot plan for development. This is why, to the journalist's question about their happiness, a pauper answers, "I say how can we be happy when we are mere wanderers without a home?" (p. 45). Stressing their plight, the unstable subject carries on, "we'd lived in five different places now, but always we'd had to move. We are looking for a place where we can live in peace. But it is hard" (p. 45). For Habila, colonised societies like Nigeria are "impotent, helpless, like a man running in his sleep with his leg crossed" (p. 63). It should be understood that such physically and mentally unstable individuals are economically disoriented, as all they want is a home, not riches and goods. It must be observed that they are naturally subject to malnutrition, school dropping, illiteracy, prostitution, and rural exodus.

Living in a poisoned environment, with the fauna and flora intoxicated and destroyed by the oil chemicals and pollutants, living under the government's military terror and the freedom fighters' postcolonial violence, the colonised societies are reduced to famine and starvation. With regard to malnutrition, Michael, the son of a poor old man called Tamuno, is the real incarnation. In fact, because of pauperisation, this very young boy of ten "looked no more than ten years old, but he might have been older, his growth stunted by poor diet. His hair was reddish and sparse, his arms were bony like his father's" (p. 7). This child and his father, whose living condition is so abject, are described as being "both dressed in the same shapeless and faded homespun shirts and trousers, their hands looked rough and callused from seawater, they smelled of fish and seemed as elemental as seaweed (p. 7). In addition to being shabbily dressed and underfed, the child of the poor has no chance for education because of poverty and political trouble; the government's chief attention is self-enrichment, military investment and their allegiance to the colonising metropolis. Due to their wretchedness, Tamuno pitifully entreats Zaq and Rufus to take his child for a better education. Rufus states thereupon: "He want us to take the boy with us when we go back to Port Harcourt. [...]—Yes. He no get good future here. Na good boy, very sharp. He go help you and your wife with any work, any work at all, and you too go send am go school" (p. 39). If Tamuno ventures into entrusting his child to people he has just met, it really testifies to the gravity of poverty staring at the colonised. The wretched Tamuno and his son called Michael, have out of misery so deeply placed their hope in the unknown journalists that when they are responded: "we'll discuss it some more and let you know what we decide before all this over" (p. 41) they are utterly disappointed. When Michael begins crying, Zaq, out of pity, is forced to say: "We'll take him. We'll find a way [...]. But I will take him. I'll find a place for him somehow. And he could be an office boy at Star. Now, you stop crying" (p. 41). The poor child sees this opportunity as heaven offered him and, "at his father's urging the boy ran to Zaq and wrapped his arms around the veteran journalist's midsection" (p. 41). It should be noted that poverty in the colonised world does not just stare at poor jobless people like Tamuno and their children; even professionals, civil servants and youths in general are also enmeshed in the economic malaise.

Poverty is so generalised and endemic in the colonised world that even civil servants live below the poverty line. This is the case of Zaq, a seasoned journalist who says: "I live in a single room. At the end of the month I'm hardly able to pay my rent" (p. 41). Like Zaq, young people in their numbers face economic ordeals. This is the case of Rufus, another journalist whose childhood and professional life are marked by economic misery. As an adolescent, he was obliged to drop school and, on his father's advice, got trained to secure a certificate to survive.

It should be underlined that in the economically torn colonised world where riches are poorly husbanded by the powers that be, youths are professionally disoriented. They are just opportunistic. This is why, at eighteen, Rufus turns disappointingly to journalism. He narrates it as follows: "I fell into journalism out of necessity, not because I had proven talent like the Max Tekena, or any ambition to be the next Zaq" (p. 70). This explains why in the colonised world, there are so many professional misfits, as the poor youths are just passionate about getting any kind of job, no matter the risks and the academic background or school profile. Being jobless, the pauperised youths whose economic opportunities are robbed by the colonising conspiracy are relegated to blue-collar jobs. The perfect illustration is Rufus' story pathetically narrated as follows: "I did odd jobs at *Whispers*, cleaning the office in the morning, washing the managing editor's car once a week, running errands, and taking pictures of "hawkers from the streets." In return I was paid a thousand naira a month, and was to sleep in the office. That was how I became journalist" (p. 71). This testifies to the joblessness and unemployment that characterise the poor colonised youths. They are ill-prepared to face life because they are not educated or poorly educated. In addition to surviving miserably through odd jobs and meagre salaries, the poor colonised populations are exposed to rural exodus, in desperate search for stability. This is once more symbolised via the life of Rufus. He recounts his painful journey to the urban centre of Port Harcourt thus: "I walked to suppress my hunger and the pain in my legs and rising cold biting at my skin, and when I got tired of walking I turned back. The men, back from their futile search for shelter, had started a fire; its flame glowed weakly, wavering in the humid wind coming off the water, briefly illuminating their anxious faces. I joined them and stood there, solemn, not talking, staring into the halfhearted fire, listening to the waves and noting how the sound they made oddly resembled the rumblings in our stomachs, waiting and hoping, but not expecting, that the boat would return" (p. 83). The most heartrending fact is that these pauperised youths who leave the hinterlands for the gentrified place following the Western landscape of urban disorder end up as "prostitutes on Bar Beach. Some ended up pregnant and homeless on the streets, and they were the lucky ones. The unlucky ones died, their bodies discovered in the water days later, washed up in faraway Lekki. Raped. Brutalized. Strangled. Stabbed" (p. 119). It is due to this unbearable immiseration that the colonised lose their sanity, get madly fixated on money possession, neglecting all the other aspects of their lives, including their physical lives. This justifies the testimony of the medical Doctor which unfolded as follows: "I set up mobile clinics in my boat, I held educational classes in churches and schools, talking to teachers and pastors and community leaders. But I soon discovered that the village's chief discontent was not over their health; they were a remarkably healthy people, actually. One day an elder looked me in the face and said, I am not ill. I am just poor. Can you give me medicine for that? We want that fire that burns day and night. He told me that, plainly, pugnaciously (pp. 151-152). And because of this destabilising, dehumanising poverty other colonised people are bound to resort to unorthodox and immoral means to alleviate their poverty and assert themselves economically. They have realised that to survive and become rich in a place of "aridity, and want and barrenness," (p. 149) they must use chiefly kidnapping and oil trafficking.

Kidnapping the oil executives and their family members in Nigerian society (ridden by unfair power relationships, unjust economic distribution of riches) is one of the best ways used by the economically exploited and marginalised subjects to regain their thieved oil dividends. In a country where many jobless university youths are "forced to take a job far below their qualifications," (p. 201) young men like Salomon, Jamabo and Bassey, the victims of the colonising conspiracy do ethically normalise kidnapping reasoning that: "It wasn't even kidnapping; I'd just be collecting payment for all the pain these people caused to me, a refund for all my investment in Koko. And that was what convinced me. The Oga had insulted me badly, he'd taken away my pride, my dignity, my manhood, and all the time I was serving him honestly, diligently. I trusted him. And another point, the money wasn't even coming out of his pocket: the oil company pays the ransom, and Bassey said that if you thought about it carefully, you'd realize that the money came from our oil, oil, so we would be getting back what was ours in the first place. Well, I started to really think. This was the chance of a lifetime" (pp. 220-221). As James Floode, the British oil official has taken Salomon's fiancée, Koko as well as his oil dividend, Salomon believes that kidnapping his wife Elizabeth Floode and demanding a huge amount of ransom is the best way of avenging the harm inflicted upon him. As they will receive "over three hundred thousand each," (p. 221) the future rich Salomon says: "With that kind of money I could get out of the country and no one would ever find me" (p. 221). If the Salomons and Jamabos seek to regain their economic wealth and health, and revenge themselves through kidnapping, others choose to do it via oil trafficking.

For his economic assertion, Rufus' father and his friend Emmanuel resort to smuggling oil, using bribery and corruption as the lubricating means. He explains it remorselessly to his son thus: "This is the only business booming in this town. I buy from little children. I buy cheap and I sell cheap. You remember your friend John? Well, Emmanuel has proved himself to be a true friend. He's the only one of my former colleagues whom I can still call a friend. He came up with this plan. We started the whole thing with his savings. It's not a bad business, really. We get by, we give the police a little something to look the other, but sooner or they'll get greedy. They'll arrest us. Or take over the whole business themselves. I don't want you to be here when that happens" (p. 69). This illegal business is carried out with children who, because of the poor living condition, are obliged to be initiated into illicit activities. This negatively impacts on their moral conduct throughout their whole existence. As they plot with adults to paradoxically thieve the oil which naturally belongs to them (which is pirated by the colonising forces), they are likely to keep on robbing and trafficking for life.

In the same vein, the unbearable economic condition which causes the colonised people to survive through illegal activities damages their religious faith and moral dignity and exposes them to drug addiction and doping. In this regard, Rufus gives this testimony about his father: "In the two days I spent at home before returning to Port Harcourt, I saw how much father had changed. He has turned his back on religion, and now smoked and drank *ogogoro* almost nonstop. He left home early in the morning in a pickup truck to go to the bush, where he and his partner bought the petrol from the kids, and returned home only after mid-night, often drunk" (p. 70). The economic malaise warrants thus the reason why many colonised people, especially youths are initiated into juvenile delinquency, felony, banditry and many other evils at an early age, which justifies the reason why colonised areas are the hotbed of insecurity. This, it needs to be recalled is the effect of the colonising conspiracy dynamically sustained by the Euro-American colonising forces. Denouncing this, Cesaire (1972) writes: "*I* am talking about natural *economies* that have been disrupted - harmonious and viable economies adapted to the indigenous population - about food crops destroyed, malnutrition permanently introduced, agricultural development oriented solely toward the benefit of the metropolitan countries, about the looting of products, the looting of raw materials" (p. 7). The colonising powers of Europe in connivance with the compliant post-independent governments are thus the reason behind the economic lethargy of Africa and many other colonised across the globe. The independence of these countries is just a farce. Informed by this failure of independence, Fanon (1963) argues that "Decolonization, which sets out to change the order of the world, is, obviously, a program of complete disorder" (p. 35). This disorder is mainly economic as the stability or instability of individuals or societies is predicated on economic conditions, riches or poverty. Closely observed, Third World countries are generally dependent on the industrialised world because of neo-colonial machinations orchestrated by the colonising monsters. Through their modern imperialism, they contour and control the poor nations' economies. Nkrumah (1963) backs this up as he states: "Imperialism is still a most powerful force to be reckoned with in Africa. It controls our economies. It operates on a worldwide scale in combinations of many different kinds: economic, political, cultural, educational, military" (p. xvi). Unfortunately, the economies of poor colonised countries are still contoured by the colonising powers. Oils, fauna and flora, land and subsoil resources and many other raw materials in poor nations are still subtly exploited by imperialist societies resulting in the lack of economic development.

Conclusion

In sum, Habila in *Oil on Water* paints the paradox of independence in Third World countries. These countries are placed on the margins of their own national riches because of the neo-colonial schemes of the capitalist monstrosity. The latter, in complicity with the leaders of the colonised world oppress and suppress the native populations economically. If in most colonised countries, "The Beautyful Ones Are Not Yet Born" since the 1960s, it is mostly due to this dynamic continuance of imperialism known today as neo-colonialism. In his text under study, the Nigerian postcolonial writer denounces this new form of colonialism which is materialised in the bilateral and multilateral relations between the Western capitalist world and the dependent or seemingly independent governments of the Third World. Through these deceitful brotherly relations, the capitalist world succeeds in impoverishing and dominating the economy of poor nations and establishes her international hegemony. It must be understood that the colonising countries act and react collectively against the disunited colonised countries through their multinationals and commercial partnerships. This is where their strength lies. Nkrumah (1963) pertinently argues that "the strength of the imperialist lies in our disunity" (p. xvi). So, the colonised societies must use the same collective actions and reactions against the oppressive forces of imperialism to wrench themselves free from the domineering system of imperialism. Furthermore, postcolonial writers and scholars like Habila are responsible for speaking for the voiceless masses by denouncing imperialist ramifications and guiding their colonised fellows to the ideal of unity. This stirs up postcolonial nationalism and unity, which resiliently work towards fagocitating neo-colonial viruses for true decolonisation to take shape.

Abstract

Post-independent nations across the globe continue to grapple not only with severe socio-political unrest, scientific and technological backwardness, and economic malaise due to the dynamic imperialist domination. In this neo-colonial era, the Western world, through its colonising multinational corporations and financial empires, continues establishing a power structure that economically marginalises the colonised world, ideologically constructed as the Third World. Conniving with the profiteer political leadership of the colonised world, Western empires form a whole colonising agglomerate that pitilessly thieves away the vital economic dividends of the already historically impoverished populations. The national riches and opportunities such as oils, diamonds, fauna and flora are still the economic stronghold of the colonising empires. Throughout the colonial networks, such as multinational companies and international organisations, with the connivance of the political leadership of the Third World, they establish their capitalist commerce to the detriment of the colonised masses. This is what Helon Habila in *Oil on Water* denounces. His novel unveils the criminal conspiracy orchestrated by the colonising Europe and the puppet Nigerian government to pirate the oil dividends of Nigeria. This postcolonial condition imperils the economic health of Nigeria. Read against the backdrop of postcolonial theory, this paper holds that the continued colonialist exploitation of the Third World by the colonising empires plunges colonised societies into chronic economic subalternity and dependency.

Keywords: Neo-colonialism, Conspiracy, Colonising World, Third World, Economic Malaise.

References

Ashcroft, B., Griffiths, G., & Tiffin, H. (2002) (Eds.). *The Empire Writes Back: Theory and Practice in postcolonial literatures.* 2nd ed. London & New York: Routledge.

Césaire, A. (1972). *Discourse on Colonialism.* New York & London: Monthly Review Press.

Du Bois, W.E.B. (1935). *Black Reconstruction: An essay toward a History of the Part Which Black Folk Played in the Attempt to Reconstruct Democracy in America, 1860-1880.* New York: Harcourt, Brace and Company.

Fanon, F. (1963). *The Wretched of the Earth.* New York: Grove Weidenfeld.

Grossberg, L. (1996). Identity and Cultural Studies: Is That All There Is? In Hall and Du Gay (Eds.), *Questions of Cultural Identity.* London: Sage Publications.

Habila, H. (2010). *Oil on Water.* London: W. W. Norton.

Memmi A. (1974). *The Colonizer and the Colonized.* London: The Orion Press.

Nkrumah, K. (1963). *Africa Must Unite.* New York: Frederick A. Praeger.

Rodney, W. (1972). *How Europe Underdeveloped Africa.* Nigeria: Panaf Press.

Said, E. (1979). *Orientalism*. New York: Vintage Books.
Spivak, G. (1985). Three Women Texts and a Critique of Imperialism. *The Chicago Journal, 12*(1), 243-261.
Spivak, G. (2003). Can the Subaltern Speak? In Ashcroft, Griffiths & Tiffin (Eds.). *The Postcolonial Studies Reader*. London & New York: Routledge.
Wa Thiong'o, N. (1993). *Moving the Centre: Struggle for Cultural Freedoms*. London: James Curry.
Wa Thiong'o, N. (2009). *Something Torn and New: An African Renaissance*. New York: Basic Civitas Books.

FOURTEEN

Santa Claus on the Cross:
A Postmodernist Reading of John Nkemngong Nkengasong's God Was African and Salman Rushdie's Fury

ETHEL JOFFI MOLUA-EWUSI

Shweder (1995), in an essay about Santa Claus on the cross, exposes the idea by Geertz (2000), an American anthropologist, who observed an experience of a visitor in Japan who wandered into a shop in Tokyo and saw the effigy of Santa Claus nailed to a cross! The image of Santa Claus on the cross is a potent metaphor in postcolonial, postmodern studies. It takes debates to different levels and great magnitudes of interpretation of discourses. In this work, it is used as a deconstructive metaphor to show how symbols lose their original connotations in the postmodern world when histories are questioned, including whether symbols still have apt messages to convey. The work will be divided into three parts, part one discusses the universalism of symbols, part two, the grafting of new histories and deconstructing these symbols. Part three reconciles new ideologies in the third space.

The Universalism of Symbols

From time immemorial, symbols have been used to convey messages. Anderson (1995) notes that in the postmodern world, symbols have become even more evident and less significant and are more widely used especially in the era where technology is trending. Symbols travel all over the world to connote, denote and convey various messages. When symbols are just a click away from our electronic devices and it is misinterpreted, it is therefore more or less intentional. In postmodernist discourse, no style dominates. There are so many cultures on the loose and on display, so people feel free to play around with them as they desire, and inventive symbols are now in universal parades; consequently, there are black, coloured and white Santas who can even be nailed to the cross.

Symbols, whether verbal or visual inform cultures in the most curious ways. The semiotics of dressing, for instance, is central to the perception of self-presentation and identity. The semiotics of the crucifix informs and symbolises Christianity, redemption and everything else that comes with the notion of Jesus on the cross. Conservatively, colonial discourse stipulates the symbol of Christianity as a discourse that represents truth beyond words and culture. Therefore, it could never be misinterpreted and certainly not played around with. However, Christianity is still one of the biggest tools of the colonisers, which has been interpreted differently by scholars across the world. When a religious symbol like the crucifix is grossly misinterpreted in a country like Japan, so many questions are left unanswered, and it can trigger many interpretations.

First of all, the American occupation of Japan after the second world war, with the bombing of Hiroshima and Nagasaki, has never fully been forgiven by the formerly colonised Japan. It is a gross satire with a tongue-in-cheek when a Santa effigy is nailed to the cross. Santa, like a martyr, becomes synonymous with Jesus. The notion of satire has been greatly used as a counter-discursive strategy in postcolonial literature which represents a situation of Santa Claus on the cross.

Satire is a device of social correction used by writers of all genres and at all times. Rushdie and Nkengasong use satire in the selected novels as a powerful counter-discursive tool to ridicule the dominant colonial discourse as well as contemporary ills. Their use of satire attempts to expose individuals, groups, institutions, societies, ideas or beliefs to ridicule or contempt. It creates humour by exposing folly. Irony and wit are the most powerful weapons of satire. Another precious weapon of the satirist is comic exaggeration which the writer attempts to interrupt and upset the original, and the reader recognises traits of the original, just like in the case of Santa Claus on the cross. The idea of Santa on the cross represents a Manichean opposition. Santa, an imaginary legend is elevated to take the position of the son of God on the cross. Within postcolonialism, writers try to overturn the colonialist mindset to favour the formally colonised.

Bombabili in *God Was African* cries out loud for the Africans to put their gods at the centre. With the coming of Christianity, the native religious systems were disrupted. The acceptance of Christianity meant the rejection of the values that held the clan together. The coloniser denounced the rites and rituals of the colonised. Many of the doctrines of Christian theology are different from and opposed to the myths and concepts of the colonised society.

Awoonor (1975, p. 22) argues that Christianity "placed God too remote from man in time and space." He further notes that the doctrine of the Trinity was difficult for the African mind to comprehend or agree with. The idea of heaven as a place where one is rewarded for certain deeds of obedience to God's laws on earth is non-existent in African religious thought. All this is counter discursive, which Bombabili adopts in *God Was African*. When Kendem asks why he still performs rituals and offers sacrifices, he answers:

> Why not? We wul not surrender. We have many gods. One big one... Fuondem is the big God, and many small God. Small God accommodate in the forest and in the hill like Nyimbong, and in the rock and in the valley, and in the waterfall like Lebialem. When I hungry, I gallivant to the forest, and harvest fruit and eat. When I wan to dring water I gallivant to Ntsembeuh and dring water. Why do you tink that I should not give goats and palm wine to the God who live in the forest and in the waterfall who give me everything? (Nkengasong, 2015, p.129)

He paints the African God as a merciful and generous provider, which starkly opposes the doctrine that the coloniser preached and he regards Christianity as the great opponent of Africa's freedom. In the above excerpt, even the English language is deconstructed to suit the purpose of the speaker.

In both novels under study, the contexts are deeply postmodern and very similar to Truett Anderson's view of postmodern studies, which connote fluctuating philosophies, changing styles, and behaviours. Above all, it brings about a psychological shift. Postmodernism even changes the way we study the past. The postmodern character, as we see in the novels, tries to adjust to shifting contexts. Much of what was once considered canonical is now negotiated. New roles are being ascribed to different situations, and what was considered as a tradition is often revised and revisited. And sometimes, of course, the negotiation escalates into conflict.

Talking about arts, Anderson (1995, p. 23) expatiates that postmodern art is characterised by "pastiche and collage." Art in a postmodern world does not belong to a unitary frame of reference, not to a project or a utopia. The plurality of perspectives leads to a "fragmentation of experience," the "collage becoming a key artistic technique of our time" (Anderson, 1995, p. 23). Styles from different periods and cultures are put together; in postmodern art, high-tech may exist side by side with antique columns and romantic ornamentation, the effects being shocking and fascinating.

In the novels under study, various cultures are put on display either through their symbols, discourse or ideology. Postmodern characters change depending on the context in which they find themselves. Rushdie paints a completely protean society occupied by Indians and other nations in the American diaspora. In the protean American society, a variety of religious beliefs exist, and characters are free to navigate in any space that they desire. There are many religious outlets which constitute the core of proteanism as seen in the passage below:

> The boy looked at him blankly. I, sir? Swearing, sir? When? This was odd. All the way, Solanka explained. At everyone within shouting distance. Motherfucker, Jew, the usual repertoire. Urdu, he added, in Urdu, to make things clear, meri madri zaban hai. Urdu is my mother tongue. Beloved blushed, deeply, the color spreading all the way to his collar line, and met Solanka's gaze with bewildered, innocent dark eyes. Sahib, if you heard it, then it must be so. But, sir, you see, I am not aware. Solanka lost patience, turned to go. It doesn't matter, he said. Road rage. You were carried away. It's not important. As he walked off along Broadway, Beloved Ali shouted after him, needily, asking to be understood: It means nothing, sahib. Me, I don't even go to the mosque. God bless America, okay? (Rushdie, 2002, p. 59)

In the above quotation, there is mention of Urdu, mosque, God, and Jew which all represent different religious outlets, thereby portraying the everchanging postmodern American society. All these religious spaces jostle for attention for their own religion to be more prolific. In this epoch, we see a globalised city. Despite the setting, most of the characters are postmodern characters, and they change frequently as the situation demands. Rushdie notes still in *Fury* that: "… These days when everything was changing it was a satellite high above the ocean, he couldn't be sure. In these days when the age of pulse was giving way to the age of tone. When the epoch of analog (which was to say also of the richness of language, of analogy) was giving way to the digital era, the final victory of the numerate over the literate" (Rushdie, 2002, p. 6).

In these days therefore, things and people are not stable. People change their visions and dreams within the spaces and just like Lifton (1995) had predicted in "The Protean Style" that "today, it is not so unusual to encounter several such shifts accomplished relatively painlessly within a year, or even a month, whether in politics, aesthetic values, or style of living. Among many groups, the rarity is the man who has gone through life holding firmly to a single ideological vision" (Lifton, 1995, p. 131).

A powerful symbol that Rushdie uses in *Fury* is the doll. Little Brain, who is a creation by Professor Solanka, instead of remaining a puppet after Solanka breathes in her, becomes human and dominates Solanka, her creator. The image of the doll that Solanka creates reminds us vividly of the colonial situation where the coloniser relegated the other to the peripheries. But in the course of time and history, the colonised symbolised by Little Brain becomes rebellious and questions the coloniser. Little Brain, a puppet, becomes human and dominates the human world, and humans instead see her as a role model. This is another Santa Claus on the cross. God, in his creation, created Adam and Eve, who were flawed shortly after. Ironically, Malik Solanka creates a doll called Little Brain who becomes very perfect and a role model to humans!

In the postmodern era, signs and symbols can be juxtaposed to graft new histories. One of the questions that this research intends to answer is: when these symbols lose their original message and a new meaning is grafted, does that new message erase the original one, or it just supplements the new knowledge?

Grafting New Histories

In the postmodern era, signs and symbols can be juxtaposed to graft new histories. One of the questions that this research intends to answer is: when these symbols lose their original message and a new meaning is grafted, does that new message erase the original one or it just supplements the new knowledge? Grafting is a borrowed term from horticulture wherein a seed is inserted in the trunk of an original tree trunk and after some time, it begins to grow. In this case, the past becomes like the trunk of the tree and new histories are grafted at the trunk. Therefore, new branches constitute their own truths that are borrowed from the main past, which remains static even though it sprouts new ideologies.

In postmodern studies, historical ideologies are challenged, reassessed and deconstructed. For a symbol to be accepted as a sign, it means that it holds a historical notion of past reality. The attributes and symbol of debasement that the colonised depicted in colonial discourse were generally accepted in the curriculum of those discourses. The colonised represented everything black and evil which stood as a direct opposite to the civil white coloniser. Images and pictures, as well as these facts, were represented in books of different fields of study. History, therefore which was written with an intention, serves as knowledge, a discourse and an ideology. In postmodernist reasoning, history is not a science therefore, it is not tested and cannot be proven without archaeological artefacts. With texts and symbols as the main proof of particular histories, they can be reconstructed, deconstructed and rewritten.

History is sometimes multifaceted, and it may not carry a crystal-clear message when communicated. History can be interpreted through different ages and generations. In postcolonial studies, history failed when it gave the power of discourse to the coloniser. Colonial history failed to recognise the colonised as humans. And therefore became an archetype and adapted stringent ideologies of identity. Postcolonialism orates the intent of the coloniser through standard and oral history. It states that history was geared towards degrading the formerly colonised and situating the coloniser on the platform to be privileged. Ironically, postcolonialism contradicts the attributes of the coloniser through counter-discourse and grafting new histories.

The question of colonised history has been a long debate in postcolonial studies. For the coloniser, history began with the coming of the coloniser to the colonised societies. History may not have been documented, but it existed in other forms such as oral tradition, archaeology, musicology and so on, most outstandingly, it is seen in a people's culture. Awoonor (1975, p. 71) propounds that "religion, worship, ritual, art and a whole way of life had been established which was distinctively African in the pure cultural and geographical sense." That is to say, if one claims that if the colonised had no history that would mean extinguishing the founding principles of its societies.

When colonialism arrived in Africa, a new history was born. It became an emergence of history according to the narrator's or the coloniser's voice because previous African histories became invisible and non-existent. Colonialism denied the history of the colonised. However, some scholars contend this was easily done due to the lack of proper written records. The colonised's history was written by the coloniser, who twisted it to the racist colonial discourse by naming the colonised with negative attributes. It is this distorted history that Bombabili in *God Was African* tries to reclaim. He attempts to restore lost African dignity by invoking and reconstructing a heroic meaningful African history. History, in this case, is a remembrance of the past. He uses intimate knowledge of his people's history through myths and legends. He is unwilling to accept their inferior position in society and resists the white man's culture proudly and openly by reinforcing historical facts on colonised consciousness. Bombabili's reclamation of history dethrones the white man's God. He argues:

> We didin knows what we was doing and we put our jujus in the fire and burn it. Is only after that we knows that God was African. Let me tell you again to and fro that God was African. And yet you pipos says that God was satanical and that our culture was babarical. And yet we didin hammer our God on the cross. We didin beat him to dead. You see, we was not babarical to our God. We show love to our God. That why we offer them sacrifice. We slaughter goat and give them to eat and we

give them raffia wine to dring. We give them good raffia wine to dring.
But you pipu say that we are satanical pipu (Nkengasong, 2015, p. 129).

The above quotation shows that Nkengasong uses even language as a counter discursive strategy. He mocks the English language and twists it to suit the context of a native African. The title *God Was African* offers a liberating and transformative paradigm of canonical identity. It foregrounds not only a counter-discursive voice but also an interrogation of history at the level of who the real creator is. In replacing the canonical Western God by contextualising God as an African, the novel attempts to formulate a history comprehensible to the postcolonial African. Bombabili searches for an authentic cultural self-awaiting retrieval and renewal beneath the contamination of white culture which claims to erase black history.

Nkengasong's return to the past is to restore truth. Nkosi (1983) postulates that the African has discovered that his history has been tactfully veiled in a shroud of mystery because if it came out that the Africans also had a culture and poetry, it would establish their humanity and their right to a fair deal. As Nkosi avers further: "It is against this background of appalling ignorance about himself, his history and his particular mould of personality, that the African is reacting so violently" (Nkosi, 1983, p. 111). Said (1993) has a similar view with Nkosi when he propounds that not only recently have Westerners become aware that what they have to say about the history and the cultures of subordinate people challengeable by the peoples themselves, people who a few years back were simply incorporated, culture, land, history, and all, into the great Western Empires, and their disciplinary discourses. This analysis shows that history can be deconstructed with time as ideas evolve and people revise their roles of subordination.

The image of God as African is as satirical as Santa Claus on the cross. One great sentiment is aroused in this case; there is a twist of irony which also becomes a counter-discursive strategy. It offers a healing therapy to the colonised psyche under the discursive power satirising the founder of Christianity.

In *Fury*, Rushdie's method of grafting colonised histories is by means of reclamation of history even if he does not go down memory lane but is preoccupied with reading history in the making:

You come at great historical moment, he told Solanka portentously. Indian people of Lilliput-Blefuscu have finally standed up for our right. Our culture is ancient and superior and will henceforth prevail. Let the fittest survive, isn't it. For one hundred years good-for-nothing Elbee cannibals drank grog-kava, glimigrim, flunec, Jack Daniel's and Coke, every kind of godless booze-and made us eat their shit. Now they can eat ours instead. Please: enjoy your stay (Rushdie, 2002, p. 206).

It is interesting to note that from the above quotation, history is not only made, but the Manichean pyramid is also overturned because the subaltern culture now has a voice instead of keeping quiet in the shadows of the subaltern space. Significantly, in the above passage, counter-discourses question and rewrite histories. In the counter-discursive age, the colonised write their own histories and give a voice to their past.

Reviewing history today, it can be brought under contest and questioning, it is presumed to be partly because of the traumatic discourse of colonialism, which has meant a loss of confidence in the colonised reference to the past. Besides, there is a lack of evidence in history books to depict how barbaric the colonised was. History books can become subjects of just ideological caricature, literature, fiction and entertainment.

Similarly, in *Fury,* Rushdie shows that history can be deconstructed with time as ideas evolve and people revise their roles of subordination. Solanka's puppets gain a voice and break free from his colonial grasp, and Rushdie says: "once again, Solanka's fictional characters began to burst out of their cages and take to the streets. From around the world came news of their images, grown gigantic, standing many stories high on city walls" (Rushdie, 2002, p. 194). The image of the cage is a great figurative device that Rushdie uses to symbolise Solanka's dominance over his creations. The fact that they have broken free from the cage denotes a counter discursive process.

Instead of Solanka being the star for his magical inventions, he becomes almost muted like the Spivakian subaltern and Rushdie (2002, pp. 84-85) says: "all this Malik Solanka witnessed from a distance with growing horror. This creature of his own imagining, born of his best self and purest endeavour, was turning before his eyes into the kind of monster of tawdry celebrity he most profoundly abhorred." Solanka remains aloof and just observes from a distance because at this point, he becomes the subaltern who cannot come out in the open to display his dissatisfaction. A great idea behind a Santa Claus on the cross situation is the idea of irony and the inversion of the Manichean pyramid. Solanka, the creator, takes the bottom of the pyramid and Little Brain ironically becomes the Self and relegates him to the background as the Other.

Solanka in all his creations, is a colonialist who claims to create and destroy histories through the characters he makes in the form of dolls and cartoons. There is a great generational gap between Solanka and his creations, especially Little Brain, because of their different historical experiences. Little Brain follows the postmodern society into which she is born and embraces new cultural practices that are profitable to her ever-changing nature, much to Solanka's disdain, as seen in the quotation below:

> She had outgrown her creator-literally; she was life-size now, and several inches taller than Solanka - and was making her own way in the world. Like Hawkeye or Sherlock Holmes or Jeeves, she had transcended the work that created her, had attained the fiction's version of freedom. She now endorsed products on television, opened supermarkets, gave after-dinner speeches, emceed gong shows. By the time Brain Street had run its course she was a full-fledged television personality... (Rushdie, 2002, p. 83).

Rushdie's figurative use of allusions to Holmes or Jeeves shows the context to which Little Brain is grown and the more she grows, the more she conflicts with her creator, Solanka. Despite Solanka's disdain over her growth towards proteanism, she still enlarges and motivates hundreds of people to escape from parental grip and fixities; to seek the greater rewards of postmodernism as traditional family practices and values gradually decline in the process of an ever-changing context. As she blooms and expands, Little Brain grows more as Rushdie narrates:

> She had become the Maya Angelou of the doll world, as relentless an autobiographer as that other caged bird, her life the model for millions of young people - its humble beginnings, its years of struggle, its triumphant overcomings; and, O, her dauntlessness in the face of poverty and cruelty!... The extraordinary thing about her fan base was its catholicity: boys dug her as much as girls, adults as much as children. She crossed all boundaries of language, race, and class. She became, variously, her admirers' ideal lover or confidante or goal. Her first book of memoirs was originally placed by the Amazon people in the nonfiction lists. The decision to move it, and the subsequent volumes, across into the world of make-believe was resisted by both readers and staff. Little Brain, they argued, was no longer a simulacrum. She was a phenomenon. The fairy's wand had touched her, and she was real (Rushdie, 2002, p. 84).

The above quotation clearly shows Rushdie's narrative technique of personification. Right in front of her creator, Little Brain surpasses the level of a stuffed doll and walks boldly into the human world without fear or favour from her creator, Solanka. Her doll-like creation, which could have been seen as a deficiency, does not destroy her dreams to rise to greater postmodern heights. Little Brain defies Solanka's command and does all that he does not want her to do.

Reconciling New and Multiple Ideologies in the Third Space

Postmodernism connotes freedom. Characters have free play in many situations. They can transcend various boundaries and misuse symbols. It is precisely this diffuse and ambiguous movement across cultures that is the subject of the present postmodern worry. The challenges therefore are far-reaching and may present various negative effects if not handled carefully. Therefore, mutating symbols are not always progressive if not handled carefully.

These changing conditions of cultures and histories have reshaped perceptions of realities. The rapid changes in postmodern society, as represented in the novels under study, connote that history and symbols appear to be fractured or fracturing. The future is gloomy and vague. There is a break in continuity due to complex mutations of ideologies. There is therefore an urgent call for a middle ground. It now seems quite incredible that anyone could have ever believed in the hierarchy of history and colonial discourse.

In the same light, Munslow (2006, p.15) notes that "we have now lost the old, modernist sense of history as the fount of wisdom or teacher of moral or intellectual certainty. What this means is that any study of what history is cannot be other than located within its social and cultural context." More so, postmodernism or deconstructive history challenges the traditional paradigm at every turn. The past becomes a text that has to be rewritten. During this era, history and symbols are in danger of being misinterpreted and overturned.

One of the major questions posed is whether these new voices that are grafted have the credibility of truth. Truth, however, is relative, and it depends on the point of view of the person in question. To the coloniser, empirical truths cannot be broken simply because the colonised have found a voice to debunk their theories. This ushers us to the notion of third spacing mostly associated with Homi Bhabha. It holds a liberating voice as characters have the liberty to navigate in-between spaces while celebrating selfhood.

This concept comes into play here when various symbols have lost their original meaning and new histories are grafted. It serves as a middle ground or confluence between the past, present and future. This concept originally connotes two spaces, but it will be deconstructed and expanded in scope in this study because it doesn't only limit analysis to the colonial and coloniser's spaces, but it offers in-betweenness to every other new ideology that emerges. It becomes a therapeutic solution to new histories. These situations find their expression in the celebration of in-betweenness. It advises characters to restrict their scope in generalisations of world symbols by engaging in an enunciation split.

Cultures and symbols would be meaningless with the increasing lack of symphony amidst historical notions. The concept of third spaces offers a prospect of mediation along cultural change lines. Without this mediation in contemporary times, symbols and cultures are subject to shifting context and, thus, can be adjusted when negotiating between past and present, old traditions and the new realities.

The quest for a third space identity is prevalent in *Fury*. Rushdie expands the notion of third spacing and creates a sense of ambiguity in the character of Little Brain. She is an embodiment of so many symbols, everchanging enough to mutate and change histories. She becomes something new and universal, a type of personality that would be unable to fit into a definition of something as narrow as tribe or race or nation. What is worth noting is how Little Brain crosses all boundaries in a quest for the third space. She merges generation, gender, and language which are all compartments of different symbols. The third space concept is extended in this case since Bhabha does not talk of more than two cultures or spaces.

Mila Milo plays a similar role in the novel *Fury*. She has multiple parentage and grows up in various settings. All these parents symbolise different cultures and spaces. She is a typical example of a postmodern character with different historical backgrounds and settings. Throughout the novel, she tries to find a balance amidst all the spaces that she occupies. So, when she comes to the States, she easily finds a place for herself, even though Solanka tries to suppress her, she does not lose herself to patriarchal domination but stands on her feet to give herself a place. The permanent creation of her identity in the third space implies, therefore a fluid concept, which is always renewed through negotiation. Salman Rushdie's words in *Shame*, "I, too, am a translated man. I have been borne across" (Rushdie, 2002, p. 24), are perhaps the most obvious evidence for the need of re-formulating the concept of identity in this context.

When Solanka leaves Mila Milo for Neela, she does not break for too long; she picks up the pieces and forges ahead with little or no signs of depression, "she had recovered from him already and was resurrected as a queen" (Rushdie, 2002, p. 155). Even as she continues to balance among spaces, the postmodern transformations are enormous, as seen below:

> The seventh veil falls away, Solanka thought. Fully clothed as Mila was

> in her daytime sportswear, she stood naked before him at last. Furia. This was the self she had never fully shown, Mila as Fury, the world-swallower, the self as pure transformative energy. In this incarnation she was simultaneously terrifying and wonderful (Rushdie, 2002, p. 155).

The excerpt reveals the various postmodern selves Mila Milo has hidden behind a veil. The image of the veil remains a recurrent symbol in postmodern studies. As Milo transforms into these spaces, she merges even emotions in the third space. Terrific meets with wonderful in the same space, and Milo reconciles these emotions. Interestingly enough, Solanka finds solace in her strength as a third-space character to somehow change his point of view. When Solanka almost crumbles with the weight of the Little Brain saga, Mila Milo comes to help:

> I know how unhappy you were-are-about the whole Little Brain saga. This is me, remember? Malik, I know that. That's what I'm saying to you here. This time you don't lose control. This time you have a better vehicle than even existed when you came up with Little Brain, and you drive it, totally. This is your chance to get right what went wrong before, and if it works, let's not be coy here, the financial upside is very, very strong (Rushdie, 2002, p. 155).

Mila Milo, as a third space character, gives out light to help others survive in the protean world. By challenging Solanka to be more flexible, she means there is a life that exists out of the margins. As she provides tangible advantages of the third space identity, Solanka starts to find new strength in her resilience, and so, "a new world was forming in him, and he had Mila to thank for the divine afflatus: the breath of life. Joy and relief coursed through him in long uncontrollable shudders... Mila had justified herself. She had provided the spur that had sent him back to work" (Rushdie, 2002, p. 120).

God Was African represents an evolving consciousness of cultural ideals. The evolution of colonised and colonial relationships marks the awakening of a special kind of discourse which is the third space celebration. The socialisation of both spaces which led to the search for the self, has resolved to a blend of both.

These cultures, which used to be very different and distinct, took attributes of each other but this does not mean that they completely lose their previous cultural identity, nor do they fully adopt the new culture. As history evolves, so do cultures and symbols. There is a mixture of both the colonised and coloniser's cultures in *God Was African*. No model can be more accurate than what Nkengasong illustrates in the novel that they entered the church shortly before the procession to the alter started. An enchanting song in Nweh was intoned, and the whole congregation rose with the solemn rhythm. In the course of the service, songs were sung in English, Nweh and Latin. The people of Nweh use hybrid lenses through which they view the changing society. They strongly attempt to negotiate the in-betweenness of both cultures that challenges any fixed concepts of identity. And thus, the third space provides possibilities to open fluid spaces and reconsider identity not as pre-given by history but as socially and discursively negotiated.

Nkengasong celebrates the third space as a privileged and superior cultural intelligence owing to the advantage of in-betweenness, the overlapping of two or more cultures or spaces and the consequent skill to negotiate the difference. Because the people of Nweh celebrate their in-betweenness, it is pertinent to note that their collective identity is not fixed but hybrid and fluid which is in a constant state of flux. In this light, there is room for negotiation and change.

Conclusion

Time and postmodernism have clearly demonstrated that the old liberal assumption of symbols that once had been considered as messages to convey information hold no further obligation towards the reference they represented. In modern times, they are perceived as weak and lacking any validity. The liberal concept of third spacing does not take into account the fact that symbols and cultures within a pluralistic society live in different circumstances originating from a variety of social, historical, and political contexts.

In a nutshell, when symbols are juxtaposed and new histories are grafted, they must be negotiated in the third space; if not, there will be a cacophony of cultures that may end up in fragmentation.

Abstract

Postmodernism involves shifting identities, and characters find it absolutely difficult to maintain a particular trend after a particular time frame. There are moves and curves and bends and carrefours along the cultural path. Too many styles take the lead, and too many voices jostle for attention. There is a cacophony of cultures as people feel free to mix cultures, so much so that some cultures lose their original connotations. However, some cultures blend perfectly while others do not; therefore, there is a problem of identity where characters try to adjust to various shifting contexts to fit into contemporary societies. The image of Santa Claus on the cross exposes many deconstructive perceptions. During the period of Cultural Revolution, Nkemngong Nkengasong and Salman Rushdie question longstanding rituals and conformist philosophies and wonder if they still have a place in postmodern society. They expose too many exciting ideas of deconstruction by grafting histories. This essay is grounded on the postmodern theory and will be supported by the postcolonial concept of third spacing. The hypothesis contends that, during the period of cultural turns and changes in the postmodern society, there are situations of contradictory things. In *God was African*, and *Fury*, orthodox principles lose their grip, and a liberating voice takes over to newness but if these identities are not negotiated in the third space, then characters instead become fragmented.

Keywords: Santa Claus, symbols, deconstruction, history, postmodern, third space.

References

Anderson, W. T. (1995). *The truth about the truth: De-confusing and reconstructing the postmodern world*. New York: Putnam.

Awoonor, K. (1975). *The breast of the earth: A survey of history, culture and literature of Africa South of the Sahara*. New York: Anchor Press.

Bhabha, H. (1990). *Nation and narration*. London and New York: Routledge.

Bhabha, H (1994). *The location of culture*. London: Routledge.

Geertz. C. J. (2000). *The interpretation of cultures*. New York: Basic Books, Inc.

Munslow, A. (2006). *Deconstructing histories*. London: Routledge.

Nkengasong, J.N. (2015). *God was African*. Langaa: Bamenda.

Nkosi, L. (1983). *Home and exile and other selections*. London: Longman,

Rushdie, S. (1983). *Shame*. London: Vintage.

Rushdie, S. (2002). *Fury*. New York: The Modern Library.

Said, E. (1993). *Culture and imperialism*. London: Chatto and Windus,

Shweder, R. (1995). "Santa Claus on the cross:" (p.72-78) *The truth about the truth: De-confusing and reconstructing the postmodern world*. New York: Putnam's Sons.

Appendix I

Sep 11, 2019 at 05:29

> Worry not about those praising Biya's meaningless speech. They are the same people who have never stood for this struggle
>
> E. Acha

👍❤ 56

👍 56   💬 5   ↗ 11

I/You/We must wake up from slumber and relcaim our country Cameroon from the ugly and deadly fangs of these demagogues and their surrogates who have confisicated and laid a false claim and a personal ownership to our fatherland, a natrurally rich nation whose rich resources are being squandered and depleted right before our very eyes. Shame shame shame on you for wasting this beautiful country Cameroon!!

Nov 7, 2016

Colours that were once a symbol of hope and the birth of a new and a prosperous Cameroon in the 80s are today a symbol of missery, shame, corruption, autocracy, theft, voilence, injustices, dystopia, sadness, fear, destruction, evil, immorality, despotism, tyranny, failure and you name the rest. If you are still in keeping of this dreadful textile in anyform, please do yourself a favour by dumping it in the bin.

If you want to be nice to yourself, use the flames on it to burn it, because those same flames have been burning and ruining your future, depriving you of the power, resources and opportunities to fulfil your potentials. Take a second brother/sister and think, interogate

Nov 28, 2016

THE PEOPLE CONSTITUTE POWER.

Unfortunately, the very headstrong man, a certain Paul BIYA and his kakistocracy fail to understand the times - they so mistake the IT age for the 90s. Who told them that military might can ever conquer a resolute people? Their numbers pale in comparison:

If the entire Buea population take to the streets and they send their military forces from Limbe. And midday Limbe and Buea, the people of Limbe also empty into the streets ... and then Muyuka, Tiko, Mamfe, Kuma, Mbonge, Ekondo Titi, Mundemba, Fontem, Tinto, Eyumojock, Akwaya, Konye, Matoh, Bakassi etc. And a similar thing happens in the North West region ... the population of all the major towns (Bamenda, Wum, Kumbo, Mbengwi, Ndop, Nkambe, Batibo, Bambui and Oshie etc)

APPENDIX

Dull way to strike #Ambazonians stay in their homes all day with doors locked expecting changes... That method aint gonna reap any changes

10:20 AM · 08 Dec 16 · Twitter Web Client

 Jan 30, 2017

This is why Biya is hidding the truth about the tragic Eseka accident. All fingers are pointing at Bollore, the frenchman with whom Biya shares all the wealth of Cameroon.

 Sep 22, 2017

John Mbah Akuroh caught up with crooked Atanga Nji Paul today at the UN building, telling him to tell Biya the truth.

 Jan 30, 2017

This is why Biya is hidding the truth about the tragic Eseka accident. All fingers are pointing at Bollore, the frenchman with whom Biya shares all the wealth of Cameroon.

 May 7, 2017

France satanic polygamous marriages of convenience with French African countries. Until the rotten umbilical cord is cut off, we shall continue to suffer from a very painful stomach ache.
France will never support the idea of a self-sufficient and self-reliant Fre... See More

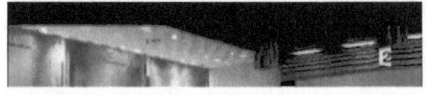

 Oct 11, 2017

Who is more dangerous? West #Cameroonian peaceful protesters or Oga Tchiroma?

APPENDIX I

 Oct 19, 2017

The Yaounde dictatorship bans the previously authorised planned march for Saturday Oct.21.

Let the entire Douala stand up as one people and defy this unjust ban. That's the only language a dictatorship understands. Let the organisers not give any reason to respect the ban. #Standupforjustice

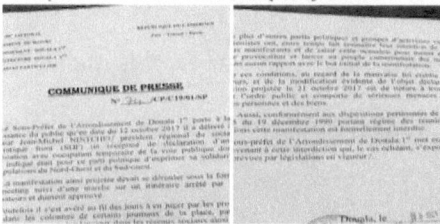

 Sep 22, 2017

Batibo takes to Street as 5 are shot in Mamfe, 2 in Santa. Reports of two killed so far from gun shots. Paul Biya must stop fooling himself. Guns will not resolve this problem.

👍❤ 11

👍 11   💬 3   ↗ 2

 May 7, 2017

Hypocrisy at its finest? Today France will be electing its 25th president, while at the same time encouraging and supporting dictatorships in Africa (like in Cameroon) to ensure the continuous payment of colonial taxes into its treasury, at the detriment of the French-Afric... See More

 Mar 29, 2017

https://www.ft.com/content/0ecbf20a-13aa-11e7-b0c1-37e417ee6c76

At 84 he is nine years younger than Robert Mugabe. And he has been in power for 35 years, two years short of the Zimbabwean leader's extravagant haul. Paul Biya, the president of Cameroon, is however, as ruthless a despot, and his role in stifling the potential of one of Africa's most promising economies, is as great. One difference between two of Africa's most enduring anachronisms is that Mr Biya has aged more quietly. The catalogue of abuses committed by his regime have received less attention for it.

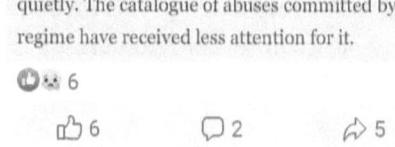

👍 6

👍 6   💬 2   ↗ 5

245

Appendix II

The unstructured interviews that were used to elicit data for this study was guided by the following questions:
- In this Covid-19 period, what greeting gesture(s) do you use when greeting
  - *A friend or a colleague?*
  - *A family member?*
  - *Your boss/ your employer/ your superior?*
  - *Your employee/ your inferiors?*
- Are you used to greeting this way before the advent of Covid-19? (yes or no)
- If no, what gesture(s) were you using before in greeting
  - *A friend or a colleague?*
  - *A family member?*
  - *Your boss/ your employer/ your superior?*
  - *Your employee/ your inferiors?*

NB: Other questions (not included in the list above) might be contextually asked to the respondents. This includes: why do you opt for using this or that strategy to greet this or that person.

List of Contributors

Camilla Arundie Tabe is Associate Professor in English language and Linguistics, and Head of the Department of English Language and Literature in the Faculty of Arts, Letters and Social Sciences at the University of Maroua. Her research domains are internet linguistics, the use of ICTs in language pedagogy and Sociolinguistics. She is co-editor of *Language, Media and Technologies: Usages, Forms and Functions* (2019) and *Teaching and Learning Language and Literature at Tertiary Level: Challenges and Proposals* (2018).

Ngong Joseph Sam holds a PhD in American Literature from the University of Maroua. He is a Senior Lecturer in the Department of English Language and Literature (FALSH) and at the Higher Teachers' Training College (ENS) at the University of Maroua. His teaching and research include American and Postcolonial Literatures.

Michael Etuge Apuge is Professor of Linguistics and holds a PhD from the University of Buea (UB), Cameroon. He is the Dean of the Faculty of Arts at the University of Buea. He has authored a book, co-edited two others, and has many scientific publications in national and international journals.

Gilbert T. Safotso is an Associate Professor of English Language and Applied Linguistics (Phonologist). He received his training at the University of Yaounde I (Cameroon), Heriot-Watt University and University of Leicester (UK). He teaches in the Department of Foreign Applied Languages, University of Dschang, Cameroon.

Ophilia A. Abianji-Menang is Senior Lecturer of Literature and researcher at the University of Maroua, Cameroon. She holds a PhD in African Literature and Civilisations from the University of Yaounde 1. She is equally a holder of the Secondary and High School Teacher Diploma with over twelve years of teaching experience in secondary and high schools in Cameroon.

LIST OF CONTRIBUTORS

Grace Nye Nformi is Senior Lecturer in the Department of English Language and Literatures of English Expression at the Higher Teacher's Training College of the University of Maroua, Cameroon. She researches American literature.

Joseph Nkwain holds a PhD in English Linguistics from the University of Yaoundé 1, Cameroon. He is currently a Senior Lecturer in the Department of Bilingual Letters at the University of Maroua, where he teaches aspects of English/French Comparative/Contrastive Studies, Translation Studies, English Usage, English Grammar and Lexicology.

Faissam Warda holds a PhD in English Language studies from the University of Maroua and a Language Teaching Diploma in Bilingual Letters (English & French). He is currently investigating the pragmatics of politeness in (the now emerging) Cameroon Francophone English (CamFE).

James N. Tasah holds a PhD in Applied linguistics from the University of Yaoundé 1. He is an Associate Professor of Applied Linguistics in the Department of English Language and Literature in the Faculty of Arts, Letters and Social Sciences of the University of Maroua, Cameroon. His research interest is in the field of Sociolinguistics.

Fombo Emmanuel holds a PhD in English Linguistics from the University of Maroua. He is a graduate assistant in the Department of English Language and Literature in the Faculty of Arts, Letters and Social Sciences at the University of Maroua. He specialises in sociolinguistics.

Etienne Langmia Forti is a Senior Lecturer of Commonwealth and Postcolonial Literatures in the Department of English Language and Literature of the Faculty of Arts, Letters and Social Sciences of the University of Maroua. His research interests include South African Literature, race and political Literature, race and identity issues in political literature.

Julius Nguafac is a doctorate student. He is currently completing his PhD thesis at the University of Dschang. He is interested in Discourse Analysis and Sociolinguistics.

Abba holds a bilingual degree in English and French from the University of Maroua, and currently a Grade 2 Secondary and High School teacher from the

Higher Teachers'Training College of the University of Maroua. He is interested in sociolinguistic studies.

Koubli Nouanwa is a Secondary School Teacher. He has taught English in the Government Teachers'Training Colleges, Government High Schools, Government Technical High Schools and Government Technical Colleges in the Far North Region for years. He is a PhD student in Commonwealth Literary Studies at the University of Maroua.

Ngonjo Victor Fuh is a Lecturer of English and a researcher at the University of Maroua, Cameroon. He holds a PhD in Sociolinguistics from the University of Yaoundé 1. He has more than 13 years of teaching experience at Secondary School and 11 years of teaching at higher education (private professional institutions).

Ethel Joffi Molua Ewusi holds a PhD in Commonwealth and American Literary Studies from the University of Yaoundé 1. She is an award-winning writer of prose and poetry. As a Senior Lecturer at the University of Maroua, she lectures Creative Writing and Literatures in English. She has published three books and academic articles in renowned international journals.

Index

Abacha, Sani 139, 141, 150, 151, 157
Abba v, x, xviii, 54, 248
Abianji-Menang, O. vi, xi, xix, 137, 139, 151, 158, 247
Adichie, Ngozi 197
advertisements 46, 163
Aidoo, Ama Ata 197
alcoholism 165
Al-Jazeera 155
Al-Shabaab 138
Ambazonia 3, 8, 13, 15, 20. See also Southern Cameroons
American Bar Association 16
ANC 173, 176, 178
Angelou, Maya vii, xii, 200, 201, 203, 204, 205, 206, 207, 208, 209, 210, 211, 212, 237
Anglophone Cameroonians 3, 5, 9, 11, 14, 17, 28
Anglophone crisis vii, ix, xvii, 1, 3, 4, 6, 7, 8, 10, 15, 16, 17, 18, 19, 20, 22, 23, 27, 28, 29, 30, 31, 33, 34, 35, 36, 130
Anglophone separatists 4, 13
Anglophone problem 1, 2, 3, 4, 5, 6, 8, 9, 11, 16, 17, 19

anti-vaxxers 75, 131
apartheid xi, xix, 161, 162, 163, 164, 165, 166, 167, 168, 169, 170, 171, 172, 173, 174, 175, 176, 177, 178, 179, 180, 181, 182, 183, 184, 185, 186, 187, 189, 190, 191, 196, 198
Apostolic Faith Church vi, x, 71, 72, 73, 82
Apostolic Faith Churches 77, 80, 82
Apuge, M. ii, v, x, xviii, 54, 247
archaeology 234
Arkansas 203, 206, 207
artificial intelligence ix, 22
Assertive Speech Act 13
autobiography 200

banditry 225
Bantustan 161
BBC News 58, 127, 132
Behabitive Speech Act 14
Belgium 3, 132
beliefs vii, xii, 23, 24, 28, 29, 33, 169, 198, 230, 232
Bhabha, Homi 238, 239, 242
Biden, Joe 94, 95
Bilingualism and Multiculturalism Com-

INDEX

mission 3
bioterrorism 74, 83
Biya, Paul vii, 12, 13, 15, 22, 28, 30, 31, 59, 61
Black Economic Empowerment 179
black feminists 202
bloggers viii, 86, 90, 91, 92, 93, 96, 98, 100, 101, 102, 103, 105
Boers 181. *See also* Afrikaners
Boko Haram xi, xviii, 20, 108, 121, 138
bourgeoisie 146, 217
Burkina Faso 72, 77, 141
business 4, 44, 62, 104, 145, 148, 224, 225

Cameroon ii, v, ix, xi, xvii, xviii, 1, 2, 3, 4, 5, 6, 7, 8, 11, 12, 13, 14, 15, 16, 17, 18, 19, 20, 21, 23, 30, 33, 34, 35, 39, 40, 41, 42, 43, 44, 45, 46, 47, 48, 49, 50, 51, 52, 53, 61, 69, 72, 77, 108, 128, 129, 130, 131, 132, 133, 134, 247, 248, 249
Cameroon Tribune 8
Canada 89, 172
capitalism 146
capitalist world, the xx, 214, 215, 226
censorship ix, 147
Centers for Disease Control and Prevention 127
childhood 20, 41, 200, 205, 222
children x, xi, 8, 14, 66, 75, 82, 108, 109, 111, 112, 113, 114, 115, 116, 120, 121, 122, 123, 142, 144, 145, 161, 163, 168, 177, 184, 185, 186, 189, 190, 192, 193, 196, 197, 203, 206, 207, 208, 222, 224, 225, 237
China 54, 55, 58, 59, 63, 64, 68, 71, 84, 85, 131

Christian faith 209
Christianity 230, 231, 235
church x, xiii, 72, 73, 77, 78, 79, 80, 81, 82, 120, 206, 207, 218, 240
civilisation 127
climate change xi, xvii, 101, 102, 124, 125, 127, 131
clinicians 74, 82
CNN 140, 155
colonial discourse 230, 233, 234, 238
colonialism 147, 181, 213, 214, 215, 218, 219, 226, 227, 234, 236
colonisation 147, 195, 215, 216
colonised peoples 213
colonised youths 223
colonising xix, xx, 213, 214, 215, 216, 217, 218, 219, 222, 223, 224, 225, 226, 227
colonising ideology 215
Commissives 6
Commissive Speech Act 12
commodity 187
communication xviii, 3, 5, 9, 19, 20, 23, 24, 32, 33, 40, 43, 50, 54, 56, 57, 68, 72, 73, 74, 75, 76, 77, 78, 80, 81, 82, 83, 87, 88, 105, 106, 107, 109, 111, 112, 114, 148, 158
Conceptual Metaphor Theory 59, 64, 65, 66, 68, 69
conflict
  armed struggle xix, 157
  civil war 16, 96, 130
  ethnic cleansing 7
  ethnic conflicts xi
  interpersonal conflict 48
  violence ix, 1, 4, 5, 6, 7, 8, 11, 12, 13, 14, 15, 16, 17, 18, 22, 129, 132, 137, 138, 139, 140, 141, 145, 147,

148, 149, 150, 151, 152, 153, 155, 156, 157, 158, 195, 196, 199, 208, 217, 219, 220, 222
consciousness 2, 185, 194, 198, 199, 212, 234, 240
conspiracy xviii, xix, 75, 84, 86, 91, 98, 102, 105, 198, 215, 218, 219, 223, 224, 225, 227
conspiracy theories xviii, 75, 84, 86, 91, 98, 102, 105
consumerism 164, 178
contamination rates 95
conviviality 44, 45
Corruption 147
Covid-19 v, vi, viii, ix, x, xi, xvii, xviii, 39, 40, 41, 42, 43, 44, 45, 46, 47, 48, 49, 50, 51, 52, 53, 54, 55, 56, 57, 58, 59, 60, 61, 62, 63, 64, 65, 66, 67, 68, 69, 70, 71, 72, 73, 74, 75, 76, 77, 78, 79, 80, 81, 82, 83, 84, 85, 86, 87, 88, 89, 90, 103, 105, 106, 107, 126, 128, 131, 133, 246
Covid-19 pandemic x, 42, 43, 44, 54, 60, 66, 67, 72, 73, 74, 75, 76, 77, 78, 79, 80, 81, 82, 83, 84, 87, 88, 105, 126, 128
crime xvii, 126, 145, 162, 165, 184
Critical Discourse Analysis 7, 88
critical theory 201
cultural change 239
cultural identity xii, 34, 240
culture xii, xiii, xviii, xx, 4, 23, 43, 113, 122, 129, 143, 159, 192, 214, 229, 230, 231, 234, 235, 236, 238, 239, 240, 241, 242
cyberbullying ix, 19

death 16, 58, 85, 94, 95, 96, 109, 110, 121, 122, 146, 156, 169, 172, 188, 189, 192, 196
deep fake images 22, 23, 27, 33, 34, 35
deforestation 127, 128, 131
democracy xix, 17, 22, 25, 36, 141, 162, 164, 165, 166, 172, 173, 174, 175, 176, 177, 178, 179, 180, 181, 182
Democratic Republic of Congo 72, 77
democratisation xvii
dependency xx, 209, 227
determination xix, 204, 214
diaspora 3, 7, 8, 20, 232
diplomacy 2, 22, 214
directive 5, 11, 15, 40
Directive Speech Act 11
discourses xviii, 1, 4, 5, 9, 11, 16, 17, 89, 229, 233, 235, 236
discrimination 5, 144, 200, 204, 211
disease x, 8, 49, 54, 56, 57, 63, 64, 69, 71, 76, 81, 85, 106, 131, 146
  AIDS 162, 189, 191
  coronavirus xviii, 39, 42, 43, 44, 45, 46, 47, 49, 51, 52, 54, 55, 60, 70, 71, 76, 77, 81, 82, 98, 104, 106, 107, 127, 131
  diarrhoea 127
  infections 55, 76, 92, 104, 167
  polio 102
  schizophrenia 185
  yellow fever 125
disinformation campaigns 27, 28, 104
diversity 106, 142, 202
drugs 86, 130, 168, 184

ecocriticism 142, 157, 159
economic crisis 125, 220

economic empowerment 187
economic exploitation 213, 214, 216, 217
Eco-terrorism 154
education xvii, xix, 2, 8, 11, 65, 76, 83, 93, 95, 111, 119, 126, 127, 131, 139, 144, 163, 166, 181, 207, 222, 249
Electra Complex 190
Emecheta, Buchi 197
empires xx, 213, 214, 215, 218, 227
employment 125, 131, 145, 155, 181
England 3, 60, 61
environment 57, 97, 111, 113, 127, 139, 142, 143, 146, 148, 151, 152, 154, 156, 157, 165, 174, 181, 205, 218, 220, 221
environmental degradation 125, 142, 147, 156, 157
ethical concerns 87
ethnic groups
  Bororo 41
ethnicity 1, 64, 111, 122. See also conflict
ethnic militia 147
ethnographic approach 90
Europe xvii, 14, 18, 39, 84, 125, 126, 128, 129, 134, 197, 215, 225, 227
Ewusi, E. vii, xii, xx, 229, 249
exploitation 34, 124, 141, 148, 154, 155, 181, 213, 214, 215, 216, 217, 218, 220, 221, 227
extrajudicial killings 141, 148

Facebook v, vii, ix, xvii, 3, 4, 9, 10, 11, 15, 17, 18, 22, 23, 25, 27, 29, 34, 35, 37, 79, 81, 129. See also social media
facial expressions 26, 74
fake news xvii, 7, 17, 36, 86, 217. See also social media
Fanon, Franz 217, 225, 227
Far North Region xviii, 110, 121, 249
Fauci, Anthony 94
feminism 187, 201, 202, 211
feminist political discourse xix, 198
fishing 127, 142, 143, 144, 145
Fombo, E. v, ix, xviii, 3, 7, 19, 22, 34, 36, 248
Food and Agricultural Organization 126
food security xi, 124, 125, 126, 128, 131
Forti, E.L. ii, vi, xi, xix, 161, 248
Foumban Conference 2
Freedom fighters 139
freedom of speech 4, 17. See also hate speech
Freud, Sigmund 185, 186, 187, 189, 190, 199
Fugard, Athol vi, xii, 184, 185, 186, 187, 188, 189, 190, 191, 197, 198, 199
Fuh, N.V. vi, x, xviii, 71, 249

Gabon 72, 77
Gambia 72, 77
Garoua 42, 52
gender equality xix, 34, 126, 189, 197
gender roles 192
genocide 12, 16, 30, 94
Germany ii, 3, 13, 58, 123
Ghana 72, 77, 122
globalisation xviii, 55, 122, 123
Gordimer, Nadine vi, xi, 161, 162, 163, 167, 168, 176, 177, 179, 180, 182
grammar 5, 23, 25, 31, 32, 33, 34, 35, 36

grandchildren 203
Great Depression, the 124
greeting techniques 39, 40, 41, 42, 44, 47, 48, 52

Harlem Renaissance 201
hate speech ix, xvii, 3, 4, 6, 7, 8, 11, 12, 14, 15, 16, 17, 18, 19, 20, 22, 23, 24, 37, 129, 130
health xvii, 20, 43, 49, 51, 54, 56, 57, 58, 60, 61, 72, 74, 75, 77, 82, 83, 86, 87, 88, 89, 90, 92, 95, 96, 97, 98, 100, 101, 104, 106, 107, 124, 125, 127, 146, 164, 166, 168, 175, 181, 218, 219, 221, 224, 227
  health equipment 86
  medical advice 84, 86
  sanitation 93, 94, 127
  vaccination 75, 93, 94, 98
healthcare 55, 72, 74, 76, 93
hegemony xii, xx, 213, 219, 226
history xiii, 60, 63, 75, 127, 139, 147, 161, 176, 177, 207, 215, 218, 233, 234, 235, 236, 238, 240, 241, 242
  oral history 234
homelessness xi, 162, 180, 220
horticulture 233
host community viii, xi, xviii, 108, 109, 111, 112, 113, 114, 116, 117, 118, 119, 121, 122
Hughes, Langston 205
humour 23, 37, 88, 230
hygiene 94, 95. *See also* health

iconography 176
identity xii, xiii, xix, xx, 27, 34, 64, 88, 108, 133, 143, 200, 201, 203, 205, 206, 209, 211, 230, 234, 235, 239, 240, 241, 248
Ideology 140, 152
illiteracy 178, 221
illocution 5
illocutionary act 5
imperialism 213, 214, 215, 226, 242
imperialists 147, 217
India 82, 95
indigenous language 110, 112. *See also* languages
Indonesia 90
inequality xi, xii, xix, xx, 107, 125, 161, 162, 166, 168, 170, 171, 173, 176, 177, 181, 182, 184, 185, 196, 197, 211
infodemic 84
Instagram xvii. *See also* social media
interactionist perspective 124
International Labour Organisation 125, 126, 128
International Monetary Fund xx
internet iv, xvii, 3, 4, 7, 12, 17, 24, 25, 37, 80, 107, 126, 247
interpretation xviii, 24, 46, 229, 242
Israel 88
Israeli-Palestinian conflict 137
Italy 85

Japan 147, 229, 230
  Hiroshima 230
  Nagasaki 230
Johnson, Boris 54, 56, 57, 59, 60, 61, 62, 63, 64, 65, 66, 67, 68, 69, 203, 205, 206, 207, 208, 209, 210
journalism 18, 22, 151, 223

INDEX

juvenile delinquency xii, 220, 225

Kentucky 193
kidnapping 139, 151, 153, 159, 224
Koza vi, viii, x, xi, xviii, 108, 109, 110, 111, 112, 113, 114, 115, 116, 117, 118, 119, 120, 121, 122, 123

language endangerment vii, xi, 109, 112
Language Endangerment and Loss 109
language loss 109, 122
languages viii, xi, 42, 108, 109, 110, 111, 112, 113, 114, 115, 116, 117, 118, 119, 120, 121, 122, 123, 128
  English v, x, xiii, xvii, xviii, 2, 3, 6, 7, 8, 17, 20, 24, 35, 37, 41, 42, 53, 54, 55, 68, 69, 87, 89, 106, 107, 119, 122, 151, 154, 156, 182, 231, 235, 241, 247, 248, 249
  French xi, 2, 3, 8, 13, 34, 35, 42, 65, 89, 110, 112, 113, 115, 116, 118, 119, 120, 137, 248
  Fulbe ix, x, 43, 44
  Fulfulde xi, 41, 42, 43, 53, 110, 111, 113, 115, 116, 119, 120
language attrition 89
language competition 114
language transmission 109
Latin xiii, 214, 241
Mafa xi, 110, 111, 112, 113, 115, 116, 119, 120, 121
language shift x, xi, xviii, 108, 109, 111, 112, 113, 120, 121, 122, 123. *See also* language endangerment
leadership 8, 147, 163, 166, 167, 173, 174, 177, 179, 214, 215, 219, 227

Lebialem 231
legitimacy xix, 148
Liberia 72, 77
libido 186, 187
lingua franca 43, 110
linguistic behaviour 41, 87
linguistic code xviii, 69
linguistic features 16, 23, 24, 26, 27, 28, 30, 31, 33, 34, 35, 87
linguistic politeness theory 51
locution 5
locutionary act 5

Macron, Emmanuel 57, 59, 61
Maghreb 126
malaria 125
malnutrition 144, 167, 221, 222, 225
Mandela, Nelson 174, 176, 177, 178
marine species 127
masks 67, 71, 74, 85, 88, 94
Mbeki, Thabo 174, 178
memes ix, 22, 23, 24, 25, 26, 27, 33, 34, 35, 37, 88, 106
metafunction 25, 26, 29, 32, 34, 35
metaphor x, xviii, 8, 20, 54, 55, 56, 57, 60, 61, 63, 64, 65, 68, 69, 98, 105, 174, 193, 194, 229
Mhlongo, Nicholas vi, xi, 161, 162, 163, 164, 165, 166, 167, 168, 169, 170, 171, 172, 173, 174, 175, 176, 177, 178, 179, 182, 183
migration xvii, xviii, xx, 108, 110, 111, 114, 123, 125, 126, 129, 131
  rural exodus xii, 220, 221, 223
militancy 139, 141, 142, 150, 152, 154, 156, 157, 159
militants 140, 142, 145, 148, 149, 150,

152, 153, 154, 155, 156, 216, 217, 221
minerals 124, 133
minority language 110, 121
misrepresentation 197, 198, 211
mobile telephones 27
morality xix, 17, 206
morphemes 5
Morrison, Toni 197, 204, 212
mortality rate 55
motherhood 190, 195
mother tongue xi, xviii, 109, 112, 122, 232. *See also* languages
multilingualism 90, 111
multinational companies 215, 227
multiracial democracy xix, 162, 164, 165, 166, 172, 173, 174, 175, 176, 177, 178, 179, 180, 181, 182
musicology 234
Muslims 73

National Dialogue 130
nationalism 219, 226
nation-building 162, 164, 166, 167, 176, 177, 179, 180, 181
nationhood 162, 166, 171, 173, 179
newspaper headlines 7, 9, 20
Nformi, Grace vii, xii, xix, 200, 248
Ngaoundere 42, 52
Ngong, J.S. ii, iii, iv, v, vi, xii, xvii, xix, 184, 247
Nguafac, J. vi, xi, xix, 124, 248
Nigeria ii, xx, 17, 18, 19, 72, 73, 77, 80, 83, 108, 112, 123, 129, 132, 133, 137, 141, 142, 146, 147, 150, 151, 154, 156, 158, 159, 215, 217, 221, 227

Niger Delta Region 142, 147, 159
Nkengasong, J. ii, vii, xii, 229, 230, 231, 235, 240, 241, 242
Nkrumah, Kwame 183, 219, 226, 227
Nkwain, Joseph vi, ix, x, xviii, 41, 53, 84, 248
Nouanwa, K. vii, xii, xix, 213, 249
novel x, 76, 87, 103, 105, 146, 147, 152, 157, 165, 171, 173, 174, 200, 201, 205, 206, 211, 227, 235, 239, 240
Nweh xiii, 241

objectification 187, 198, 199
oil spills 144, 146
oligarchy 161
online communication 3, 9, 24, 75
oppression 196, 200, 201, 202, 215, 219
organised crime xvii

Pakistan 133, 137
patriarchal organisation 203
Peace Security Report 130
performative speech acts 11, 14
perlocution 5
perlocutionary act 5
perlocutionary perspectives 5, 17
petroleum 141, 142, 144, 145, 147, 153, 156, 157
pharmaceutical 91, 95
phonology 5
Poland 88, 89, 106
polio 102
political leaders 11, 13, 147, 176
political misinformation 24
pollutants 220, 221
pollution 127, 139, 142, 143, 147, 152,

INDEX

156
population xviii, xix, 3, 16, 27, 42, 54, 55, 63, 66, 69, 73, 80, 101, 109, 111, 126, 131, 144, 147, 165, 167, 173, 176, 177, 181, 182, 184, 216, 218, 221, 225
pornography 24
Port Harcourt 141, 145, 153, 156, 222, 223, 225
postcolonial literature 215, 230
postmodern 229, 231, 232, 233, 237, 238, 239, 240, 242
Postmodernism 231, 238, 241
poverty 126, 127, 129, 133, 139, 144, 145, 147, 148, 152, 161, 162, 164, 165, 167, 168, 169, 170, 171, 172, 173, 174, 175, 176, 178, 180, 181, 195, 220, 221, 222, 224, 225, 237
Pragma-stylistics 86, 87
pragmatic analysis 4
Pragmatics v, ix, 18, 19, 39, 53, 87
prebendalism 147
prisoners of war 141
private newspapers 8
propaganda 16, 17, 18, 95, 96, 97, 98, 101, 103, 139, 151, 154, 155
prostitution 220, 221
psychic energy 187
psychoanalysis 186, 187, 198, 199
psychological disorder 85
psychological stressors 84
psychosis xviii
public health 72, 74, 89, 107, 124

racial stigma 200, 209, 210, 211
racism xvii, xix, xx, 158, 162, 200, 201, 205, 206, 207, 208, 209, 210

rebels 139, 140, 150, 155
reconciliation 176, 182
refugee children x, xi, 108, 109, 111, 113, 114, 116, 121, 122, 123
religion 73, 82, 206, 211, 225, 232, 234
religious ceremonies 73
religious symbol 230
repression xi, 141, 148, 150, 157, 185
resistance vii, 112, 122, 143, 150, 151, 156, 201, 209, 215, 217
rituals x, xviii, 39, 40, 41, 51, 52, 230, 231, 241
Rockefeller Foundation 78
Rushdie, S. vii, xii, 229, 230, 232, 235, 236, 237, 239, 240, 241, 242

Safotso, G. ii, vi, xi, xix, 124, 128, 133, 247
Santa Claus vii, xii, 229, 230, 233, 235, 236, 241, 242
Saro-Wiwa, Ken 141
secession 1, 2, 3, 4, 130
Second World War 94, 124
semiotic perspective 33, 37
semiotics 25, 230
sexual energy 187
slavery 193, 194, 196, 197, 201, 215
slave trade 211, 213
social inequality xi, xix, 107, 162, 173, 176, 177, 181, 182
socialisation 108, 109, 240
social media xvii, 1, 3, 4, 5, 6, 7, 11, 15, 16, 17, 18, 19, 20, 22, 23, 28, 33, 34, 35, 37, 74, 75, 77, 79, 80, 81, 82, 89, 90, 129
Tik Tok xvii
Twitter vii, 3, 4, 9, 10, 11, 15, 17, 18,

20, 24, 36, 89, 107
social networks 24, 110, 151, 159
socioeconomic issues xviii, 122
sociolinguistic integration 108
sociopragmatics 39
South Africa xi, xix, 3, 97, 99, 104, 132, 161, 162, 163, 164, 165, 166, 167, 168, 170, 171, 172, 173, 174, 175, 176, 177, 178, 179, 180, 181, 182, 183, 185, 186, 188, 190, 191, 196, 199
  Afrikaner Nationalist Party 161
  Afrikaners 161
  Johannesburg 163, 167, 177, 178, 190
  Soweto 169, 170, 171, 172, 173, 175, 177
Southern Cameroons 2, 22, 28
Spain 85, 88, 106
speech act 1, 5, 6, 11, 12, 13, 14, 15, 17, 19, 36
Speech Act Theory 5, 19, 86, 105
spirituality 73, 93, 94, 206
stability 16, 17, 73, 223, 225
status xvii, 50, 89, 96, 103, 109, 113, 139, 179, 180, 184, 187, 192, 211
stereotypes 129, 192, 198, 199
stigmatisation 210
subaltern 214, 215, 218, 236
Subjectivity 219
symbolism 30, 32, 168, 171
symbols xii, 24, 33, 77, 138, 139, 141, 148, 229, 231, 233, 238, 239, 240, 241, 242

Tabe, C.A. iii, iv, v, ix, x, xvii, 1, 7, 8, 20, 39, 41, 42, 43, 53, 69, 247
Taiwan 76, 83

Tasah, James ii, vi, x, xviii, 7, 20, 108, 111, 123, 248
terrorism xix, xx, 1, 20, 96, 126, 137, 138, 139, 140, 141, 142, 143, 145, 147, 148, 149, 150, 151, 152, 154, 155, 156, 157, 158, 159, 160. *See also* conflict
Togo 72, 77
Tokyo 229
tourism 88, 89, 106, 107
township 168, 169, 170, 171, 172, 175, 179
toxins 91, 96, 218, 220, 221
traditional media 24. *See also* social media
Trump, Donald 57, 58, 59, 61, 62, 63, 64, 65, 66, 71
Tutu, Desmond 161, 183

underdevelopment xx, 147, 213, 215
unemployment xi, 139, 147, 162, 163, 164, 165, 166, 167, 180, 223
United Kingdom 73, 81
United Nations Office on Drugs and Crime 126, 134, 160
United Nations Security Council 138

vaccine hesitancy 74, 102
vaccines x, xviii, 74, 75, 76, 83, 85, 86, 91, 92, 95, 96, 97, 98, 99, 100, 101, 102, 103, 104, 105
variable 50
vegetation 144
verdictive 11, 12, 15
Verdictive Speech Act 11
virtual state 3
visual language 30, 33

Warda, F. v, ix, xviii, 39, 248
warfare 36, 138, 139, 140, 141, 154, 158, 159
Wa Thiong'o, Ngugi 214, 215, 219, 228
WhatsApp xvii, 3, 4, 77, 79, 80, 81, 106
Wilson, August vi, xii, 137, 152, 160, 184, 185, 191, 192, 193, 194, 195, 196, 197, 198, 199
Winfrey, Oprah 196
womanhood 194, 197, 199. *See also* feminism
World Bank xx, 128, 133, 134, 214
World Health Organisation 70, 71, 86, 127, 131

YouTube xvii, 4, 80, 81, 82

Zoom 80, 81